CHARLEY'S WAR

UNDERGROUND AND
OVER THE TOP

CHARLEY'S WAR: Underground and Over The Top
ISBN: 9781845767976

Published by
Titan Books
A division of Titan Publishing Group Ltd
144 Southwark Street
London SE1 0UP

A CIP catalogue record for this title is available from the British Library.

This edition first published: October 2009
2 4 6 8 10 9 7 5 3 1

Printed in Spain.

Also available from Titan Books:
Charley's War: 2 June 1916 – 1 August 1916 (ISBN: 9781840236279)
Charley's War: 1 August 1916 – 17 October 1916 (ISBN: 9781840239294)
Charley's War: 17 October 1916 – 21 February 1917 (ISBN: 9781845762704)
Charley's War: Blue's Story – 21 February 1917 (ISBN: 9781845763237)
Charley's War: Return to The Front – April 1917 (ISBN: 9781845767969)

Grateful thanks to Pat Mills, Trucie Henderson, and Yvonne Oliver for their help and support in the production of this book.

Cover image: 'Digging out the wounded from the trenches' (1914 - 1918)
Image: Wellcome Library, London.

Photo credits:
Photographs used in this volume have been sourced from images in the public domain, from the US Library of Congress and the Photos of the Great War website (www.gwpda.org).

What did you think of this book? We love to hear from our readers.
Please email us at: readerfeedback@titanemail.com,
or write to us at the above address.

To receive advance information, news, competitions, and exclusive Titan offers online, please register as a member by clicking the "sign up" button on our website:
www.titanbooks.com

Much of the comic strip source material used by Titan Books in this edition is exceedingly rare. As such, we hope that readers appreciate that the quality of reproduction achievable can vary.

CHARLEY'S WAR

UNDERGROUND AND OVER THE TOP

PAT MILLS
JOE COLQUHOUN

Titan Books

MINER'S STRIKE

The Secret War Beneath The Trenches

by Steve White

"FOR, LOOK YOU, THE MINES IS NOT ACCORDING TO THE DISCIPLINES OF THE WAR"
Henry V, Act III, Scene 2

20 DECEMBER 1914

With the First World War only five months old, stagnation had already begun to settle in on the Western Front. In northern France, close to the Belgian border, Indian troops of the Sirhind Brigade serving with the British were entrenched close to the village of Festubert. They had no idea the Germans had sunk ten small mine shafts under their lines and filled them with explosives.

The resulting blast caused pandemonium at the front. Survivors fled to the rear, spreading fear and paranoia like a virus, and sending morale plummeting. The troops refused to return to the forward trenches, living in terror of a more insidious enemy than artillery or machine guns. They could hear shells falling or guns firing, but the new German tactics undermined not just the trenches in a physical sense, but the mental confidence of the soldiers. Minds already stretched by battle fatigue and the everyday threat of death by enemy fire now had to contend with a new terror – one that was unpredictable and, apparently, undetectable.

The British General Headquarters (GHQ) needed a response to this new form of warfare and ordered similar attacks against the German lines as a retaliatory measure. However, British engineers were not up to the task; they had neither the manpower nor the skills to conduct operations at the level of their opponents. There was also mistrust of any mining efforts for fear that not only might they draw German retaliation but could also add further to the growing medieval stultification of the frontlines – at a time when British commanders were still hoping for a return to manoeuvre warfare that had typified the opening battles of the war. But something needed to be done and, fortunately, the British had just the man for the job.

SIR JOHN NORTON-GRIFFITHS

Born 13 July 1871, Sir John Norton-Griffiths had left for Australia at the age of 17, where he became a mining engineer, then moved on to South Africa in time to take part in various Colonial wars. He continued to hone his engineering skills in Portuguese West Africa (now Angola) and the United States before returning to Britain to become a Conservative MP.

A flamboyant entrepreneur, he also established his own engineering firm, refining the art of 'clay-kicking' – a technique used for boring small tunnels in which the diggers sat with their backs against a wooden rest and used their feet to control a type of spade.

With the outbreak of war, Norton-Griffiths funded the formation of his own regiment of Colonial troops willing to fight for Britain, but he was soon suggesting to the War Office that the Army form specialised mining units.

After the attacks of 20 December, he was sent off on a fact-finding tour of the Western Front by the War Office. In February 1915, Norton-Griffiths was given the go-ahead to form units of civilian miners and used eighteen of his own redundant workers to form his first unit of Royal Engineers Tunnelling Companies. Nine more

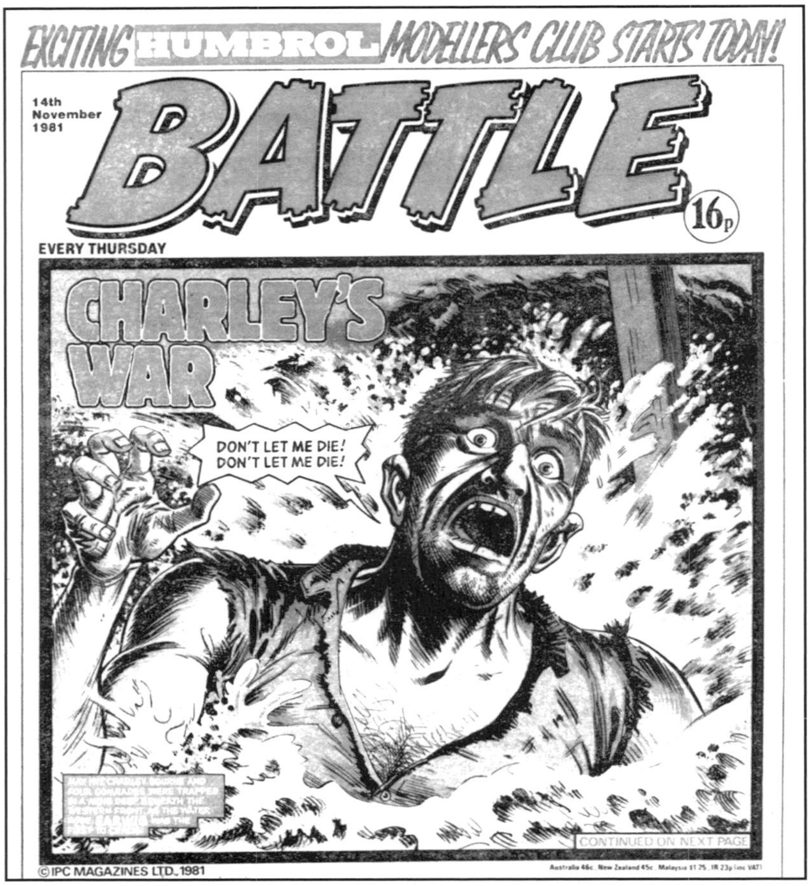

EXCITING HUMBROL MODELLERS CLUB STARTS TODAY!
14th November 1981
BATTLE
16p
EVERY THURSDAY
CHARLEY'S WAR
DON'T LET ME DIE! DON'T LET ME DIE!
CONTINUED ON NEXT PAGE
© IPC MAGAZINES LTD. 1981

ABOVE: Flooding in the mines was just one danger for the British tunnellers below the Messines Ridge.

LOOKS LIKE SNELL PULLED IT OFF, AFTER ALL. IN A FEW DAYS WE'LL... HALF A MOMENT! WHAT WAS THAT?
HIMMEL!
HECK!

ABOVE:
Charley 'clay-kicking' to dig the Bakerloo Mine.

followed and were soon on their way to France.

There were problems: the recruits, some as old as sixty, were ill-prepared for the frontline. Undisciplined and with no formal military training, Army commanders did not welcome them and Norton-Griffiths had a hard time keeping order. He was also busy recruiting new members – miners from Wales and northern England, tunnel and sewage workers from London, and the like – from regular units already serving with the BEF. Driving around the front in a Rolls Royce, he sometimes used cases of fine wines to bribe offices into releasing desirable candidates!

THE DIGGERS

Norton-Griffiths wasn't the only prescient engineer. In Sydney, Australia, a geology professor, Tannatt William Edgeworth David, proposed the formation of the Australian Mining Corps. The Corps was comprised of three companies of approximately 300 men each; the first was recruited principally from New South Wales; the second from South Australia and Victoria; and the third from Western Australia and Tasmania. Like their British counterpart, many were experienced miners who had worked all over the world; few had prior military service.

Australian engineers played a minor role at the disastrous operation at Gallipoli before arriving in France in May 1916. As well as relatively advanced equipment such as 'geotelephones' and electric pumps and generators, they also brought another important asset: an understanding of geology.

The Australians found themselves operating in several distinct geological environments; at the northern end of the line, in Belgium, from the coast to Ypres, they were contending with sandy loams, dunes, shale, blue clay and even quicksands; further south, they faced layers of chalk. David, now serving with the Army, drilled boreholes to identify the stratigraphy of the various rocks and soils. and drew up detailed geological references and water tables that allowed the miners to operate far more effectively.

HAND TO HAND

By July 1916, the three Australian companies joined twenty-five British, three Canadian, and a single New Zealand engineering company. Equipment had also improved, aided considerably by a variety of Australian and French devices such as the 'Wombat' – a compressed air-powered drill for boring much-needed air holes – and new, more sensitive 'geotelephone' listening devices for detecting the enemy digging underground.

However, conditions remained at best difficult for the miners of both sides. Civilian miners were used to working in larger tunnels, and with better equipment. But now they also found the mine entrances being targeted by enemy artillery, threatening entombment and slow death by suffocation.

But far more psychologically testing was the threat of countermining. If digging was detected, a small charge called a camouflet was used to destroy the opposition's mine, so the miners needed to work in silence to avoid detection whilst listening for the enemy. 'Quiet' electric pumps were developed to minimise noise at the workface.

The real fear was that if you could hear the other side's miners, they could hear you – and it would become a race and a real test of nerve to see who could fire their charges first. Sometimes the opposing mineshafts were even close enough for one side to break through into the other's, and then there would be close-quarter fighting with rifles, bayonets, pistols, spades, and picks.

THE SOMME AND BEYOND

By the middle of 1916 a technology race was underway between the two sides, while the miners themselves were becoming more skilled and more experienced. The placement of explosives and their resulting effects were becoming more accurately formulated and the Allied companies were learning a lot from captured German mines.

The first real test of strength came at the Battle of the Somme (see *Charley's War* Volume 1). With only three months notice, nineteen mines of various sizes were constructed under key positions along the German line and all but one successfully fired. However, the poor strategic thinking and tactical handling of the British Army squandered any hope of monopolising on this success.

By the end of 1916, 750 Allied and 696 German mines had been exploded. In contrast, 1917 saw the detonation of just 117 British and 106 German mines.

1916 had seen the Battle of Verdun bleed out the French Army and after the disastrous Second Battle of Aisne in

WORK ON "BAKERLOO" MINE CONTINUED, DAY AFTER DAY, ROUND THE CLOCK. THE CLAY-KICKERS WORKED DOUBLE SHIFTS SO THE MINE WOULD BE READY ON TIME.

THE HUMMING OF THE PUMP MOTORS DROWNED THE SOUND OF THE GERMANS DIGGING.

SLOWLY BUT SURELY, THE ENEMY TUNNEL DREW CLOSER

NEWCASTLE MINE.

SYDNEY MINE.

PERTH MINE.

THE SNOUT MINE.

THE BLAST WAS SO SAVAGE, ITS ROAR WAS HEARD ACROSS THE CHANNEL AT TEN DOWNING STREET!

ABOVE: The British mines under the Messines Ridge are blown – all except two.

ABOVE RIGHT: German prisoners at Messines Ridge. Although the date of the photograph is uncertain, it seems likely that these men were the lucky survivors of the British mining operation. (Image: Library of Congress.)

BELOW RIGHT: Joe Colquhoun's stunning depiction of the detonation of the British mines beneath the Messines Ridge as featured on the cover of *Battle*.

BELOW: British troops and German prisoners in the remains of a German trench that has been mined in 1915, evidence of the success of the tactic. (Photo from *The War Illustrated*, 24 July 1915.)

April 1917 some forty-nine French infantry divisions were wracked by dissent and mutiny. The British were required to fill the gaps left by the exhausted French, whose engineering works were not only unfamiliar to them but, in some cases, in poor repair and damaged by German fire.

The British miners were also hampered by poor co-ordination with other arms such as infantry and artillery. Many mines were dug but deemed superfluous after heavy artillery barrages had battered the German lines.

In the Allies' favour was the tightening grip of their economic blockade against the German fatherland. By the end of 1916, around 125,000 German miners had been recalled from the frontline to augment the civilian workers at home, leaving the Allies to take the upper hand in the mining war. The decisive blow would be struck at the Battle of Messines on 7 June 1917.

HILL 60 AND THE CATERPILLAR

In May 1915, the Germans had seized the ridge close to the village of Messines, in West Flanders, and by the beginning of 1916 it remained a salient bulging into the British frontline. The ridge itself included 'Hill 60', a hill made from the spoil left by the construction of a nearby railway line. To its south were two other artificial mounds called the 'Caterpillar' and the 'Dump'. These hills lay over a soft, wet soil of several layers of clay, sand, quicksand and blue clay.

The entire ridge had been heavily fortified by the Germans and GHQ decided that the best way to clear them off was by undermining them.

The plan was to dig wenty-one mines below the length of the entire ridge and detonate 455 tonnes of explosives to create an artificial earthquake that would shake the Germans loose. The Germans, meanwhile, were confident that their own engineers outclassed the British and conducted a furious countermining operation against the Australian, British and Canadian miners. The Allied tunnellers fought back, 'shouldering' the Germans away from the principal mines using smaller, shallow 'intermediates'.

By November 1916, Australian miners heard the Germans nearby. Using extreme caution and silence, they continued to work, but the Germans could still be heard digging as close as twenty feet to one of their mines. Charges for a camouflet were laid and, with the Germans believed to be no more than ten feet away, exploded on 19 December. The explosion, so deep behind their lines, shook German confidence and their mining operations were temporarily abandoned.

Countermining against the allies continued despite this attack and the Germans managed to trap two Australian 'listeners' for forty-eight hours in May, and destroyed one of the mines on 24 August. However, their efforts failed to stop the work by the Allied miners, who sank some eight kilometres of tunnels beneath Hill 60 and the Caterpillar.

With pumps and men working twenty-four hours, averaging three to four metres a day, the mines were readied by 7 June. Amazingly, all this work went undetected by the Germans, who seemed to have no clue as to what was about to be unleashed beneath their feet. The explosives were set, the detonators for all twenty-one mines linked to a single circuit that was tested and re-tested by the Royal Engineers and their Australian counterparts.

At 3.10am, 7 June, the explosives were triggered. It was said that the resulting blasts were heard by British Prime Minster David Lloyd-George as he sat in his office in London, and in the few seconds it took for all the mines to explode, day became night and the ground shook as though from an earthquake – exactly the effect the engineers had been hoping for.

Although two of the mines failed to explode, it didn't really matter – the surprise was total. German casualties are unknown but were believed in the region of 10,000 killed, the casualties exasperated by the fact that the troops at the Front were just being relieved by new formations and both groups happened to be on the ridge when it was blown. The ridge, its fortifications and the village of Messines were all destroyed.

The stunned, disorientated, terrified Germans had no time to recover. The noise and dust clouds were roiling away when over 2,400 guns were fired by British artillery, a prelude to a barrage that lasted all day and fired over six millions shells.

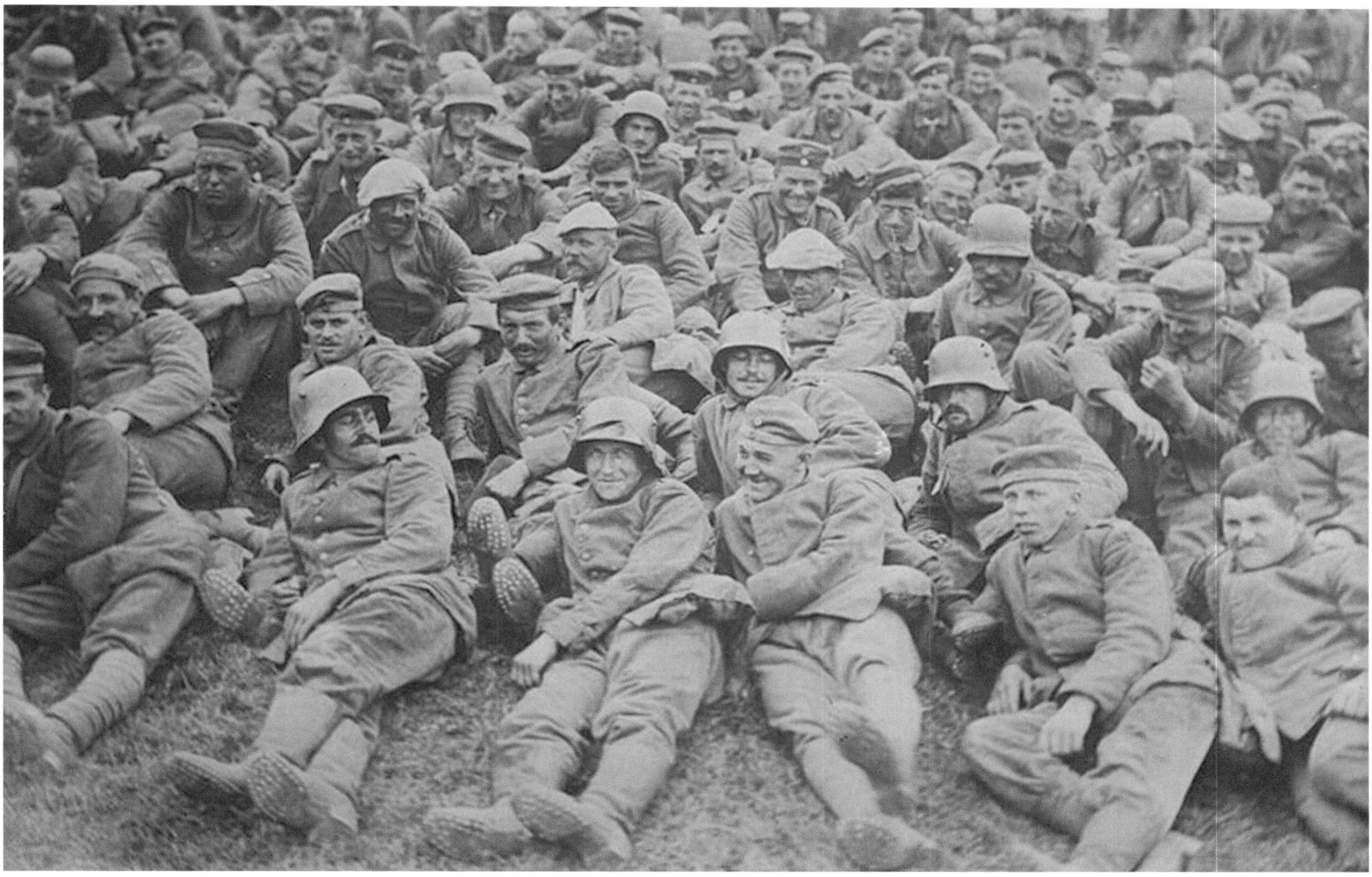

The onslaught had the desired effect. The Allied assault took the ridge with ease and the whole Messines front was in their hands by 9.00am, sustaining only modest casualties and capturing over 7,000 prisoners, many still in a state of shock.

The German commanders were not best pleased with their geologists, who had assured them the ridge could not be cratered. Those over 40 years old were sent back to Berlin; for the under 40s, it was the frontline.

The attack on Messines Ridge was the high watermark of the mining war. No similar operations were undertaken even though the Western Front remained stagnated until the spring of 1918, and the engineers and miners found themselves consigned to digging trenches, fortifications and roads.

AFTERSHOCK

Although the Royal Engineers created secret maps of the mines, the locations of the two that failed to explode on 7 June were apparently lost in the mists of time. However, one made its presence felt when lightning struck an electric pylon inadvertently built over the mine, triggering it on 17 June 1955. The explosion left a massive crater but the only casualty was an unfortunate cow.

The whereabouts of the last mine remain unknown. ✢

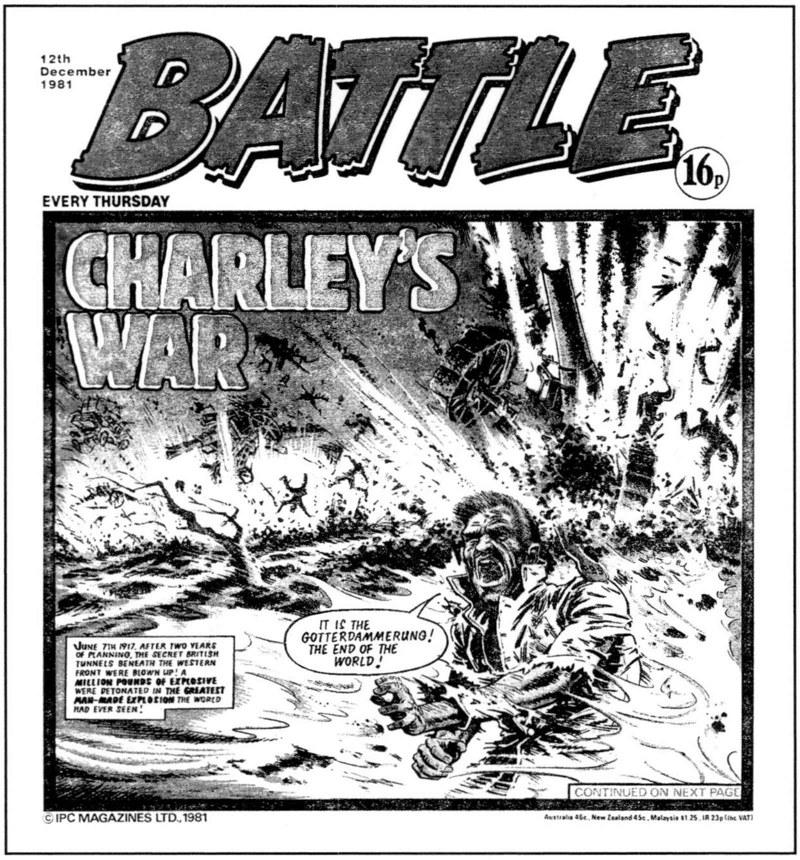
12th December 1981
BATTLE
16p
EVERY THURSDAY
CHARLEY'S WAR
JUNE 7TH 1917. AFTER TWO YEARS OF PLANNING, THE SECRET BRITISH TUNNELS BENEATH THE WESTERN FRONT WERE BLOWN UP! A MILLION POUNDS OF EXPLOSIVE WERE DETONATED IN THE GREATEST MAN-MADE EXPLOSION THE WORLD HAD EVER SEEN!
IT IS THE GOTTERDAMMERUNG! THE END OF THE WORLD!
CONTINUED ON NEXT PAGE
© IPC MAGAZINES LTD., 1981

• There is no permanent memorial on the Western Front to the extraordinary work of the Royal Engineers tunnellers. More information on a fund for the erection of a permanent memorial can be found at www.tunnellersmemorial.com

PREVIOUSLY IN *CHARLEY'S WAR*

SUDDENLY...
LOOK OUT! IT'S AN OVER!

ABOVE: A stray shell destroys a lorry load of Australian troops in Ypres.

BELOW: Captain Snell is chosen to finish off the digging of Bakerloo tunnel deep beneath enemy lines.

BELOW RIGHT: Laden down with supplies, Charley and his comrades enter the shattered city of Ypres.

YOU SOUND JUST THE CHAP WE'RE LOOKING FOR, SNELL! I'LL ARRANGE FOR YOU AND YOUR MEN TO BE TEMPORARILY SECONDED TO THE ONE-HUNDRED-AND-SEVENTY-FIFTH COMPANY

2 June 1916: Charley Bourne, who has joined the army aged sixteen (two years under the official age for conscription), is sent with his unit to France several weeks before the Battle of the Somme.

1 July 1916: The Battle of the Somme begins. Charley and his comrades spare a German soldier they find, but he is shot in cold blood by Lieutenant Snell.

2 July – 14 July 1916: Charley, "Ginger" Jones and "Lonely" are captured. Lonely reveals the secret of the lost platoon, his old unit. During the escape, Charley inhales poison gas and becomes gravely ill.

14 July 1916: Charley, Ginger and Lonely meet a group of British cavalrymen. Lonely bravely sacrifices himself during a German attack.

1 August 1916: On Charley's seventeenth birthday, the British forces accidentally begin shelling their own side. Charley volunteers to be a communications runner to try to end the bombardment, but is delayed by Snell. Lieutenant Thomas orders Charley's unit to retreat, and is later arrested for cowardice.

August 1916: Charley refuses his order to execute Lieutenant Thomas (who is killed in any case, aged twenty-two). Charley and his comrade "Weeper" are sentenced to fourteen days punishment, strapped to the wheel of a field gun.

September 1916: Ginger is killed by a stray shell, causing Charley to temporarily break down. Charley's unit is reinforced by tanks, and on 15 September Charley is joined by his cowardly brother-in-law, "Oiley". Oiley deliberately injures himself to be sent home, and Charley covers for him.

October 1916: Charley is wounded during the battle against the "Judgement Troopers", but sent back to the lines. Eventually, Colonel Zeiss' plan is halted by the German High Command, but before he can celebrate, Charley is badly injured by shrapnel from a stray shell.

November 1916: Charley, an "unknown soldier" suffering from amnesia, is recuperating in a military hospital when Sergeant Tozer arrives and recognises him.

February 18, 1917: Charley survives a U-Boat attack on the *York Castle*, the hospital ship returning him home.

March 1917: Charley meets a French Foreign Legion deserter, "Blue", and helps him hide as Blue tells him the grim story of the Battle of Verdun. Eventually, Blue escapes his pursuers, but decides to return to his unit. Charley, likewise, knows that he will soon have to return to the war.

April 1917: Charley rejoins his regiment and is reunited with old comrades Weeper and his longtime sergeant, Old Bill, as it moves up from Flanders to Ypres. There are plenty of new faces, including conscripts made unwelcome by some volunteer soldiers. There are new officers too – including, to Charley's horror, Lieutenant Snell, now company commander and a temporary captain. The company's duties vary from clearance work to road repairs and prisoner transfer – all of it dangerous, made all the more miserable by Snell's interference and fellow soldiers like the sadistic killer Grogan. Attacked by German troops, snipers, gas attacks and even from the air, Ypres is hell on Earth...

May 1917: After some weeks in reserve trenches, Charley begins a twenty mile march out of the line to billets, Snell leading them on the horse Warrior. Old Bill loses his sergeant's stripes after the march, and even life away from the Front proves harsh for those that earn Snell's wrath. But worse is to come, as Snell is ordered to take charge of a tunnel intended to undermine German guns at Messines…✢

COLLECT PART 1 OF AN EXCITING D-DAY LANDING GAME!
30th May 1981
BATTLE
15p
EVERY THURSDAY
CHARLEY'S WAR
APRIL 1917. CHARLEY BOURNE AND HIS COMRADES CARRIED SUPPLIES UP TO THE FRONT-LINE... THROUGH YPRES, A GHOSTLY, RUINED CITY SHELLED NIGHT AND DAY BY THE GERMANS. THOUSANDS OF SOLDIERS HAD ALREADY DIED IN THE YPRES SALIENT IN TWO EARLIER BATTLES. TO THE BRITISH TOMMY, YPRES WOULD ALWAYS BE KNOWN AS "WIPERS"!
CONTINUED ON NEXT PAG
Australia 45c., New Zealand 45c., Malays
©IPC Magazines Ltd., 1981

CHARLEY'S WAR

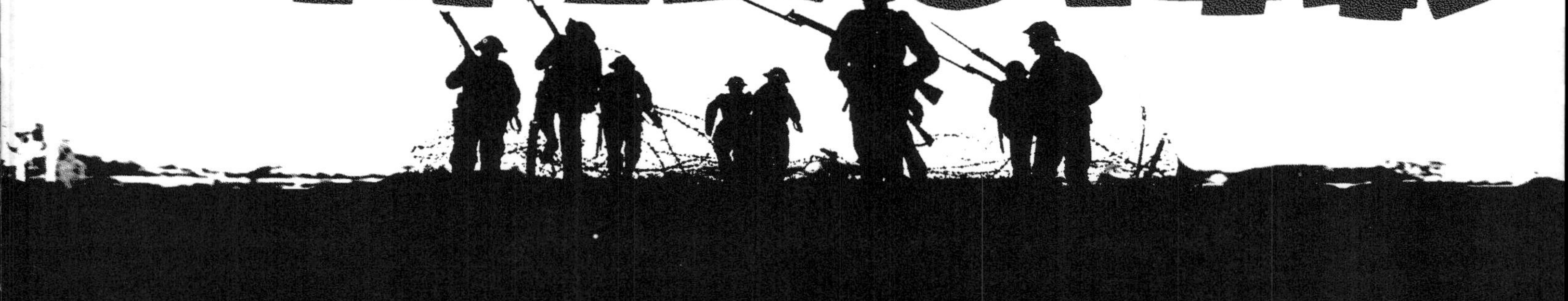

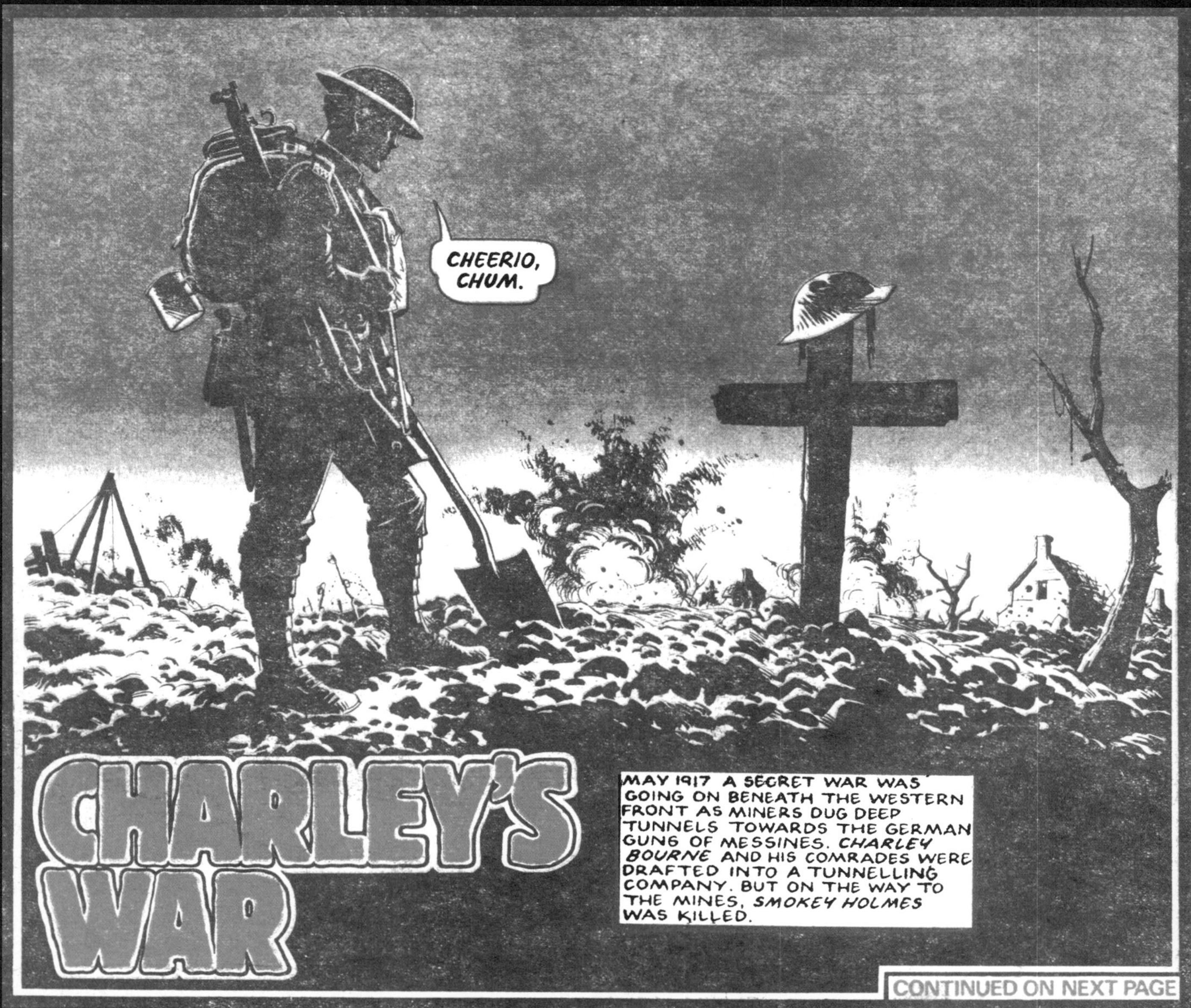
CHEERIO, CHUM.
CHARLEY'S WAR
MAY 1917 A SECRET WAR WAS GOING ON BENEATH THE WESTERN FRONT AS MINERS DUG DEEP TUNNELS TOWARDS THE GERMAN GUNS OF MESSINES. CHARLEY BOURNE AND HIS COMRADES WERE DRAFTED INTO A TUNNELLING COMPANY. BUT ON THE WAY TO THE MINES, SMOKEY HOLMES WAS KILLED.

CONTINUED ON NEXT PAGE

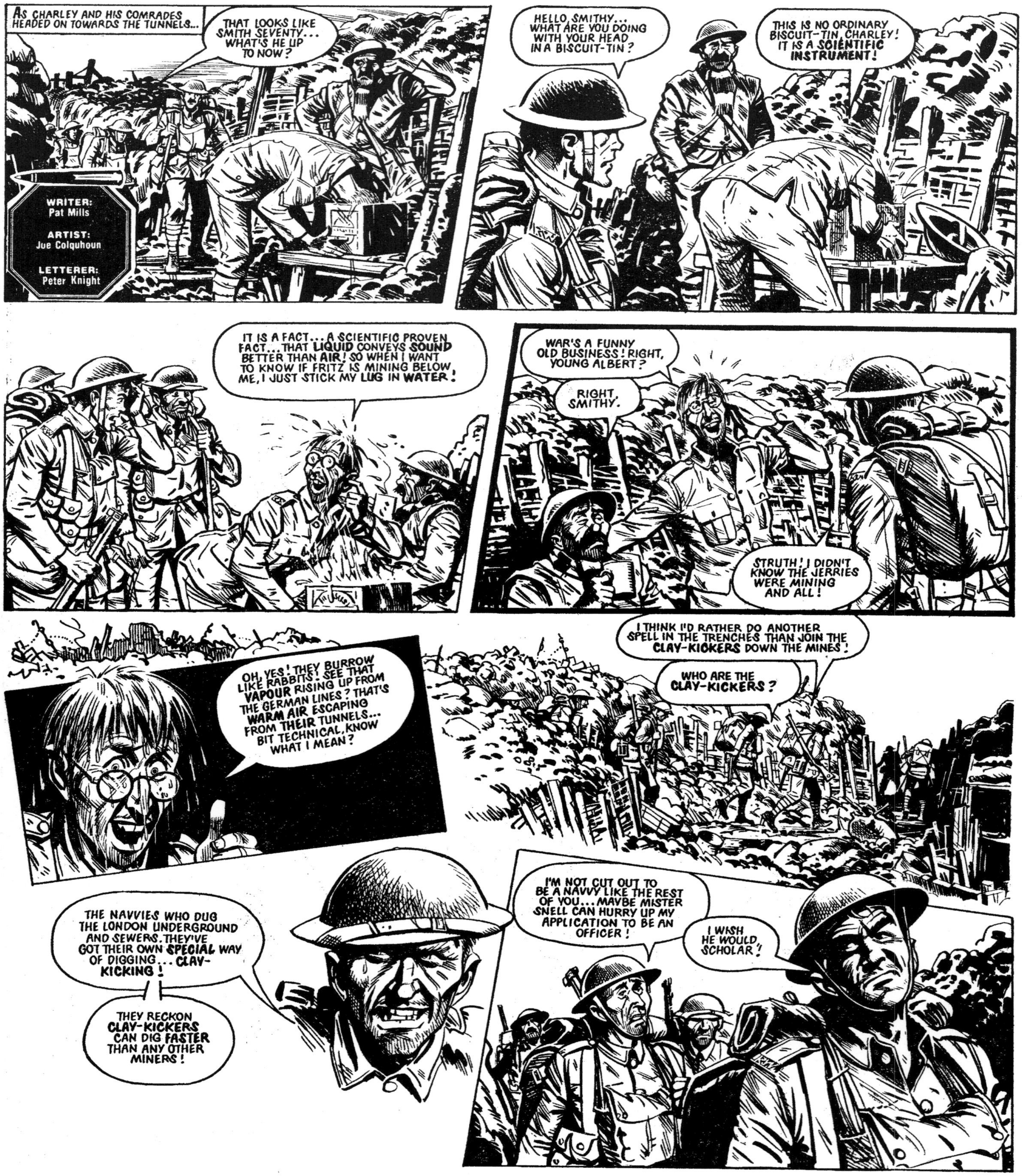
As Charley and his comrades headed on towards the tunnels...
That looks like Smith Seventy... what's he up to now?
WRITER: Pat Mills
ARTIST: Jue Colquhoun
LETTERER: Peter Knight
Hello, Smithy... what are you doing with your head in a biscuit-tin?
This is no ordinary biscuit-tin, Charley! It is a SCIENTIFIC INSTRUMENT!
It is a fact... a scientific proven fact... that LIQUID conveys SOUND better than AIR! So when I want to know if Fritz is mining below me, I just stick my LUG in WATER!
War's a funny old business! Right, young Albert?
Right, Smithy.
Struth! I didn't know the Jerries were mining and all!
Oh, yes! They burrow like rabbits! See that VAPOUR rising up from the German lines? That's WARM AIR escaping from THEIR tunnels... bit technical, know what I mean?
I think I'd rather do another spell in the trenches than join the CLAY-KICKERS down the mines!
Who are the CLAY-KICKERS?
The navvies who dug the London underground and sewers. They've got their own SPECIAL way of digging... CLAY-KICKING!
They reckon CLAY-KICKERS can dig FASTER than any other miners!
I'm not cut out to be a navvy like the rest of you... maybe Mister Snell can hurry up my application to be an officer!
I wish he would, Scholar!

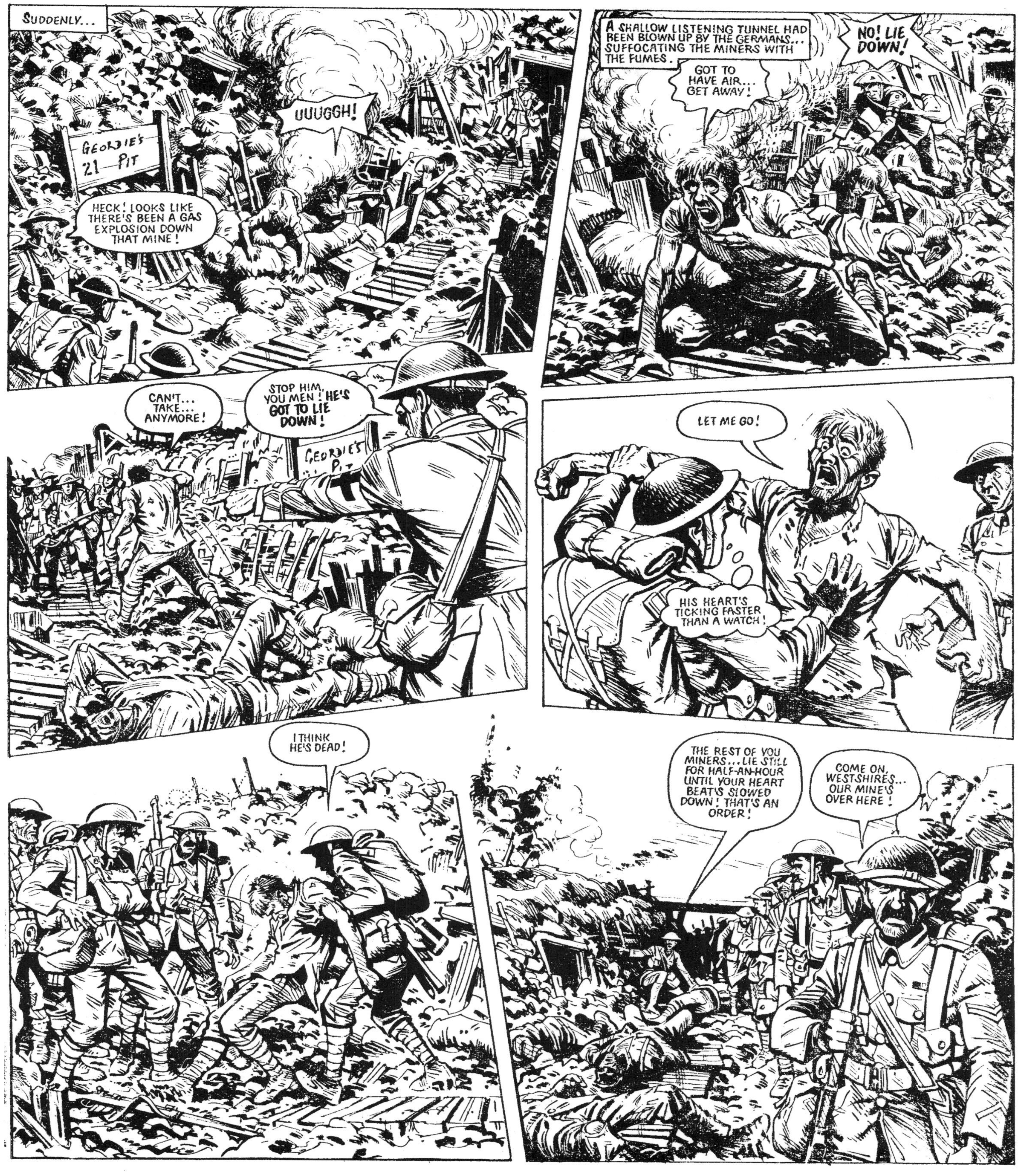
SUDDENLY...
GEORDIE'S 21 PIT
UUUGGH!
HECK! LOOKS LIKE THERE'S BEEN A GAS EXPLOSION DOWN THAT MINE!
A SHALLOW LISTENING TUNNEL HAD BEEN BLOWN UP BY THE GERMANS... SUFFOCATING THE MINERS WITH THE FUMES.
GOT TO HAVE AIR... GET AWAY!
NO! LIE DOWN!
CAN'T... TAKE... ANYMORE!
STOP HIM, YOU MEN! HE'S GOT TO LIE DOWN!
GEORDIE'S PIT
LET ME GO!
HIS HEART'S TICKING FASTER THAN A WATCH!
I THINK HE'S DEAD!
THE REST OF YOU MINERS... LIE STILL FOR HALF-AN-HOUR UNTIL YOUR HEART BEAT'S SLOWED DOWN! THAT'S AN ORDER!
COME ON, WESTSHIRES... OUR MINE'S OVER HERE!

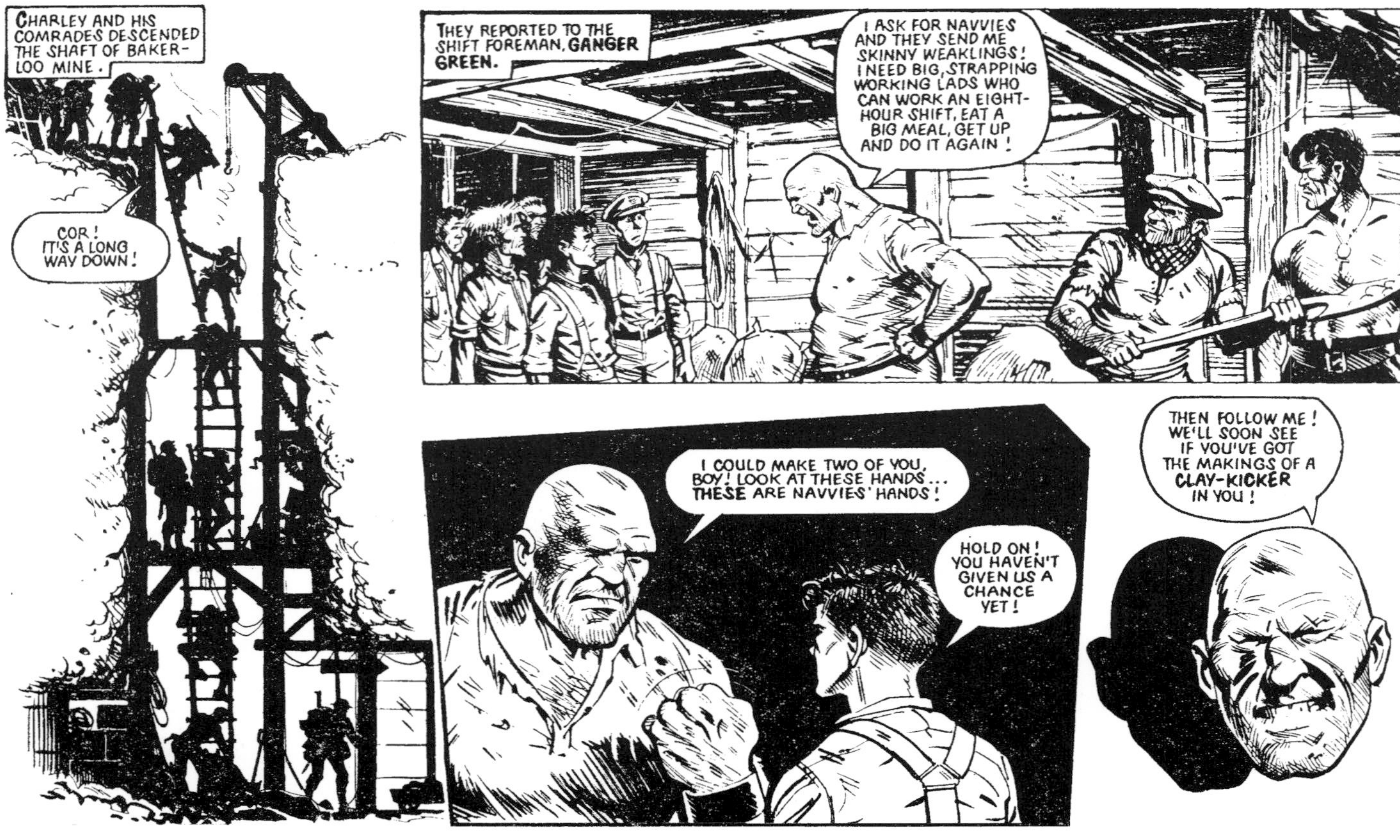
CHARLEY AND HIS COMRADES DESCENDED THE SHAFT OF BAKER-LOO MINE.
COR! IT'S A LONG WAY DOWN!
THEY REPORTED TO THE SHIFT FOREMAN, GANGER GREEN.
I ASK FOR NAVVIES AND THEY SEND ME SKINNY WEAKLINGS! I NEED BIG, STRAPPING WORKING LADS WHO CAN WORK AN EIGHT-HOUR SHIFT, EAT A BIG MEAL, GET UP AND DO IT AGAIN!
I COULD MAKE TWO OF YOU, BOY! LOOK AT THESE HANDS... THESE ARE NAVVIES' HANDS!
HOLD ON! YOU HAVEN'T GIVEN US A CHANCE YET!
THEN FOLLOW ME! WE'LL SOON SEE IF YOU'VE GOT THE MAKINGS OF A CLAY-KICKER IN YOU!

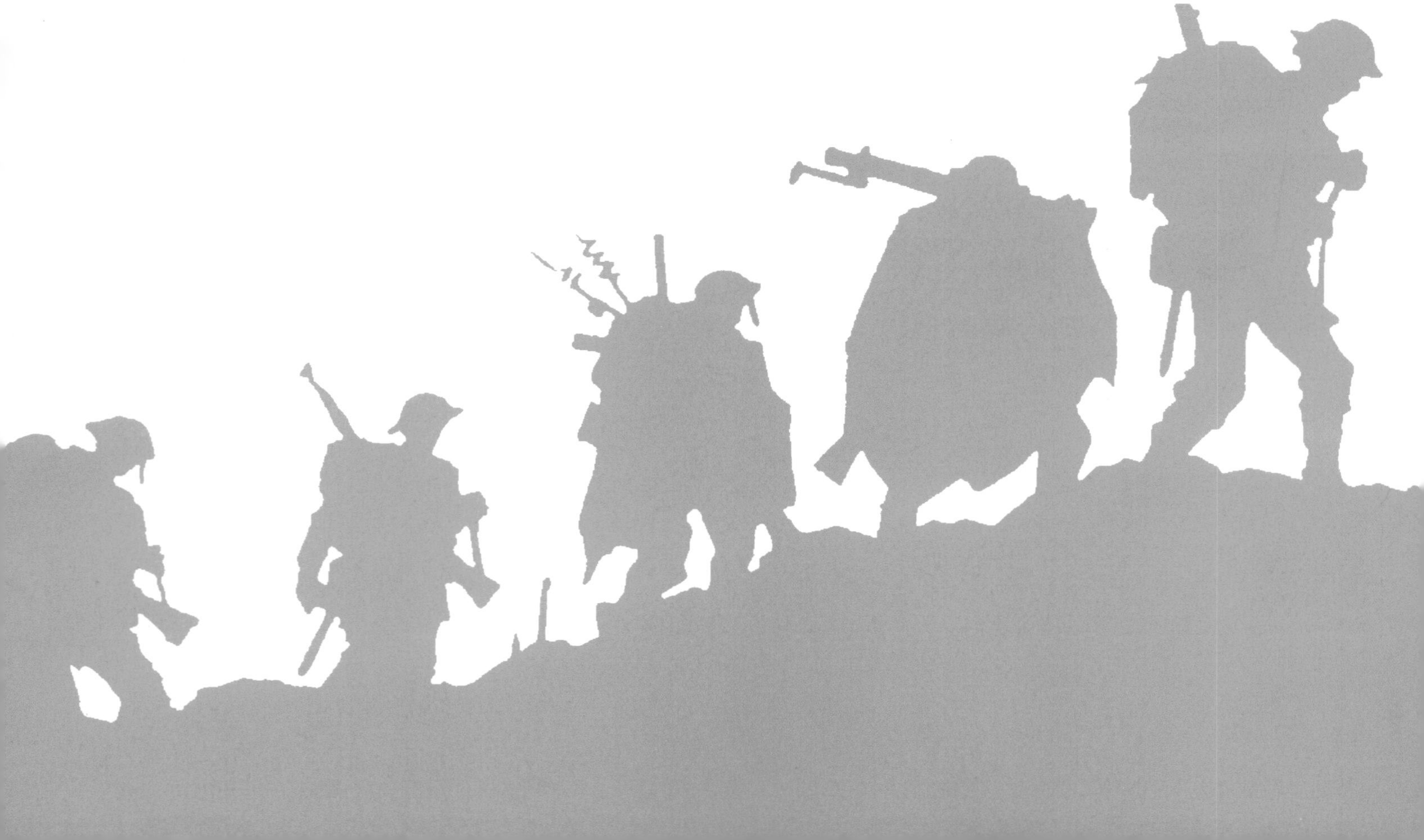

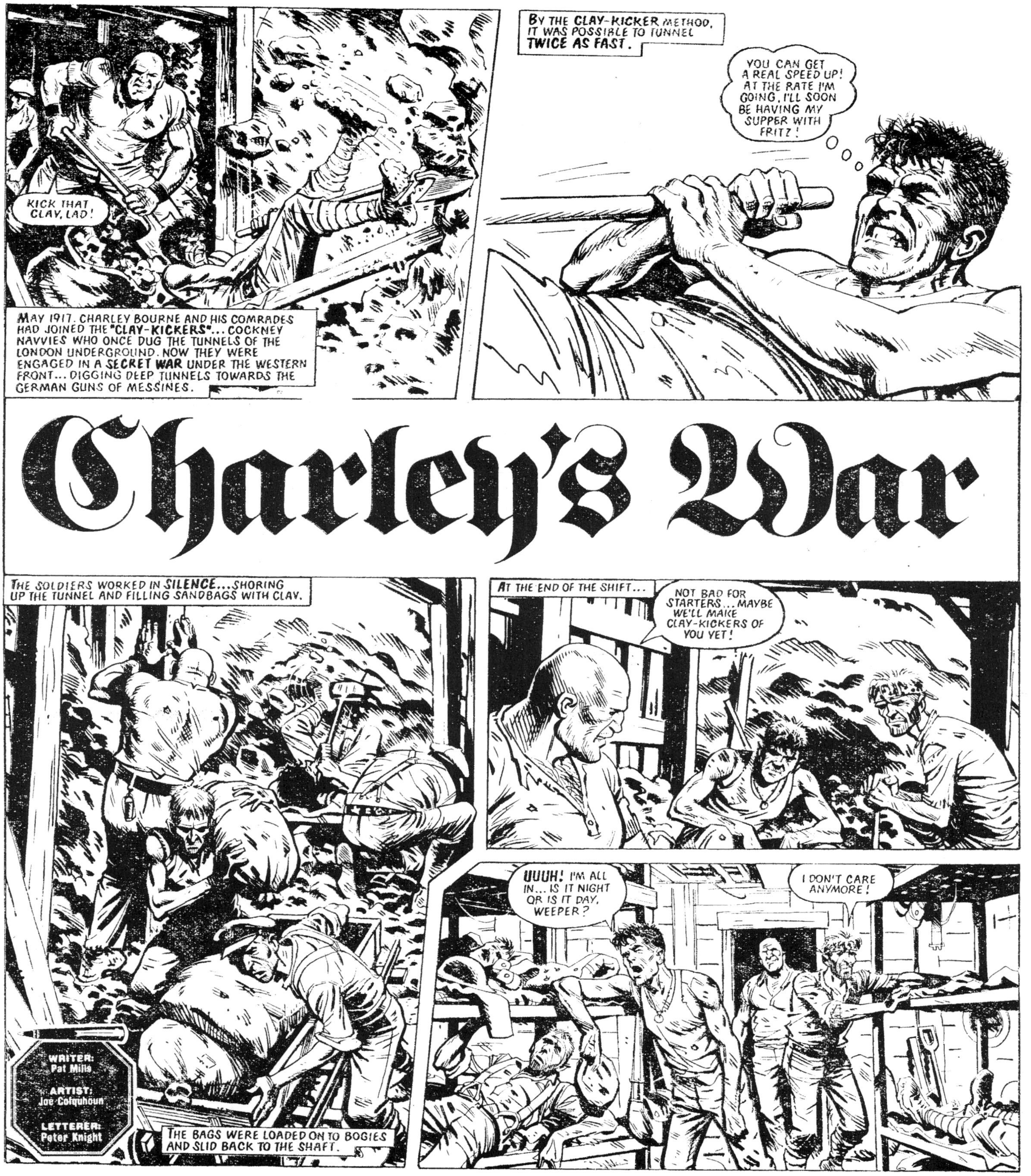

KICK THAT CLAY, LAD!
MAY 1917. CHARLEY BOURNE AND HIS COMRADES HAD JOINED THE "CLAY-KICKERS"... COCKNEY NAVVIES WHO ONCE DUG THE TUNNELS OF THE LONDON UNDERGROUND. NOW THEY WERE ENGAGED IN A SECRET WAR UNDER THE WESTERN FRONT... DIGGING DEEP TUNNELS TOWARDS THE GERMAN GUNS OF MESSINES.
BY THE CLAY-KICKER METHOD, IT WAS POSSIBLE TO TUNNEL TWICE AS FAST.
YOU CAN GET A REAL SPEED UP! AT THE RATE I'M GOING, I'LL SOON BE HAVING MY SUPPER WITH FRITZ!
Charley's War
THE SOLDIERS WORKED IN SILENCE... SHORING UP THE TUNNEL AND FILLING SANDBAGS WITH CLAY.
WRITER: Pat Mills
ARTIST: Joe Colquhoun
LETTERER: Peter Knight
THE BAGS WERE LOADED ON TO BOGIES AND SLID BACK TO THE SHAFT.
AT THE END OF THE SHIFT...
NOT BAD FOR STARTERS... MAYBE WE'LL MAKE CLAY-KICKERS OF YOU YET!
UUUH! I'M ALL IN... IS IT NIGHT OR IS IT DAY, WEEPER?
I DON'T CARE ANYMORE!

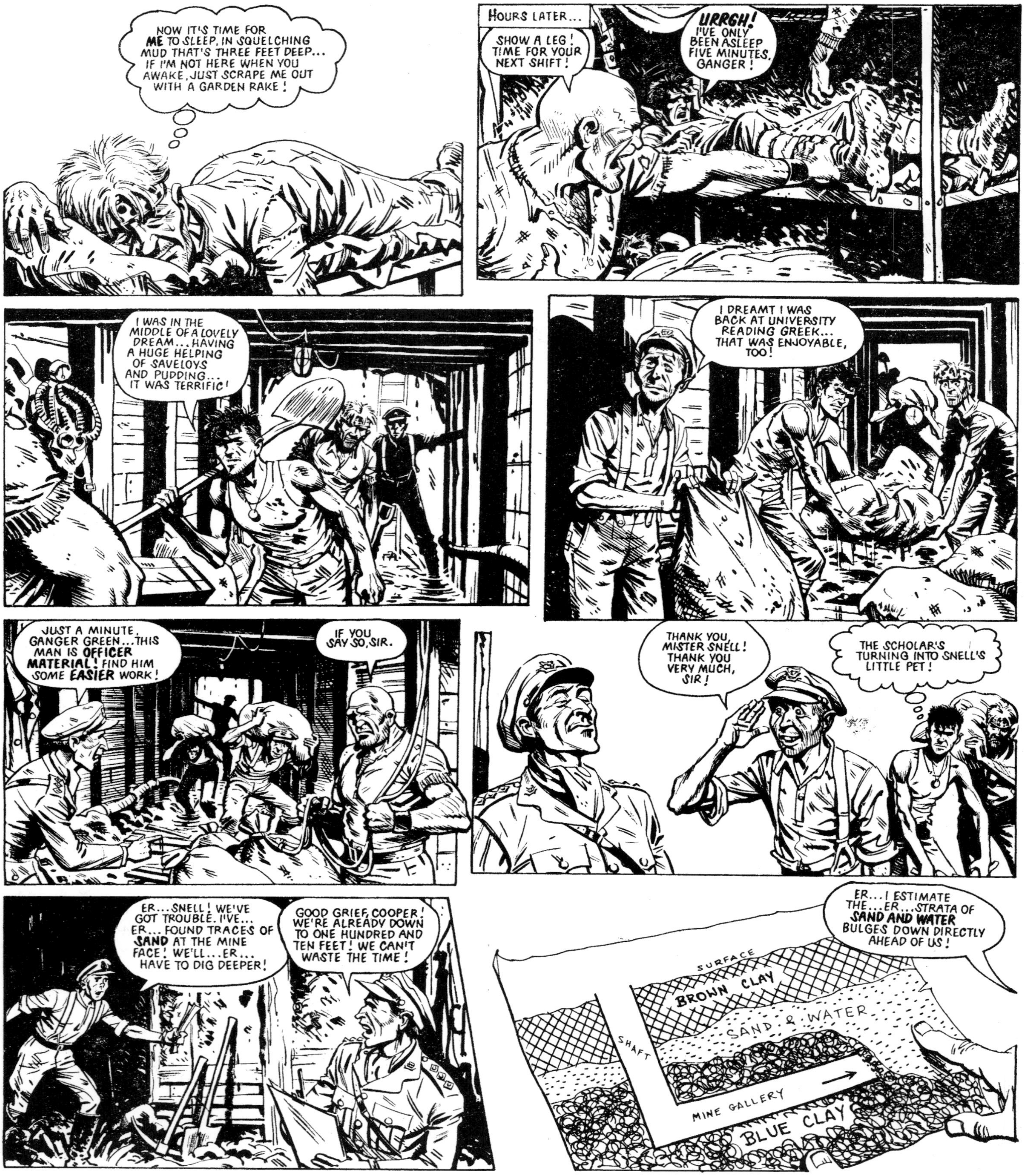
NOW IT'S TIME FOR ME TO SLEEP, IN SQUELCHING MUD THAT'S THREE FEET DEEP... IF I'M NOT HERE WHEN YOU AWAKE, JUST SCRAPE ME OUT WITH A GARDEN RAKE!
HOURS LATER...
SHOW A LEG! TIME FOR YOUR NEXT SHIFT!
URRGH! I'VE ONLY BEEN ASLEEP FIVE MINUTES, GANGER!
I WAS IN THE MIDDLE OF A LOVELY DREAM... HAVING A HUGE HELPING OF SAVELOYS AND PUDDING... IT WAS TERRIFIC!
I DREAMT I WAS BACK AT UNIVERSITY READING GREEK... THAT WAS ENJOYABLE, TOO!
JUST A MINUTE, GANGER GREEN... THIS MAN IS OFFICER MATERIAL! FIND HIM SOME EASIER WORK!
IF YOU SAY SO, SIR.
THANK YOU, MISTER SNELL! THANK YOU VERY MUCH, SIR!
THE SCHOLAR'S TURNING INTO SNELL'S LITTLE PET!
ER... SNELL! WE'VE GOT TROUBLE. I'VE... ER... FOUND TRACES OF SAND AT THE MINE FACE! WE'LL... ER... HAVE TO DIG DEEPER!
GOOD GRIEF, COOPER! WE'RE ALREADY DOWN TO ONE HUNDRED AND TEN FEET! WE CAN'T WASTE THE TIME!
ER... I ESTIMATE THE... ER... STRATA OF SAND AND WATER BULGES DOWN DIRECTLY AHEAD OF US!
SURFACE
BROWN CLAY
SAND & WATER
SHAFT
MINE GALLERY
BLUE CLAY

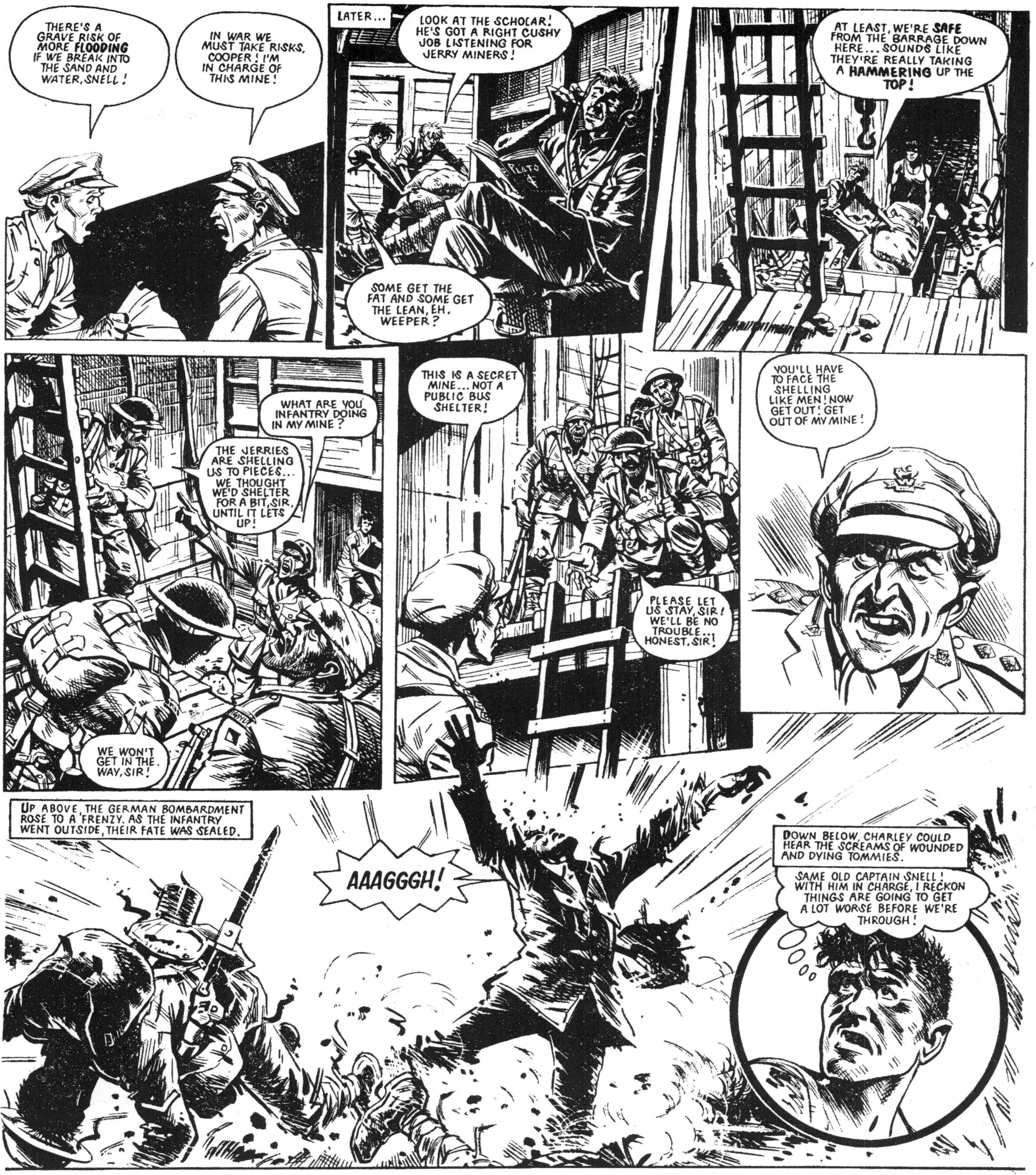
THERE'S A GRAVE RISK OF MORE **FLOODING** IF WE BREAK INTO THE SAND AND WATER, SNELL!
IN WAR WE MUST TAKE RISKS, COOPER! I'M IN CHARGE OF THIS MINE!
LATER...
LOOK AT THE SCHOLAR! HE'S GOT A RIGHT CUSHY JOB LISTENING FOR JERRY MINERS!
PLATO
SOME GET THE FAT AND SOME GET THE LEAN, EH, WEEPER?
AT LEAST, WE'RE **SAFE** FROM THE BARRAGE DOWN HERE... SOUNDS LIKE THEY'RE REALLY TAKING A **HAMMERING** UP THE **TOP**!
WHAT ARE YOU INFANTRY DOING IN MY MINE?
THE JERRIES ARE SHELLING US TO PIECES... WE THOUGHT WE'D SHELTER FOR A BIT, SIR, UNTIL IT LETS UP!
WE WON'T GET IN THE WAY, SIR!
THIS IS A SECRET MINE... NOT A PUBLIC BUS SHELTER!
PLEASE LET US STAY, SIR! WE'LL BE NO TROUBLE... HONEST, SIR!
YOU'LL HAVE TO FACE THE SHELLING LIKE MEN! NOW GET OUT! GET OUT OF MY MINE!
UP ABOVE, THE GERMAN BOMBARDMENT ROSE TO A FRENZY. AS THE INFANTRY WENT OUTSIDE, THEIR FATE WAS SEALED.
AAAGGGH!
DOWN BELOW, CHARLEY COULD HEAR THE SCREAMS OF WOUNDED AND DYING TOMMIES.
SAME OLD CAPTAIN SNELL! WITH HIM IN CHARGE, I RECKON THINGS ARE GOING TO GET A LOT WORSE BEFORE WE'RE THROUGH!

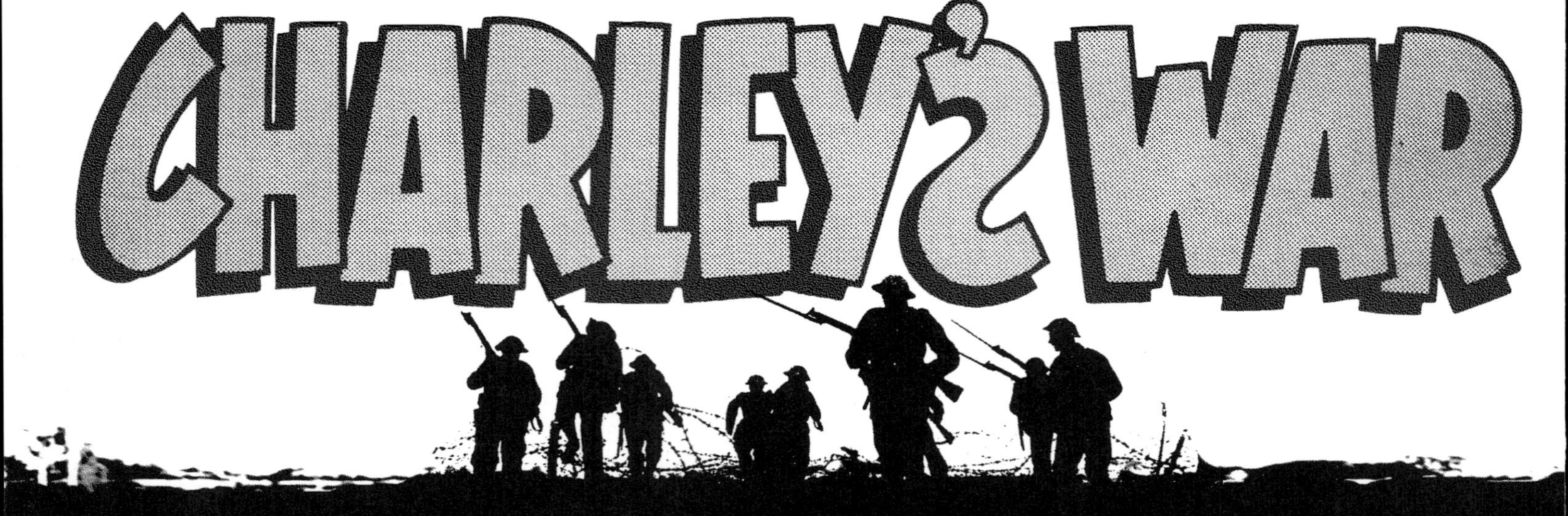
CHARLEY'S WAR

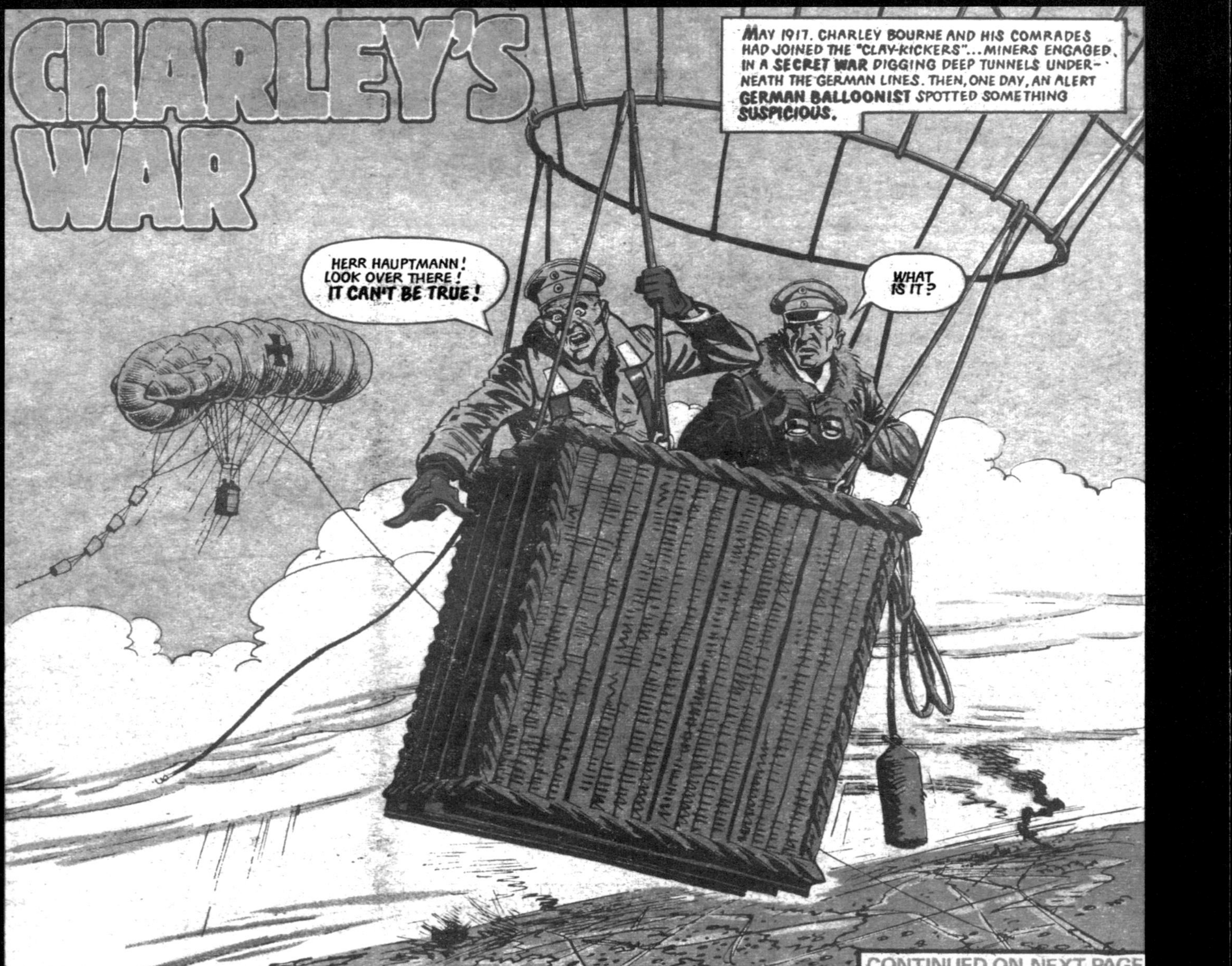
CHARLEY'S WAR
MAY 1917. CHARLEY BOURNE AND HIS COMRADES HAD JOINED THE "CLAY-KICKERS"... MINERS ENGAGED IN A SECRET WAR DIGGING DEEP TUNNELS UNDERNEATH THE GERMAN LINES. THEN, ONE DAY, AN ALERT GERMAN BALLOONIST SPOTTED SOMETHING SUSPICIOUS.
HERR HAUPTMANN! LOOK OVER THERE! IT CAN'T BE TRUE!
WHAT IS IT?

CONTINUED ON NEXT PAGE

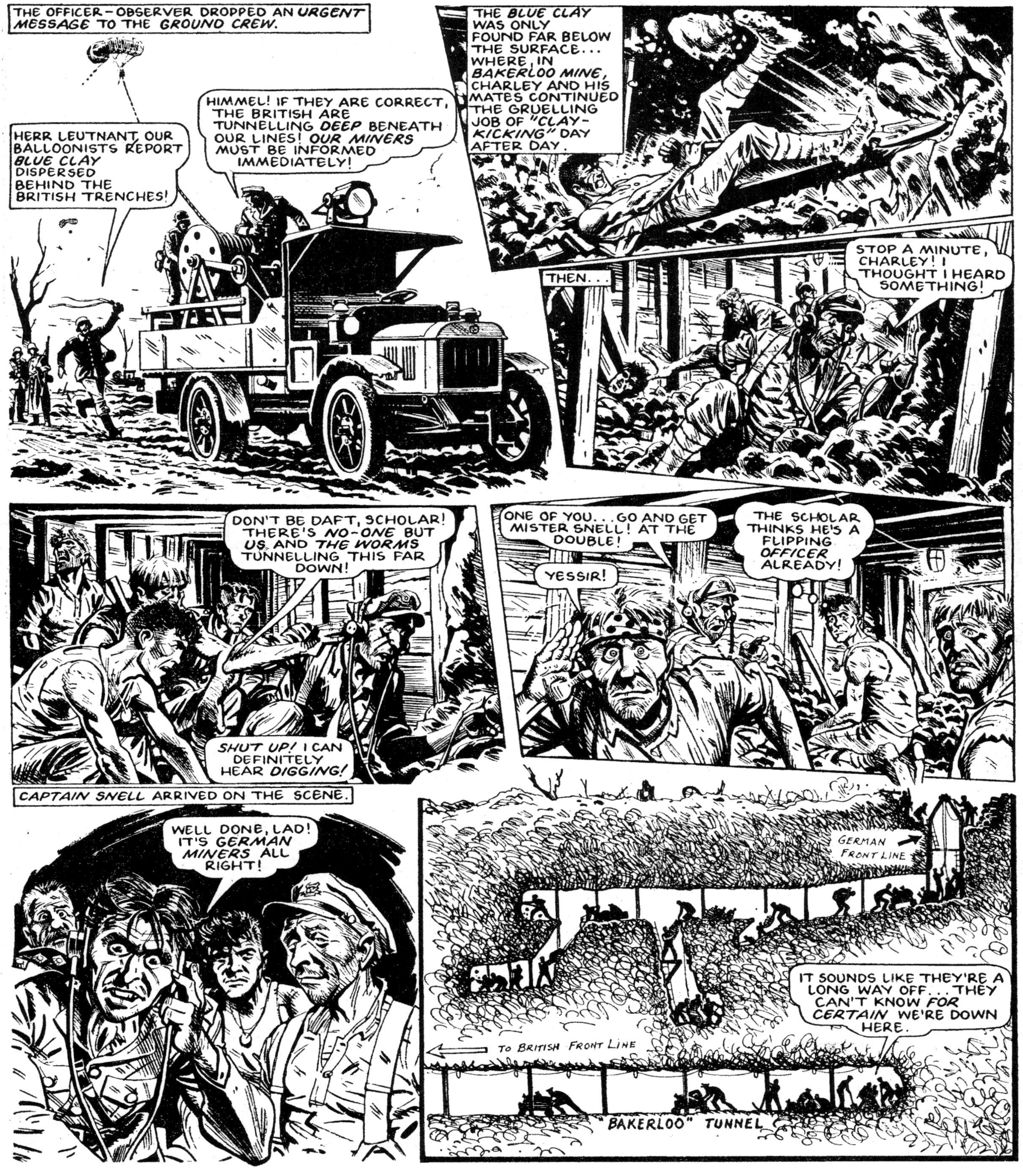
THE OFFICER-OBSERVER DROPPED AN URGENT MESSAGE TO THE GROUND CREW.
HERR LEUTNANT, OUR BALLOONISTS REPORT BLUE CLAY DISPERSED BEHIND THE BRITISH TRENCHES!
HIMMEL! IF THEY ARE CORRECT, THE BRITISH ARE TUNNELLING DEEP BENEATH OUR LINES! OUR MINERS MUST BE INFORMED IMMEDIATELY!
THE BLUE CLAY WAS ONLY FOUND FAR BELOW THE SURFACE... WHERE, IN BAKERLOO MINE, CHARLEY AND HIS MATES CONTINUED THE GRUELLING JOB OF "CLAY-KICKING" DAY AFTER DAY.
THEN...
STOP A MINUTE, CHARLEY! I THOUGHT I HEARD SOMETHING!
DON'T BE DAFT, SCHOLAR! THERE'S NO-ONE BUT US AND THE WORMS TUNNELLING THIS FAR DOWN!
SHUT UP! I CAN DEFINITELY HEAR DIGGING!
ONE OF YOU... GO AND GET MISTER SNELL! AT THE DOUBLE!
YESSIR!
THE SCHOLAR THINKS HE'S A FLIPPING OFFICER ALREADY!
CAPTAIN SNELL ARRIVED ON THE SCENE.
WELL DONE, LAD! IT'S GERMAN MINERS ALL RIGHT!
GERMAN FRONT LINE
TO BRITISH FRONT LINE
IT SOUNDS LIKE THEY'RE A LONG WAY OFF... THEY CAN'T KNOW FOR CERTAIN WE'RE DOWN HERE.
"BAKERLOO" TUNNEL

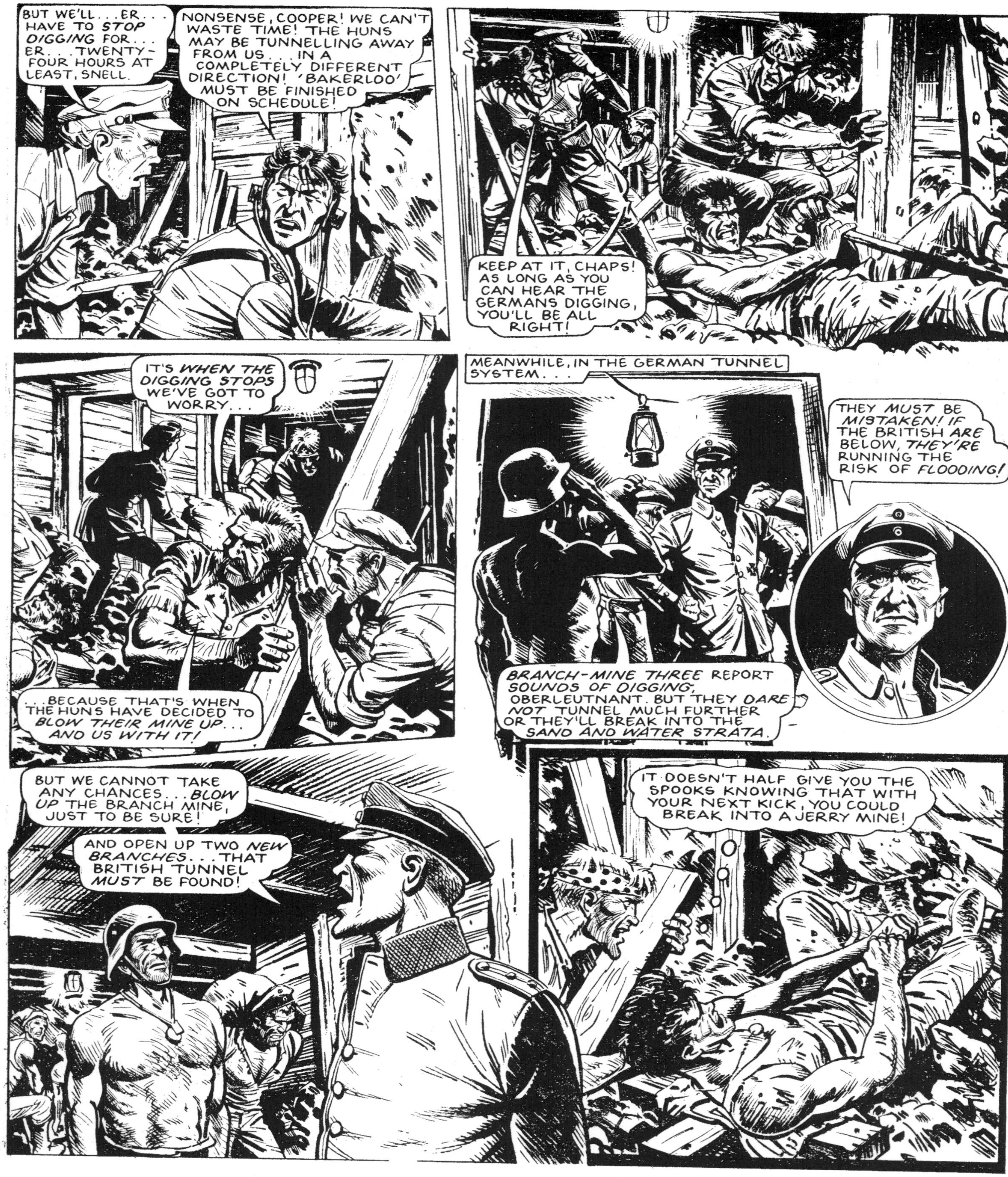

BUT WE'LL... ER... HAVE TO STOP DIGGING FOR... ER... TWENTY-FOUR HOURS AT LEAST, SNELL.
NONSENSE, COOPER! WE CAN'T WASTE TIME! THE HUNS MAY BE TUNNELLING AWAY FROM US... IN A COMPLETELY DIFFERENT DIRECTION! 'BAKERLOO' MUST BE FINISHED ON SCHEDULE!
KEEP AT IT, CHAPS! AS LONG AS YOU CAN HEAR THE GERMANS DIGGING, YOU'LL BE ALL RIGHT!
IT'S WHEN THE DIGGING STOPS WE'VE GOT TO WORRY...
...BECAUSE THAT'S WHEN THE HUNS HAVE DECIDED TO BLOW THEIR MINE UP... AND US WITH IT!
MEANWHILE, IN THE GERMAN TUNNEL SYSTEM...
BRANCH-MINE THREE REPORT SOUNDS OF DIGGING, OBERLEUTNANT. BUT THEY DARE NOT TUNNEL MUCH FURTHER OR THEY'LL BREAK INTO THE SAND AND WATER STRATA.
THEY MUST BE MISTAKEN! IF THE BRITISH ARE BELOW, THEY'RE RUNNING THE RISK OF FLOODING!
BUT WE CANNOT TAKE ANY CHANCES... BLOW UP THE BRANCH MINE, JUST TO BE SURE!
AND OPEN UP TWO NEW BRANCHES... THAT BRITISH TUNNEL MUST BE FOUND!
IT DOESN'T HALF GIVE YOU THE SPOOKS KNOWING THAT WITH YOUR NEXT KICK, YOU COULD BREAK INTO A JERRY MINE!

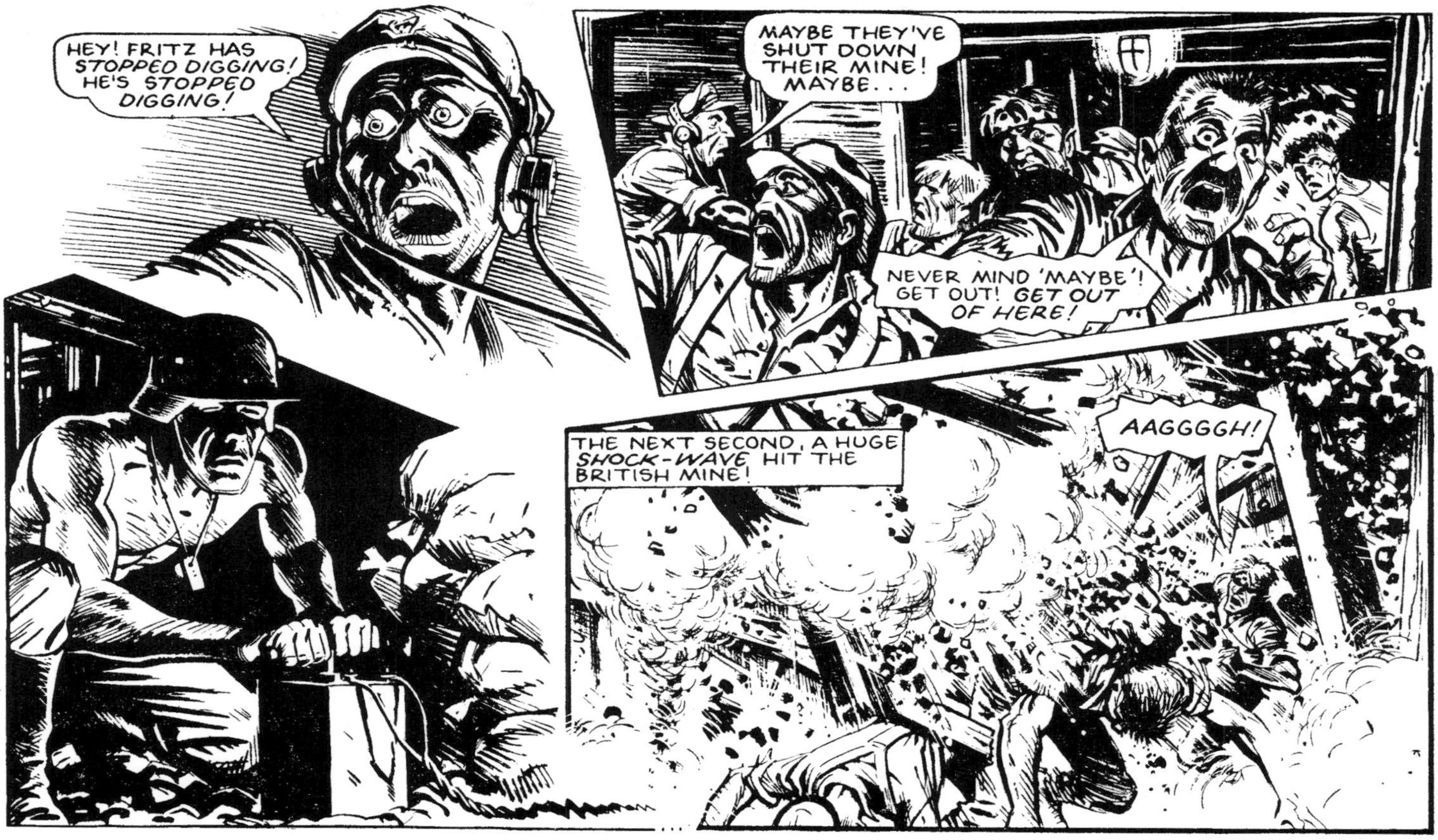
HEY! FRITZ HAS STOPPED DIGGING! HE'S STOPPED DIGGING!
MAYBE THEY'VE SHUT DOWN THEIR MINE! MAYBE...
NEVER MIND 'MAYBE'! GET OUT! GET OUT OF HERE!
THE NEXT SECOND, A HUGE SHOCK-WAVE HIT THE BRITISH MINE!
AAGGGGH!

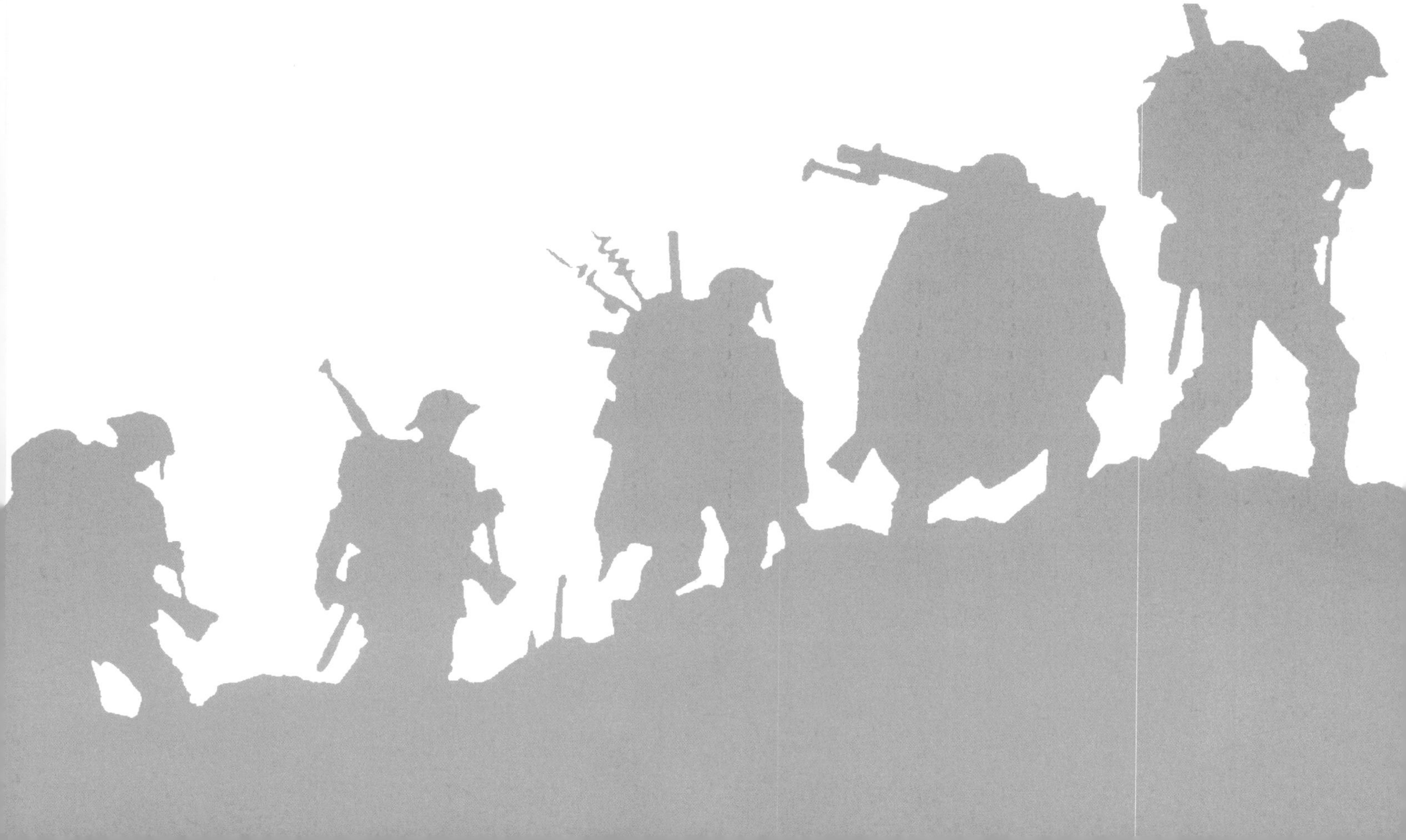

Charley's War

MAY 1917. DEEP BENEATH THE WESTERN FRONT, A SECRET TUNNELLING WAR WAS GOING ON. THE GERMANS HAD DELIBERATELY BLOWN UP ONE OF THEIR OWN MINES, CAUSING A SHOCK~WAVE WHICH HIT CHARLEY BOURNE'S TUNNEL.

THE WHOLE MINE'S CAVING IN...!

AAHHHHH!

IN THE SUFFOCATING DARKNESS, THE SURVIVORS TRIED TO FIND EACH OTHER.

IT'S DARKER THAN A CINEMA IN HERE... WHO'S THIS?

ME, YOU FOOL! EARWIG!

WRITER:
Pat Mills

ARTIST:
Joe Colquhoun

LETTERER:
Mike Peters

THE SURVIVORS WERE CHARLEY, EARWIG, BUDGIE BROWN, THE SCHOLAR AND WEEPER.

WEEPER'S UNCONSCIOUS... SAPPER DOWD AND SAPPER KEARNEY ARE DEAD! SO WE'RE ON OUR OWN!

WISH WE HAD A LIGHT.

THE WATER LEVEL'S RISING! WHAT SHALL WE DO?

YOU'RE MEANT TO BE OFFICER MATERIAL, SCHOLAR... YOU TELL US. YOU MAKE A DECISION.

ER..., WELL. ER...

PERHAPS WE SHOULD TRY AND DIG THROUGH. WHAT DO YOU THINK, CHARLEY?

NO! IF WE DO, WE'LL JUST LET MORE WATER IN. WE'LL HAVE TO BLOCK IT AS BEST WE CAN AND SIT TIGHT TILL HELP ARRIVES.

IF HELP ARRIVES!

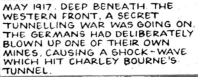

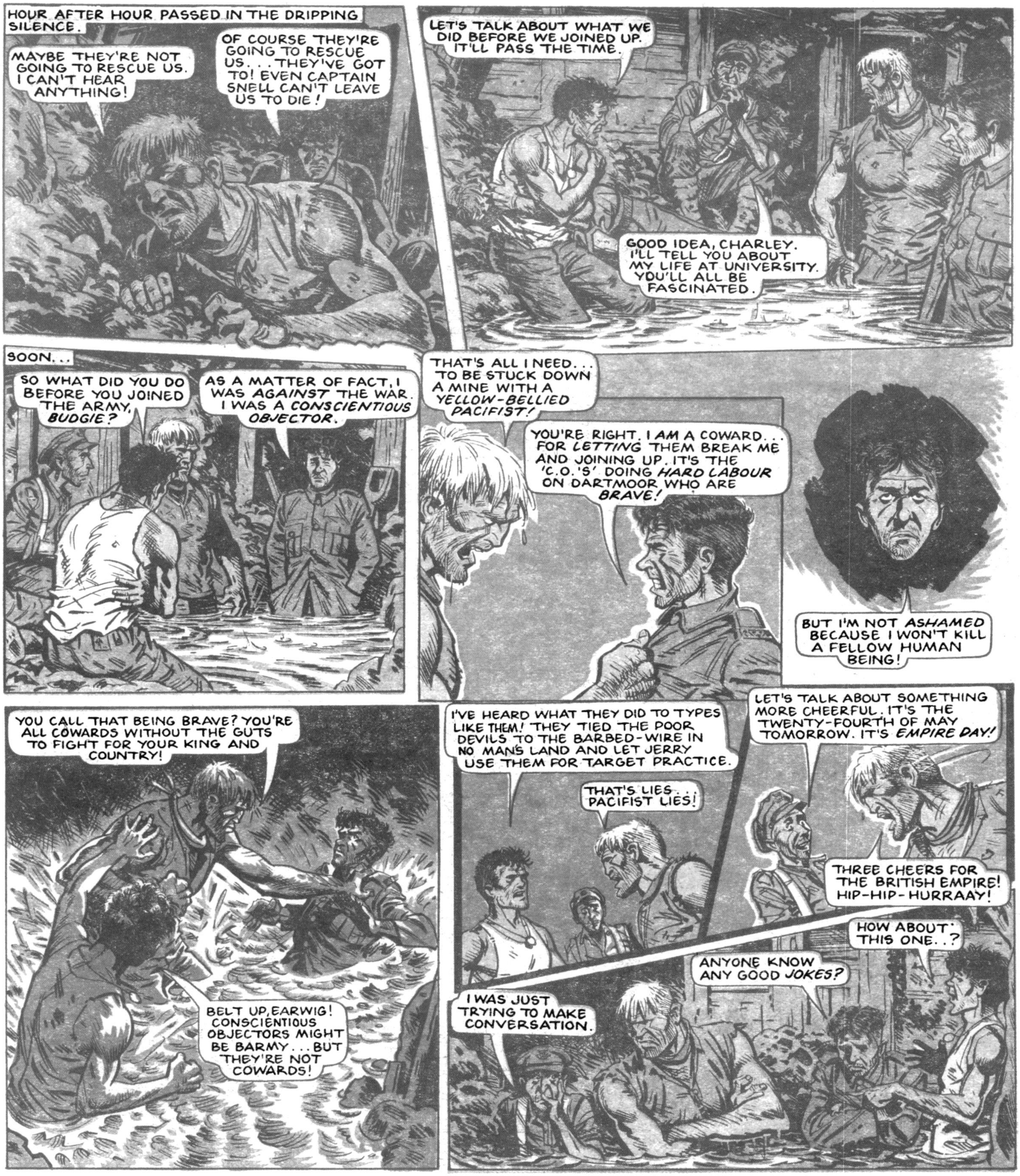

HOUR AFTER HOUR PASSED IN THE DRIPPING SILENCE.
MAYBE THEY'RE NOT GOING TO RESCUE US. I CAN'T HEAR ANYTHING!
OF COURSE THEY'RE GOING TO RESCUE US. . . THEY'VE GOT TO! EVEN CAPTAIN SNELL CAN'T LEAVE US TO DIE!
LET'S TALK ABOUT WHAT WE DID BEFORE WE JOINED UP. IT'LL PASS THE TIME.
GOOD IDEA, CHARLEY. I'LL TELL YOU ABOUT MY LIFE AT UNIVERSITY. YOU'LL ALL BE FASCINATED.
SOON. . .
SO WHAT DID YOU DO BEFORE YOU JOINED THE ARMY, BUDGIE?
AS A MATTER OF FACT, I WAS AGAINST THE WAR. I WAS A CONSCIENTIOUS OBJECTOR.
THAT'S ALL I NEED. . . TO BE STUCK DOWN A MINE WITH A YELLOW-BELLIED PACIFIST!
YOU'RE RIGHT. I AM A COWARD. . . FOR LETTING THEM BREAK ME AND JOINING UP. IT'S THE 'C.O.'S' DOING HARD LABOUR ON DARTMOOR WHO ARE BRAVE!
BUT I'M NOT ASHAMED BECAUSE I WON'T KILL A FELLOW HUMAN BEING!
YOU CALL THAT BEING BRAVE? YOU'RE ALL COWARDS WITHOUT THE GUTS TO FIGHT FOR YOUR KING AND COUNTRY!
BELT UP, EARWIG! CONSCIENTIOUS OBJECTORS MIGHT BE BARMY . . . BUT THEY'RE NOT COWARDS!
I'VE HEARD WHAT THEY DID TO TYPES LIKE THEM! THEY TIED THE POOR DEVILS TO THE BARBED-WIRE IN NO MAN'S LAND AND LET JERRY USE THEM FOR TARGET PRACTICE.
THAT'S LIES. . . PACIFIST LIES!
LET'S TALK ABOUT SOMETHING MORE CHEERFUL. IT'S THE TWENTY-FOURTH OF MAY TOMORROW. IT'S EMPIRE DAY!
THREE CHEERS FOR THE BRITISH EMPIRE! HIP-HIP-HURRAAY!
I WAS JUST TRYING TO MAKE CONVERSATION.
ANYONE KNOW ANY GOOD JOKES?
HOW ABOUT THIS ONE. .?

THIS TOMMY'S ABOUT TO GO DOWN A CAPTURED JERRY DUG-OUT. WITH A HAND-GRENADE IN HIS HAND, HE SHOUTS DOWN THE STAIRS... 'ANYBODY THERE?'

UP COMES THE REPLY 'NEIN!'... 'NINE, EH?' SAYS 'TOMMY. 'WELL, SHARE THIS AMONG YOU!' AND CHUCKS THE GRENADE DOWN THE STEPS!

HA! HA! I SAY... THAT'S NOT BAD, CHARLEY.

THE WATER LEVEL'S STILL RISING!

WEEPER'S COMING ROUND!

LET'S HAVE A SING-SONG...

I'M C-C-C-COLD, CHARLEY!

OH, THE MOON SHINES BRIGHT ON CHARLIE CHAPLIN, HIS BOOTS ARE CRACKING FOR WANT OF BLACKING, AND HIS BAGGY TROUSERS THEY WANT MENDING, BEFORE WE SEND HIM TO THE DARDANELLES!

SHUT UP! SHUT UP! YOU'RE SINGING AND CRACKING JOKES AND WE'RE GOING TO DIE! CAN'T YOU GET IT THROUGH YOUR THICK HEADS? WE'RE GOING TO DIE!

I DON'T WANT TO DIE! I DON'T WANT TO DIE! I DON'T WANT TO DIE!

CHARLEY'S WAR

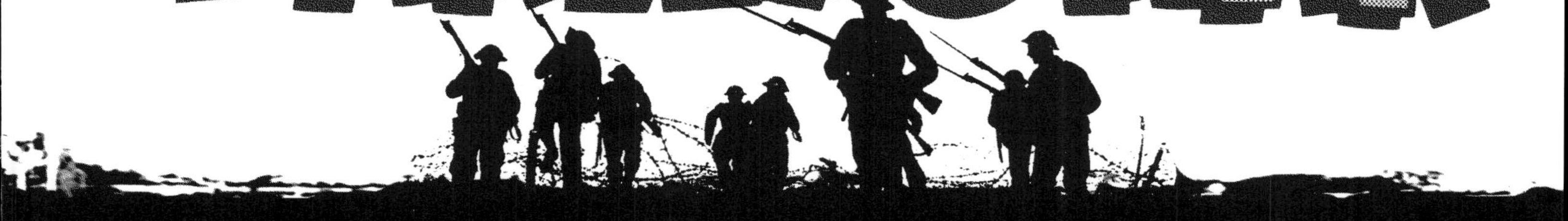

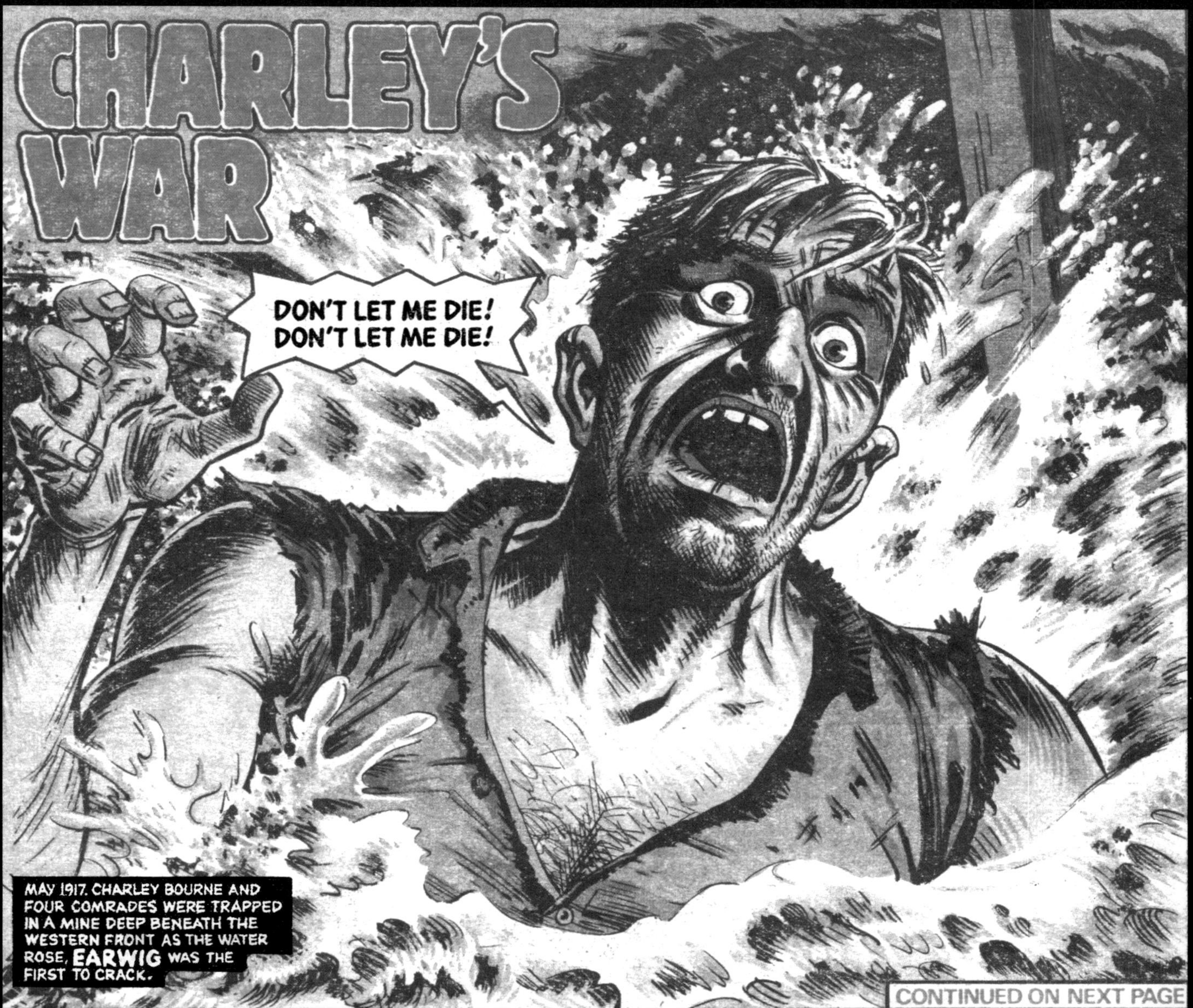
CHARLEY'S WAR
DON'T LET ME DIE! DON'T LET ME DIE!
MAY 1917. CHARLEY BOURNE AND FOUR COMRADES WERE TRAPPED IN A MINE DEEP BENEATH THE WESTERN FRONT AS THE WATER ROSE, EARWIG WAS THE FIRST TO CRACK.

CONTINUED ON NEXT PAGE

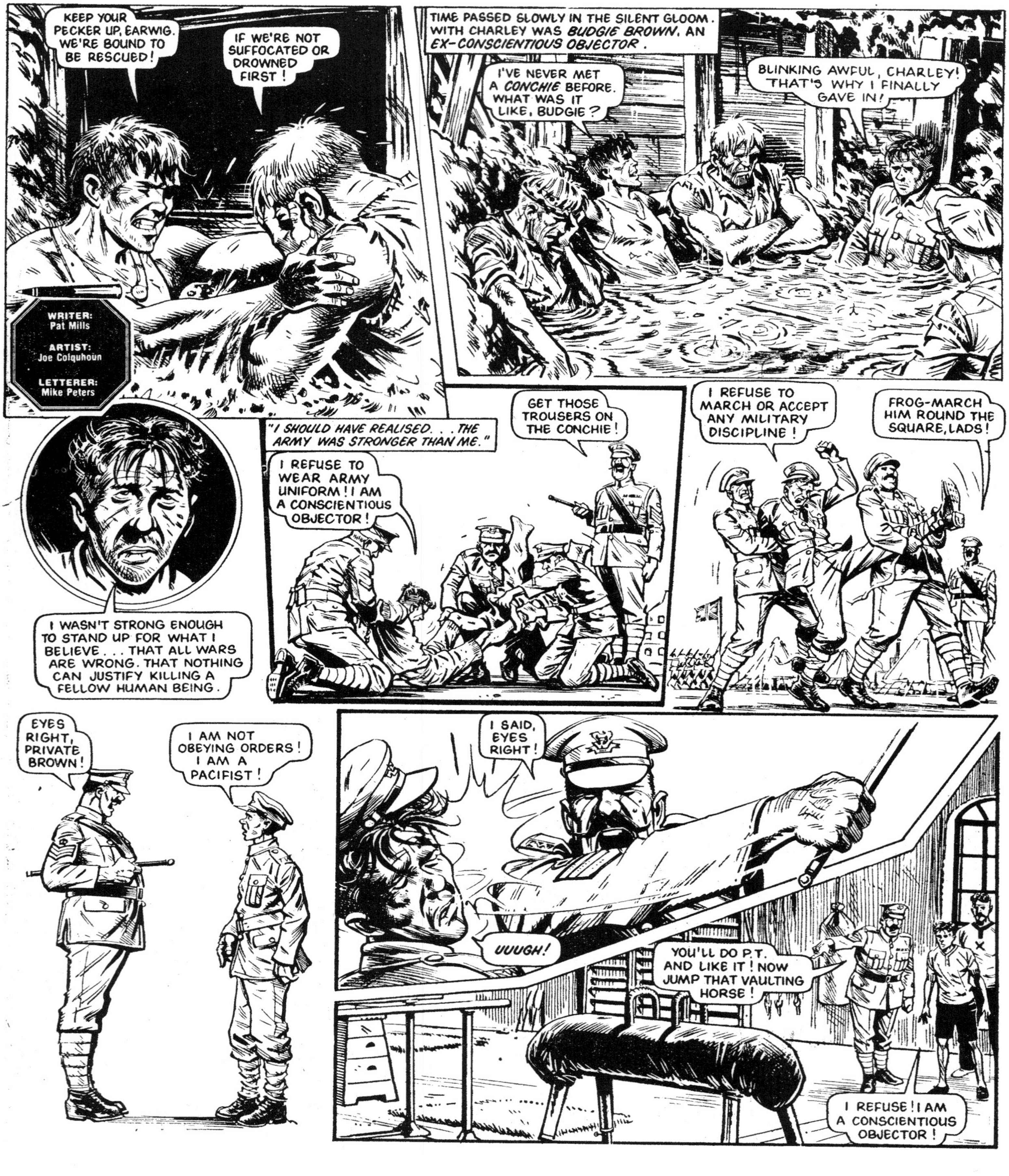
KEEP YOUR PECKER UP, EARWIG. WE'RE BOUND TO BE RESCUED!
IF WE'RE NOT SUFFOCATED OR DROWNED FIRST!
WRITER: Pat Mills
ARTIST: Joe Colquhoun
LETTERER: Mike Peters
TIME PASSED SLOWLY IN THE SILENT GLOOM. WITH CHARLEY WAS BUDGIE BROWN, AN EX-CONSCIENTIOUS OBJECTOR.
I'VE NEVER MET A CONCHIE BEFORE. WHAT WAS IT LIKE, BUDGIE?
BLINKING AWFUL, CHARLEY! THAT'S WHY I FINALLY GAVE IN!
I WASN'T STRONG ENOUGH TO STAND UP FOR WHAT I BELIEVE... THAT ALL WARS ARE WRONG. THAT NOTHING CAN JUSTIFY KILLING A FELLOW HUMAN BEING.
"I SHOULD HAVE REALISED... THE ARMY WAS STRONGER THAN ME."
I REFUSE TO WEAR ARMY UNIFORM! I AM A CONSCIENTIOUS OBJECTOR!
GET THOSE TROUSERS ON THE CONCHIE!
I REFUSE TO MARCH OR ACCEPT ANY MILITARY DISCIPLINE!
FROG-MARCH HIM ROUND THE SQUARE, LADS!
EYES RIGHT, PRIVATE BROWN!
I AM NOT OBEYING ORDERS! I AM A PACIFIST!
I SAID, EYES RIGHT!
UUUGH!
YOU'LL DO P.T. AND LIKE IT! NOW JUMP THAT VAULTING HORSE!
I REFUSE! I AM A CONSCIENTIOUS OBJECTOR!

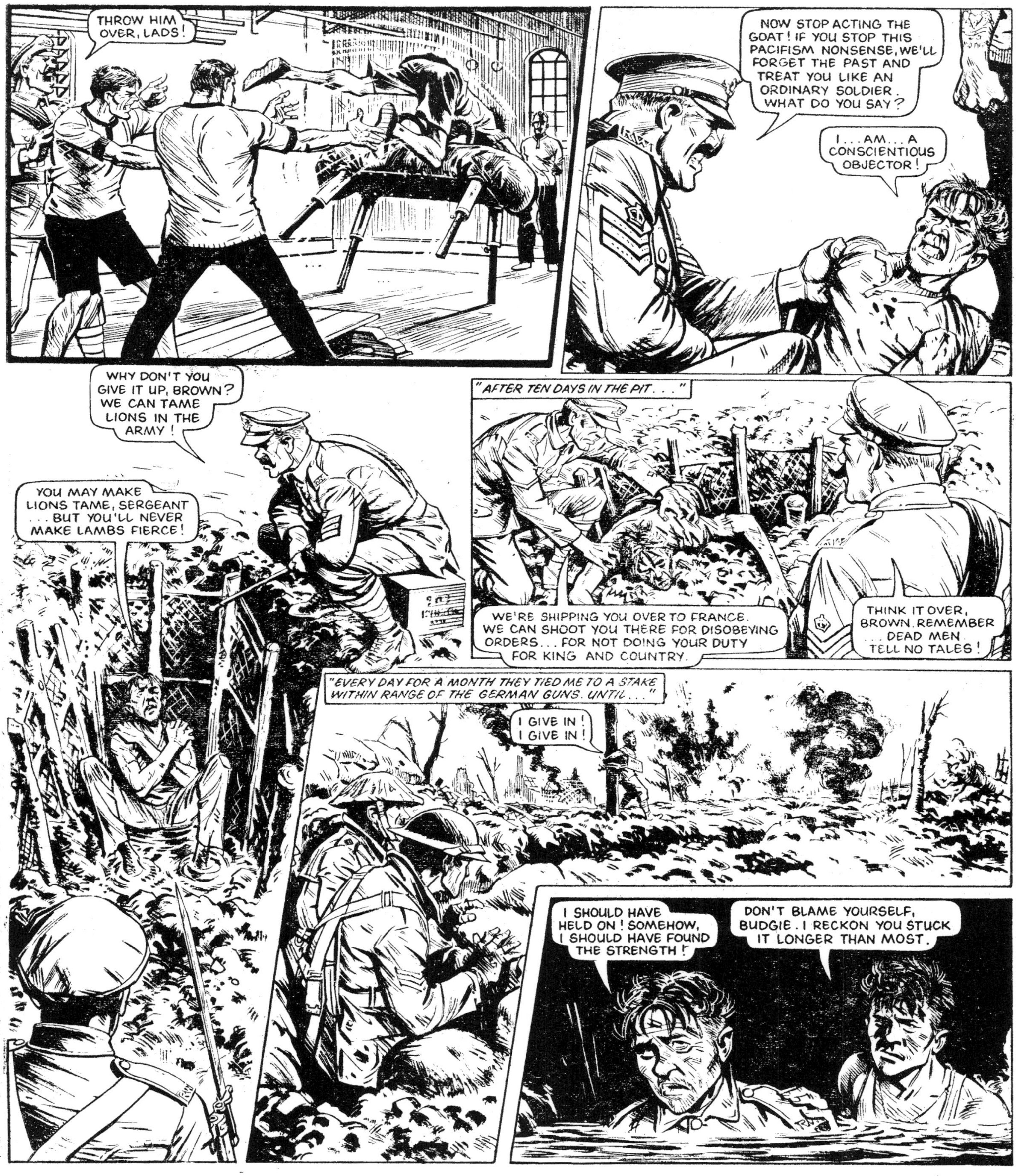
THROW HIM OVER, LADS!
NOW STOP ACTING THE GOAT! IF YOU STOP THIS PACIFISM NONSENSE, WE'LL FORGET THE PAST AND TREAT YOU LIKE AN ORDINARY SOLDIER. WHAT DO YOU SAY?
I... AM... A CONSCIENTIOUS OBJECTOR!
WHY DON'T YOU GIVE IT UP, BROWN? WE CAN TAME LIONS IN THE ARMY!
YOU MAY MAKE LIONS TAME, SERGEANT ... BUT YOU'LL NEVER MAKE LAMBS FIERCE!
"AFTER TEN DAYS IN THE PIT..."
WE'RE SHIPPING YOU OVER TO FRANCE. WE CAN SHOOT YOU THERE FOR DISOBEYING ORDERS... FOR NOT DOING YOUR DUTY FOR KING AND COUNTRY.
THINK IT OVER, BROWN. REMEMBER ... DEAD MEN TELL NO TALES!
"EVERY DAY FOR A MONTH THEY TIED ME TO A STAKE WITHIN RANGE OF THE GERMAN GUNS. UNTIL..."
I GIVE IN! I GIVE IN!
I SHOULD HAVE HELD ON! SOMEHOW, I SHOULD HAVE FOUND THE STRENGTH!
DON'T BLAME YOURSELF, BUDGIE. I RECKON YOU STUCK IT LONGER THAN MOST.

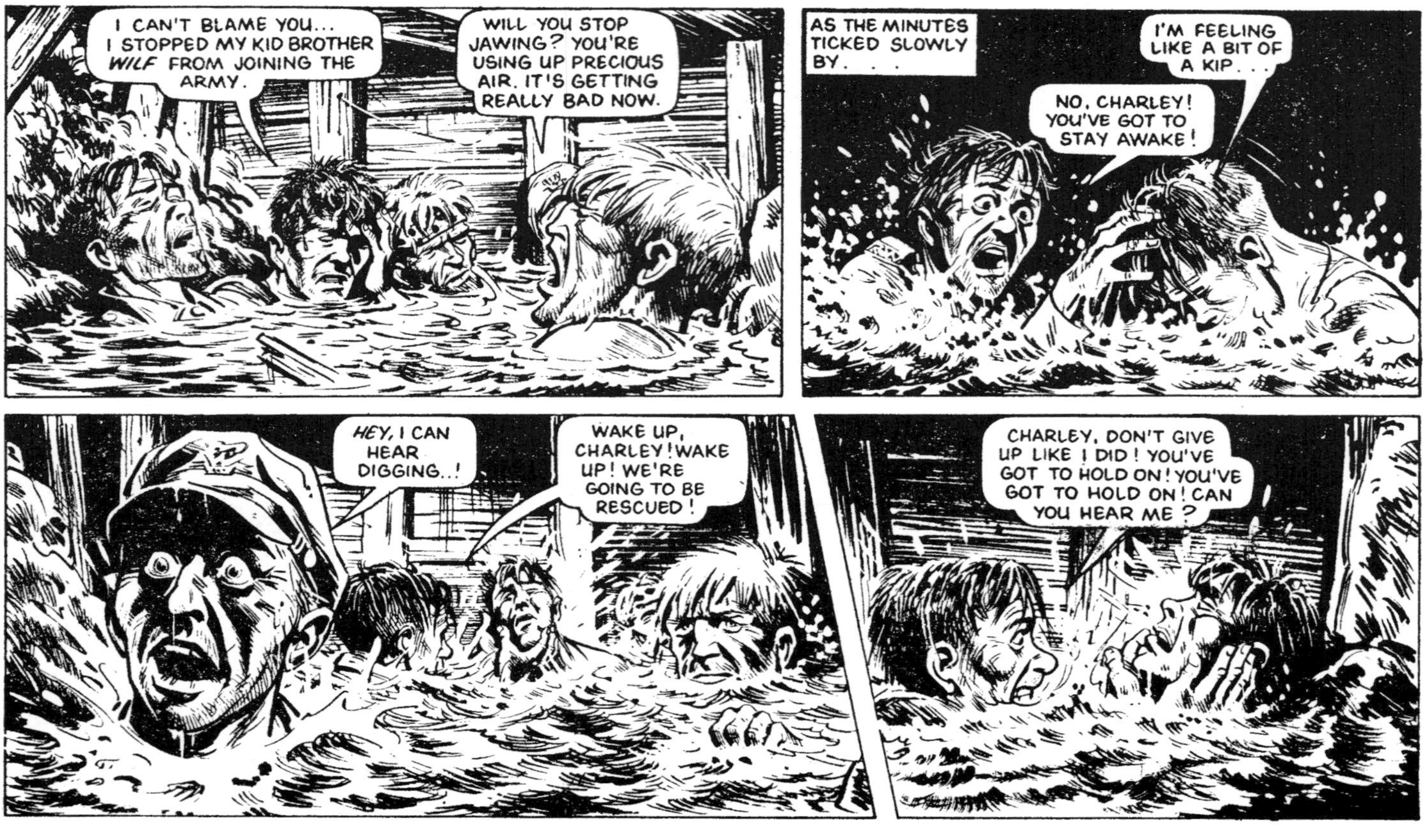
I CAN'T BLAME YOU... I STOPPED MY KID BROTHER *WILF* FROM JOINING THE ARMY.
WILL YOU STOP JAWING? YOU'RE USING UP PRECIOUS AIR. IT'S GETTING REALLY BAD NOW.
AS THE MINUTES TICKED SLOWLY BY. . .
I'M FEELING LIKE A BIT OF A KIP. . .
NO, CHARLEY! YOU'VE GOT TO STAY AWAKE!
HEY, I CAN HEAR DIGGING..!
WAKE UP, CHARLEY! WAKE UP! WE'RE GOING TO BE RESCUED!
CHARLEY, DON'T GIVE UP LIKE I DID! YOU'VE GOT TO HOLD ON! YOU'VE GOT TO HOLD ON! CAN YOU HEAR ME?

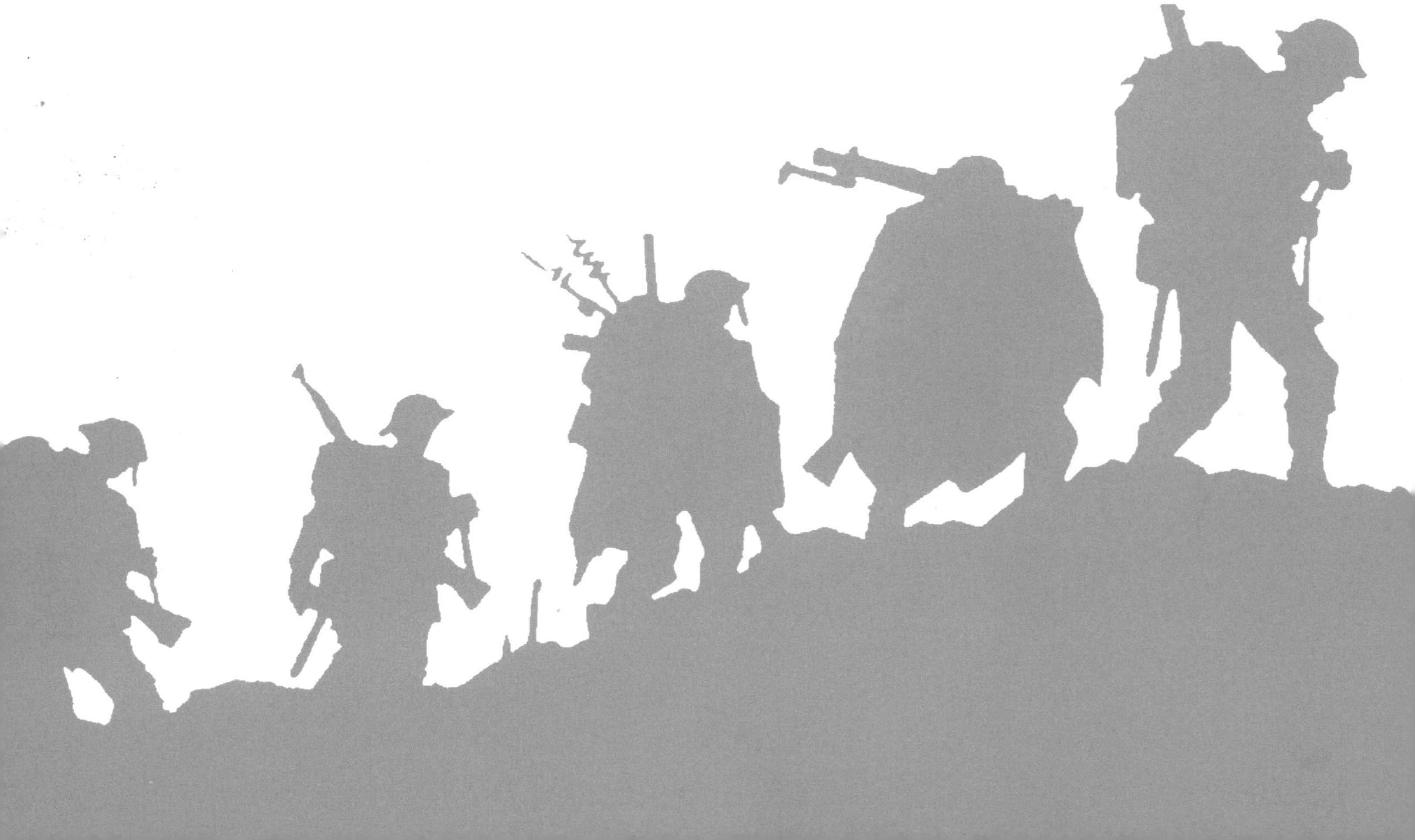

Charley's War

MAY 1917. IN A MINE DEEP BENEATH THE WESTERN FRONT, *CHARLEY BOURNE* AND FOUR COMRADES WERE TRAPPED. AS THE AIR BECAME UNBREATHABLE, *BUDGIE BROWN*. . . AN EX-CONSCIENTIOUS OBJECTOR . . . DESPERATELY TRIED TO KEEP CHARLEY AWAKE.

HOLD ON, CHARLEY. . . WE'RE GOING TO MAKE IT! HELP'S ON IT'S WAY!

THE WATER LEVEL'S DROPPING!

I CAN SEE A CHINK OF LIGHT!

COME ON!

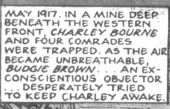

WRITER: Pat Mills
ARTIST: Joe Colquhoun
LETTERER: Mike Peters

EASY DOES IT, LADS . . .EASY!

NOW THEY'RE RESCUED, SNELL, WE'LL . . .ER . . . HAVE TO SHUT DOWN THE MINE. THE . . .ER . . . GERMANS MUST KNOW WE'RE HERE.

DON'T BE RIDICULOUS, COOPER. THE HUNS BLEW THEIR MINE UP 'BLIND'.

WE CAN'T DIG DEEPER THAN ANOTHER . . .ER . . . SEVEN FEET IN THE TIME LEFT. IT'LL STILL BE LIKE WORKING IN A . . .ER . . .DRAIN.

THESE CHAPS ARE SEWER WORKERS . . .THEY'RE USED TO IT. IF WE USE *EVERY PUMP* WE'VE GOT, WE'LL MANAGE. 'BAKERLOO' *WILL* BE FINISHED ON TIME!

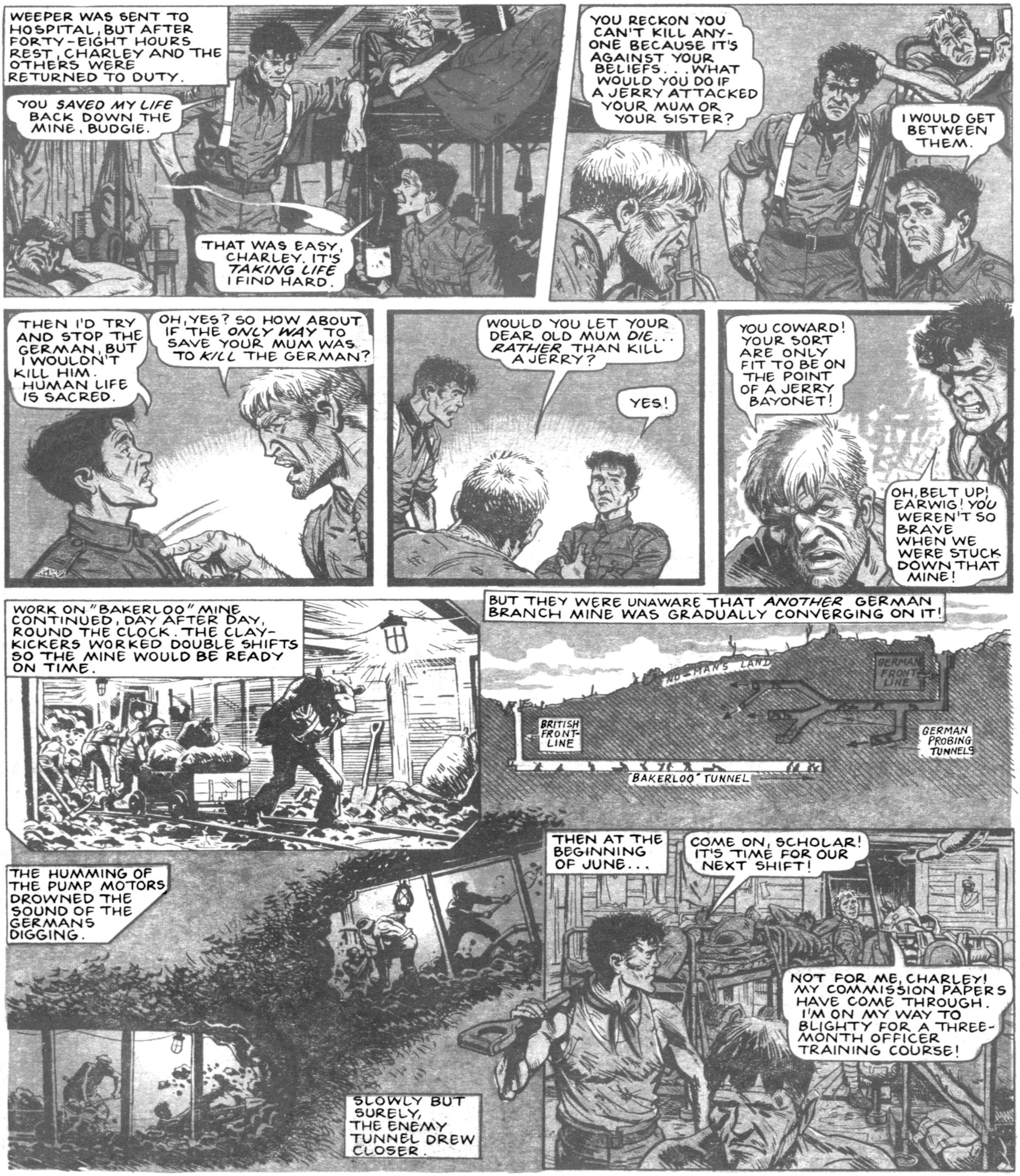

WEEPER WAS SENT TO HOSPITAL, BUT AFTER FORTY-EIGHT HOURS REST, CHARLEY AND THE OTHERS WERE RETURNED TO DUTY.
YOU SAVED MY LIFE BACK DOWN THE MINE, BUDGIE.
THAT WAS EASY, CHARLEY. IT'S TAKING LIFE I FIND HARD.
YOU RECKON YOU CAN'T KILL ANYONE BECAUSE IT'S AGAINST YOUR BELIEFS... WHAT WOULD YOU DO IF A JERRY ATTACKED YOUR MUM OR YOUR SISTER?
I WOULD GET BETWEEN THEM.
THEN I'D TRY AND STOP THE GERMAN, BUT I WOULDN'T KILL HIM. HUMAN LIFE IS SACRED.
OH, YES? SO HOW ABOUT IF THE ONLY WAY TO SAVE YOUR MUM WAS TO KILL THE GERMAN?
WOULD YOU LET YOUR DEAR OLD MUM DIE... RATHER THAN KILL A JERRY?
YES!
YOU COWARD! YOUR SORT ARE ONLY FIT TO BE ON THE POINT OF A JERRY BAYONET!
OH, BELT UP! EARWIG! YOU WEREN'T SO BRAVE WHEN WE WERE STUCK DOWN THAT MINE!
WORK ON "BAKERLOO" MINE CONTINUED, DAY AFTER DAY, ROUND THE CLOCK. THE CLAY-KICKERS WORKED DOUBLE SHIFTS SO THE MINE WOULD BE READY ON TIME.
BUT THEY WERE UNAWARE THAT ANOTHER GERMAN BRANCH MINE WAS GRADUALLY CONVERGING ON IT!
NO-MAN'S LAND
GERMAN FRONT LINE
BRITISH FRONT-LINE
GERMAN PROBING TUNNELS
"BAKERLOO" TUNNEL
THE HUMMING OF THE PUMP MOTORS DROWNED THE SOUND OF THE GERMANS DIGGING.
SLOWLY BUT SURELY, THE ENEMY TUNNEL DREW CLOSER.
THEN AT THE BEGINNING OF JUNE...
COME ON, SCHOLAR! IT'S TIME FOR OUR NEXT SHIFT!
NOT FOR ME, CHARLEY! MY COMMISSION PAPERS HAVE COME THROUGH. I'M ON MY WAY TO BLIGHTY FOR A THREE-MONTH OFFICER TRAINING COURSE!

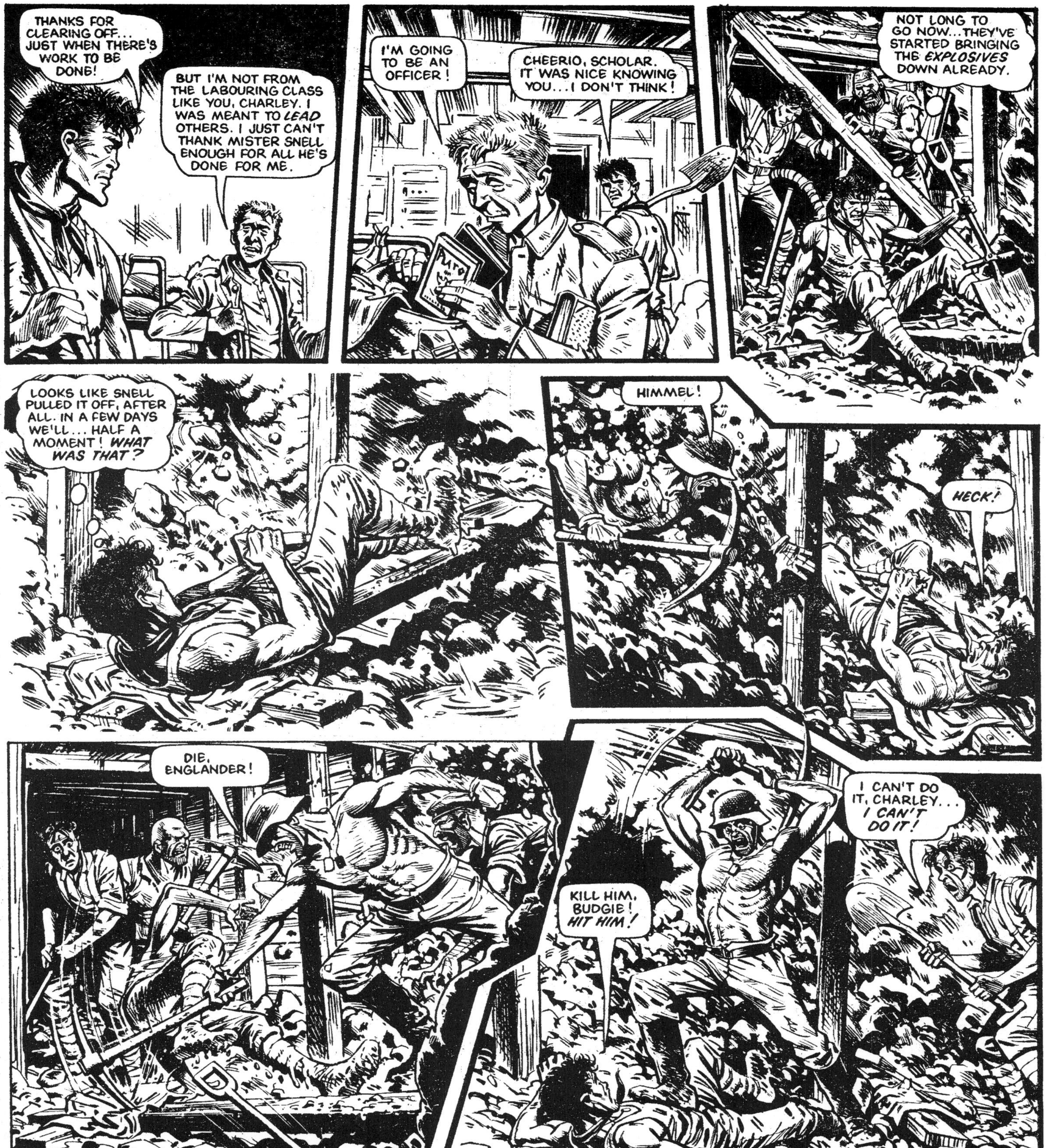
THANKS FOR CLEARING OFF... JUST WHEN THERE'S WORK TO BE DONE!
BUT I'M NOT FROM THE LABOURING CLASS LIKE YOU, CHARLEY. I WAS MEANT TO *LEAD* OTHERS. I JUST CAN'T THANK MISTER SNELL ENOUGH FOR ALL HE'S DONE FOR ME.
I'M GOING TO BE AN OFFICER!
CHEERIO, SCHOLAR. IT WAS NICE KNOWING YOU... I DON'T THINK!
NOT LONG TO GO NOW... THEY'VE STARTED BRINGING THE *EXPLOSIVES* DOWN ALREADY.
LOOKS LIKE SNELL PULLED IT OFF, AFTER ALL. IN A FEW DAYS WE'LL... HALF A MOMENT! *WHAT WAS THAT?*
HIMMEL!
HECK!
DIE, ENGLANDER!
KILL HIM, BUDGIE! *HIT HIM!*
I CAN'T DO IT, CHARLEY... *I CAN'T DO IT!*

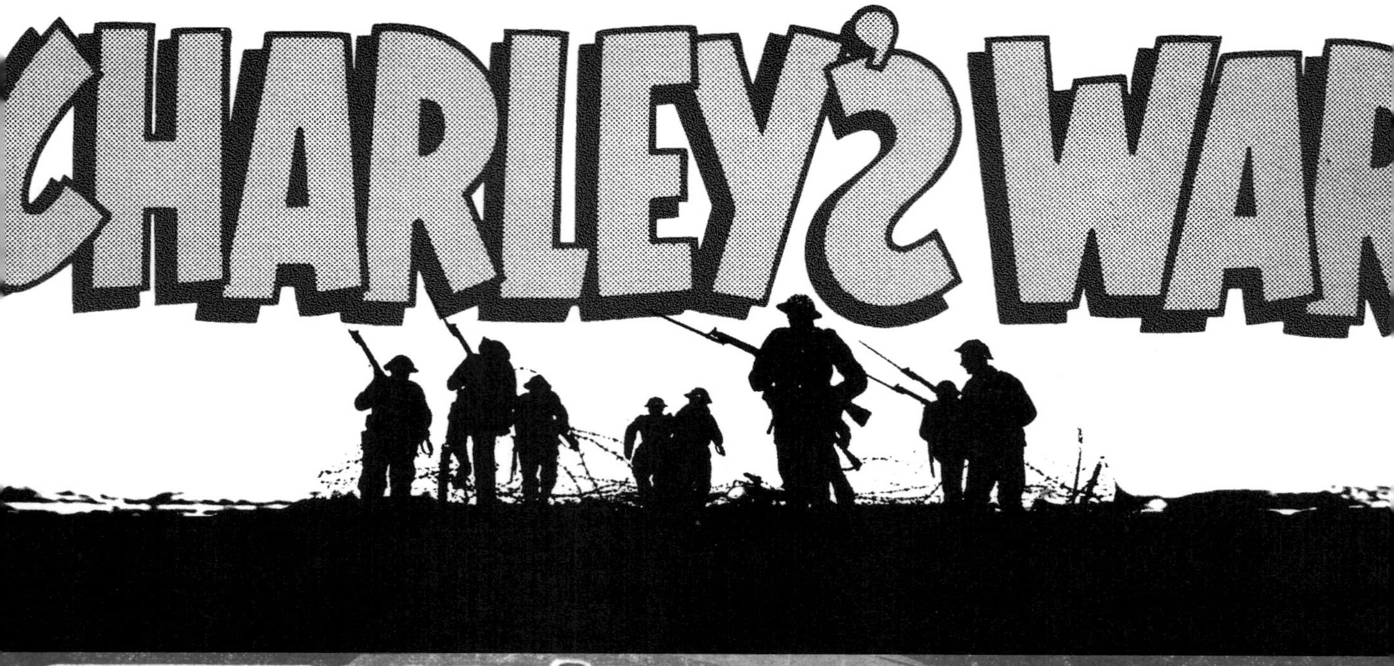
CHARLEY'S WAR

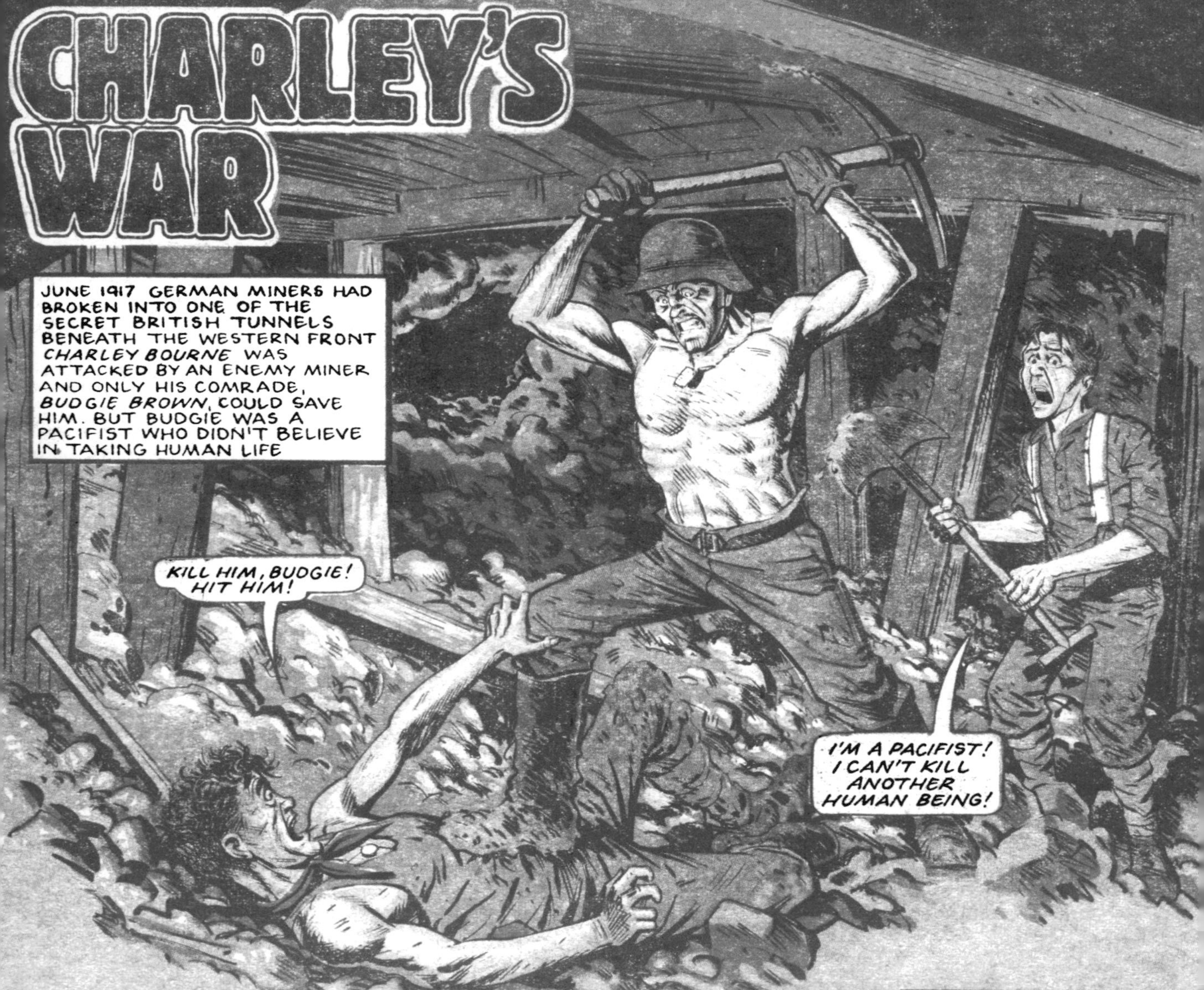
CHARLEY'S WAR
JUNE 1917 GERMAN MINERS HAD BROKEN INTO ONE OF THE SECRET BRITISH TUNNELS BENEATH THE WESTERN FRONT CHARLEY BOURNE WAS ATTACKED BY AN ENEMY MINER AND ONLY HIS COMRADE, BUDGIE BROWN, COULD SAVE HIM. BUT BUDGIE WAS A PACIFIST WHO DIDN'T BELIEVE IN TAKING HUMAN LIFE
KILL HIM, BUDGIE! HIT HIM!
I'M A PACIFIST! I CAN'T KILL ANOTHER HUMAN BEING!

CONTINUED ON NEXT PAGE

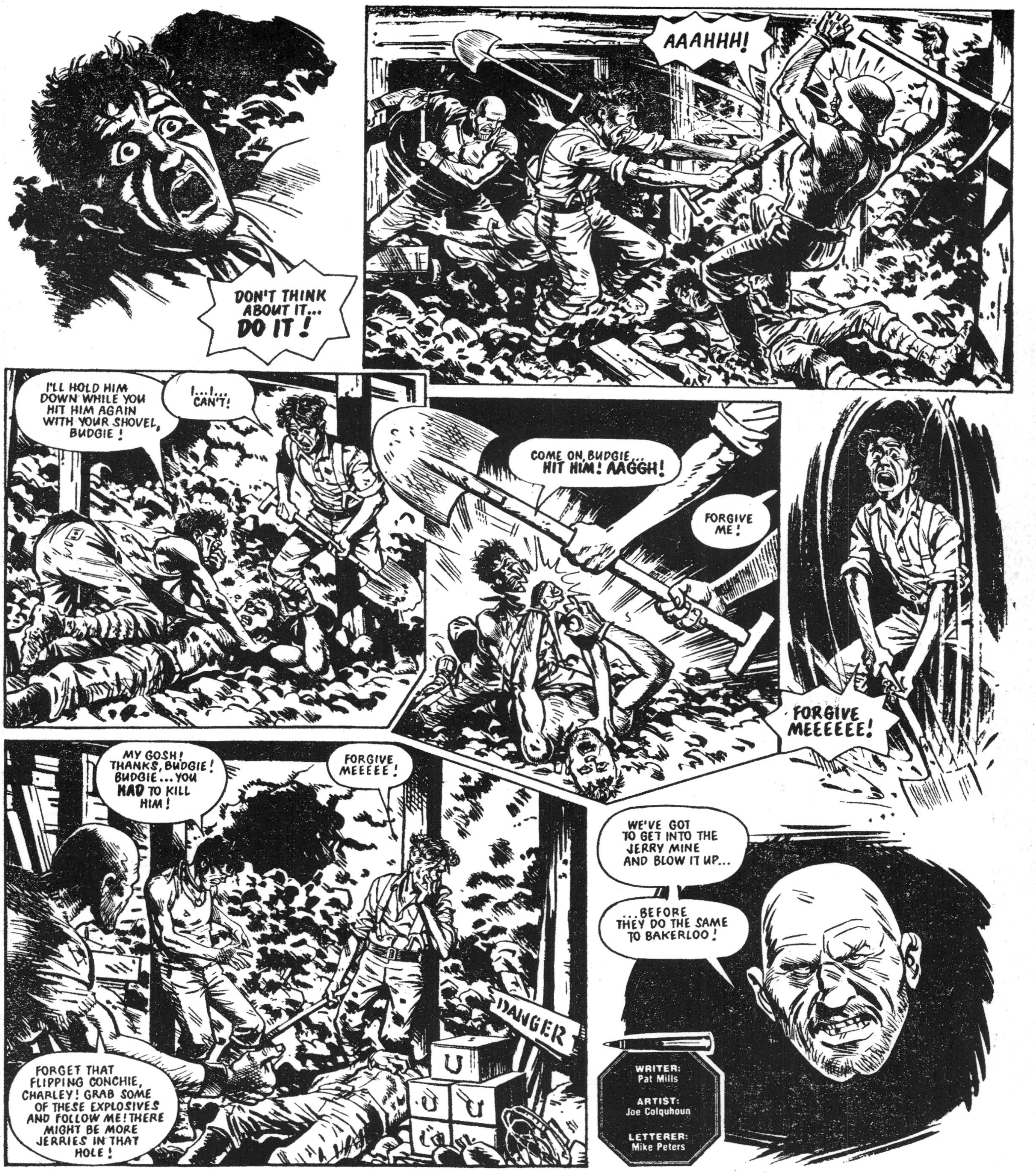
DON'T THINK ABOUT IT... DO IT!
AAAHHH!
I'LL HOLD HIM DOWN WHILE YOU HIT HIM AGAIN WITH YOUR SHOVEL, BUDGIE!
I...I... CAN'T!
COME ON, BUDGIE... HIT HIM! AAGGH!
FORGIVE ME!
FORGIVE MEEEEEE!
MY GOSH! THANKS, BUDGIE! BUDGIE... YOU HAD TO KILL HIM!
FORGIVE MEEEEE!
DANGER
FORGET THAT FLIPPING CONCHIE, CHARLEY! GRAB SOME OF THESE EXPLOSIVES AND FOLLOW ME! THERE MIGHT BE MORE JERRIES IN THAT HOLE!
WE'VE GOT TO GET INTO THE JERRY MINE AND BLOW IT UP...
...BEFORE THEY DO THE SAME TO BAKERLOO!
WRITER: Pat Mills
ARTIST: Joe Colquhoun
LETTERER: Mike Peters

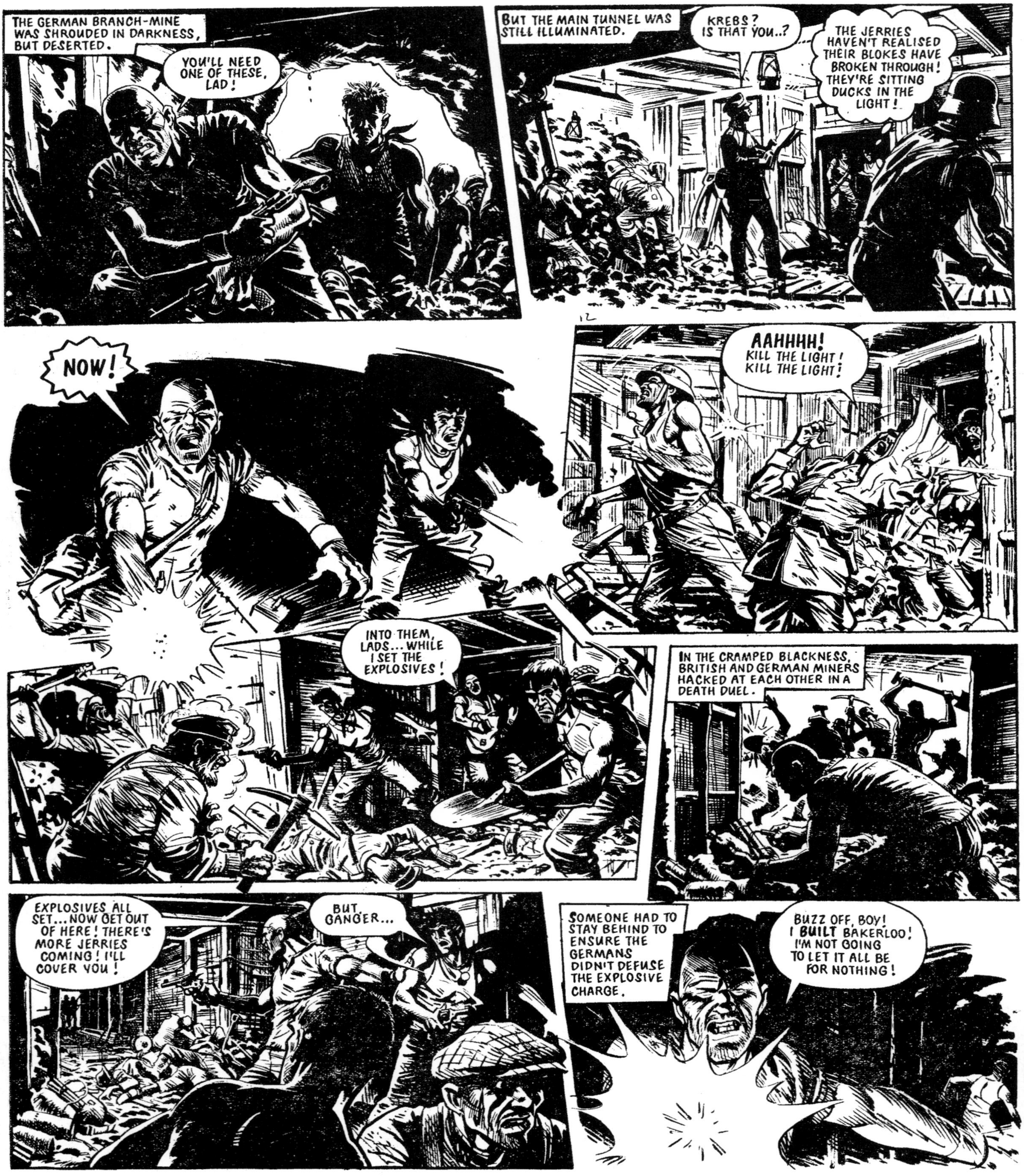
THE GERMAN BRANCH-MINE WAS SHROUDED IN DARKNESS, BUT DESERTED.
YOU'LL NEED ONE OF THESE, LAD!
BUT THE MAIN TUNNEL WAS STILL ILLUMINATED.
KREBS? IS THAT YOU..?
THE JERRIES HAVEN'T REALISED THEIR BLOKES HAVE BROKEN THROUGH! THEY'RE SITTING DUCKS IN THE LIGHT!
NOW!
AAHHHH! KILL THE LIGHT! KILL THE LIGHT!
INTO THEM, LADS... WHILE I SET THE EXPLOSIVES!
IN THE CRAMPED BLACKNESS, BRITISH AND GERMAN MINERS HACKED AT EACH OTHER IN A DEATH DUEL.
EXPLOSIVES ALL SET... NOW GET OUT OF HERE! THERE'S MORE JERRIES COMING! I'LL COVER YOU!
BUT, GANGER...
SOMEONE HAD TO STAY BEHIND TO ENSURE THE GERMANS DIDN'T DEFUSE THE EXPLOSIVE CHARGE.
BUZZ OFF, BOY! I BUILT BAKERLOO! I'M NOT GOING TO LET IT ALL BE FOR NOTHING!

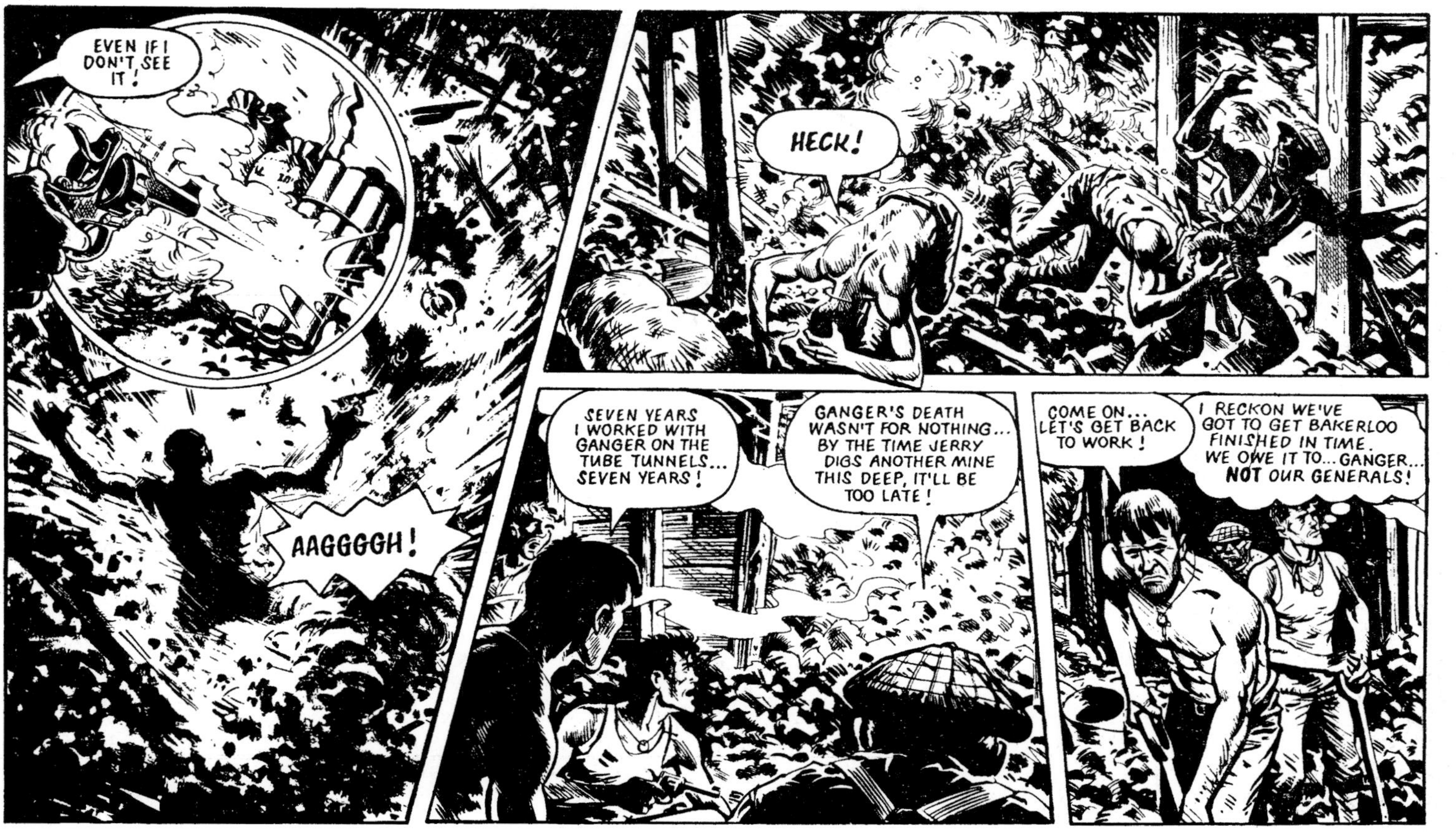
EVEN IF I DON'T SEE IT!
HECK!
AAGGGGH!
SEVEN YEARS I WORKED WITH GANGER ON THE TUBE TUNNELS... SEVEN YEARS!
GANGER'S DEATH WASN'T FOR NOTHING... BY THE TIME JERRY DIGS ANOTHER MINE THIS DEEP, IT'LL BE TOO LATE!
COME ON... LET'S GET BACK TO WORK!
I RECKON WE'VE GOT TO GET BAKERLOO FINISHED IN TIME. WE OWE IT TO... GANGER... NOT OUR GENERALS!

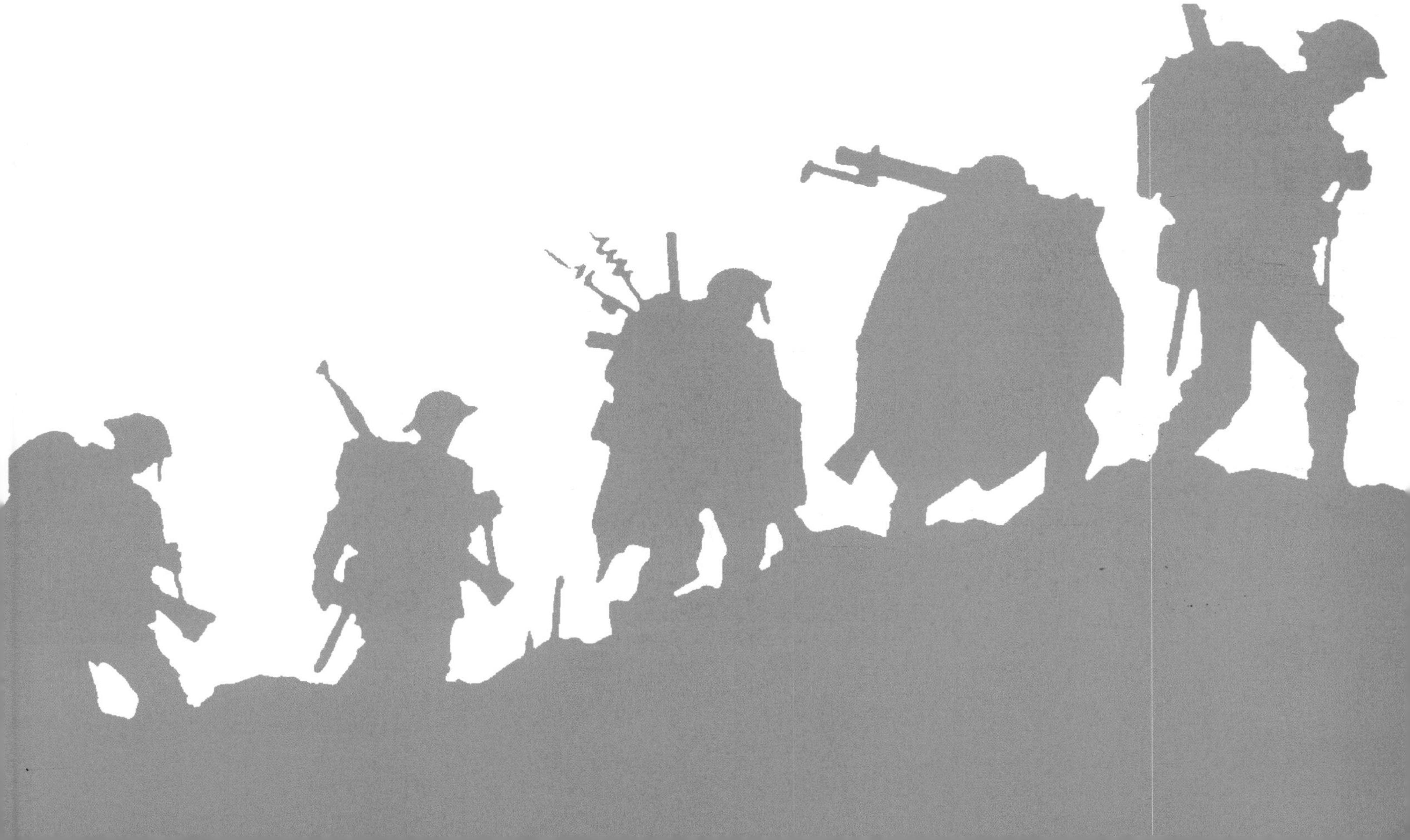

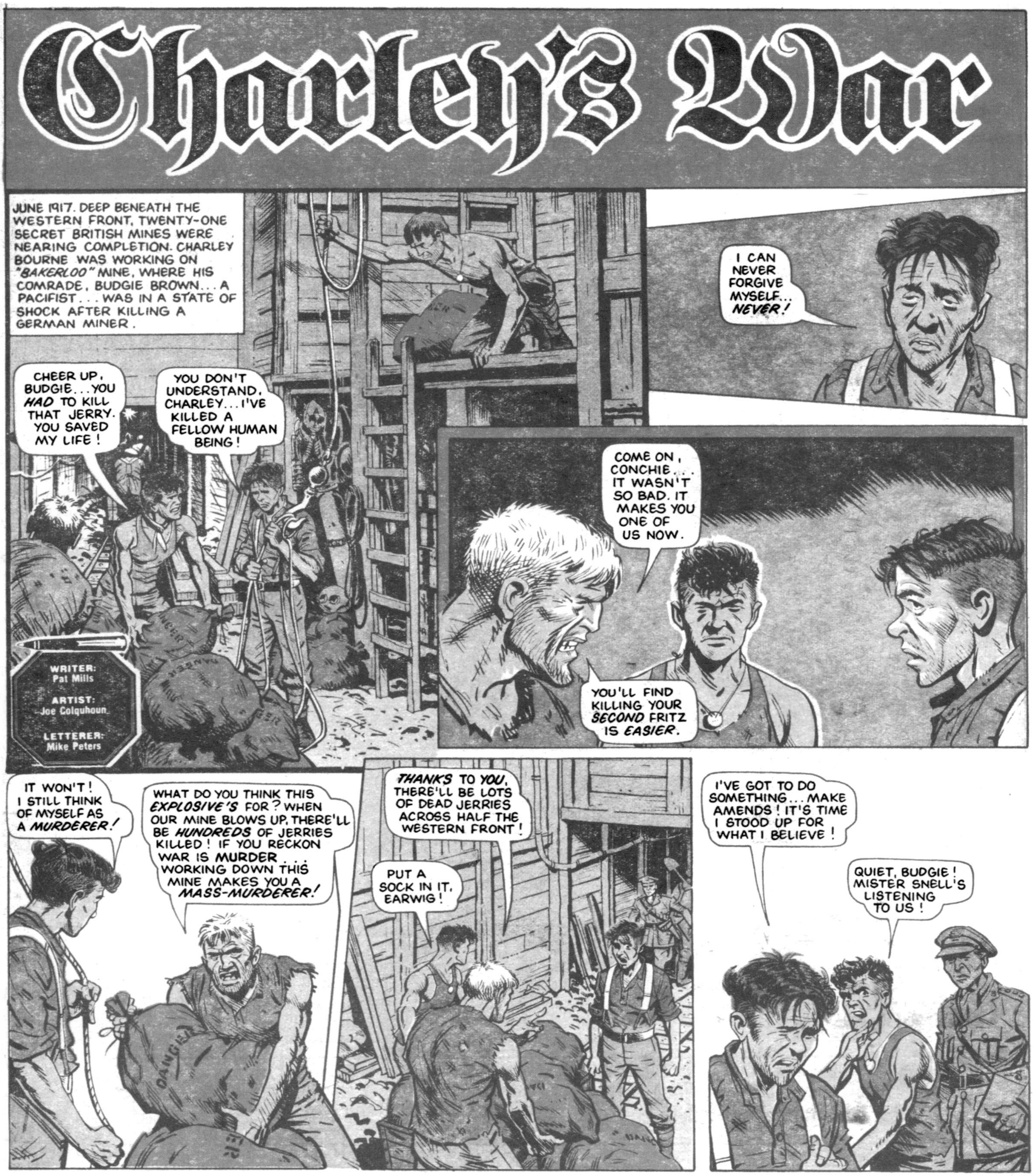
Charley's War
JUNE 1917. DEEP BENEATH THE WESTERN FRONT, TWENTY-ONE SECRET BRITISH MINES WERE NEARING COMPLETION. CHARLEY BOURNE WAS WORKING ON "BAKERLOO" MINE, WHERE HIS COMRADE, BUDGIE BROWN... A PACIFIST... WAS IN A STATE OF SHOCK AFTER KILLING A GERMAN MINER.
CHEER UP, BUDGIE... YOU HAD TO KILL THAT JERRY. YOU SAVED MY LIFE!
YOU DON'T UNDERSTAND, CHARLEY... I'VE KILLED A FELLOW HUMAN BEING!
WRITER: Pat Mills
ARTIST: Joe Colquhoun
LETTERER: Mike Peters
I CAN NEVER FORGIVE MYSELF... NEVER!
COME ON, CONCHIE... IT WASN'T SO BAD. IT MAKES YOU ONE OF US NOW.
YOU'LL FIND KILLING YOUR SECOND FRITZ IS EASIER.
IT WON'T! I STILL THINK OF MYSELF AS A MURDERER!
WHAT DO YOU THINK THIS EXPLOSIVE'S FOR? WHEN OUR MINE BLOWS UP, THERE'LL BE HUNDREDS OF JERRIES KILLED! IF YOU RECKON WAR IS MURDER... WORKING DOWN THIS MINE MAKES YOU A MASS-MURDERER!
THANKS TO YOU, THERE'LL BE LOTS OF DEAD JERRIES ACROSS HALF THE WESTERN FRONT!
PUT A SOCK IN IT, EARWIG!
I'VE GOT TO DO SOMETHING... MAKE AMENDS! IT'S TIME I STOOD UP FOR WHAT I BELIEVE!
QUIET, BUDGIE! MISTER SNELL'S LISTENING TO US!

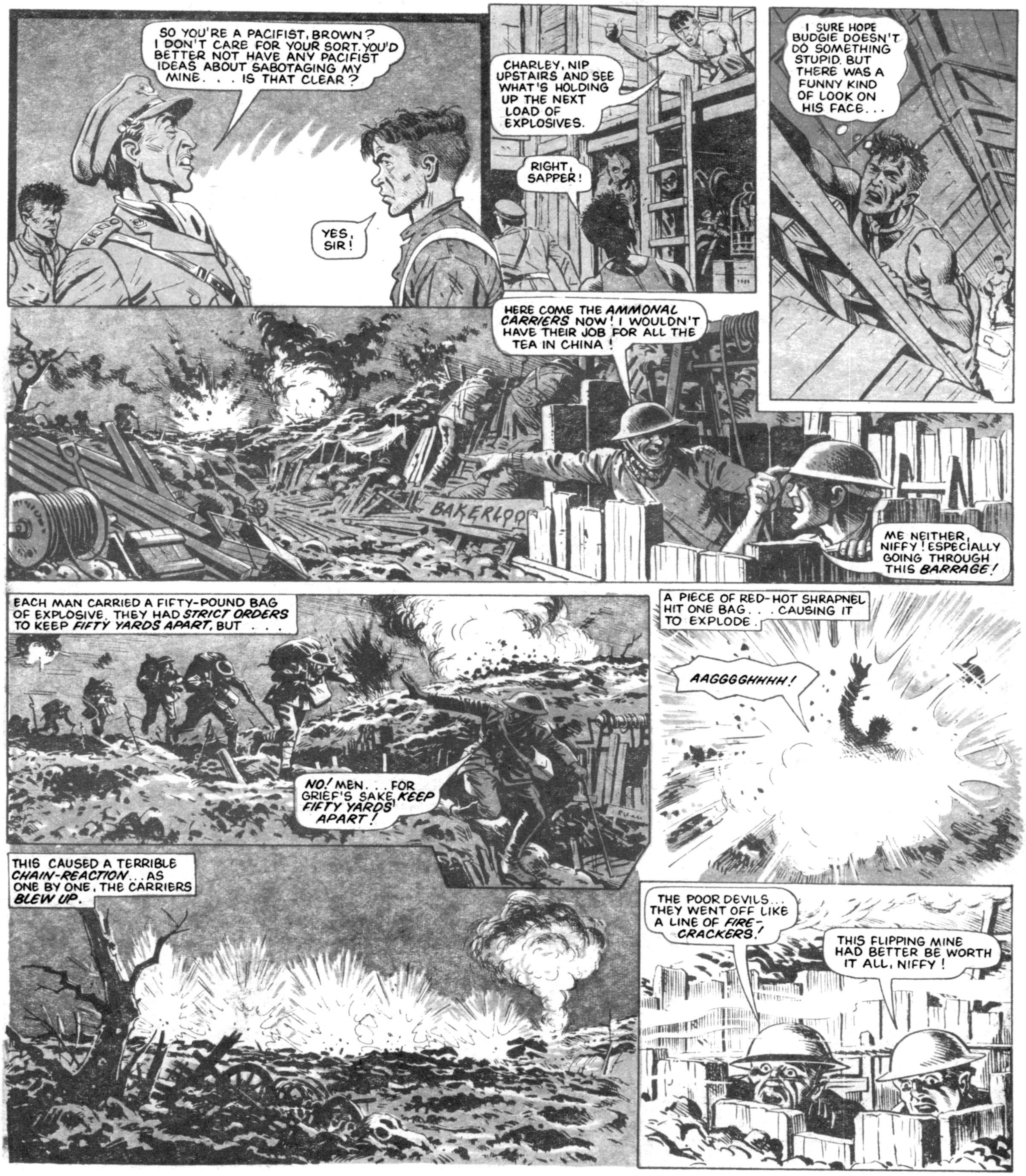

SO YOU'RE A PACIFIST, BROWN? I DON'T CARE FOR YOUR SORT. YOU'D BETTER NOT HAVE ANY PACIFIST IDEAS ABOUT SABOTAGING MY MINE. . . IS THAT CLEAR?
YES, SIR!
CHARLEY, NIP UPSTAIRS AND SEE WHAT'S HOLDING UP THE NEXT LOAD OF EXPLOSIVES.
RIGHT, SAPPER!
I SURE HOPE BUDGIE DOESN'T DO SOMETHING STUPID. BUT THERE WAS A FUNNY KIND OF LOOK ON HIS FACE . . .
HERE COME THE AMMONAL CARRIERS NOW! I WOULDN'T HAVE THEIR JOB FOR ALL THE TEA IN CHINA!
BAKERLOO
ME NEITHER, NIFFY! ESPECIALLY GOING THROUGH THIS BARRAGE!
EACH MAN CARRIED A FIFTY-POUND BAG OF EXPLOSIVE. THEY HAD STRICT ORDERS TO KEEP FIFTY YARDS APART, BUT . . .
NO! MEN. . . FOR GRIEF'S SAKE, KEEP FIFTY YARDS APART!
A PIECE OF RED-HOT SHRAPNEL HIT ONE BAG. . . CAUSING IT TO EXPLODE.
AAGGGGHHHH!
THIS CAUSED A TERRIBLE CHAIN-REACTION... AS ONE BY ONE, THE CARRIERS BLEW UP.
THE POOR DEVILS... THEY WENT OFF LIKE A LINE OF FIRE-CRACKERS!
THIS FLIPPING MINE HAD BETTER BE WORTH IT ALL, NIFFY!

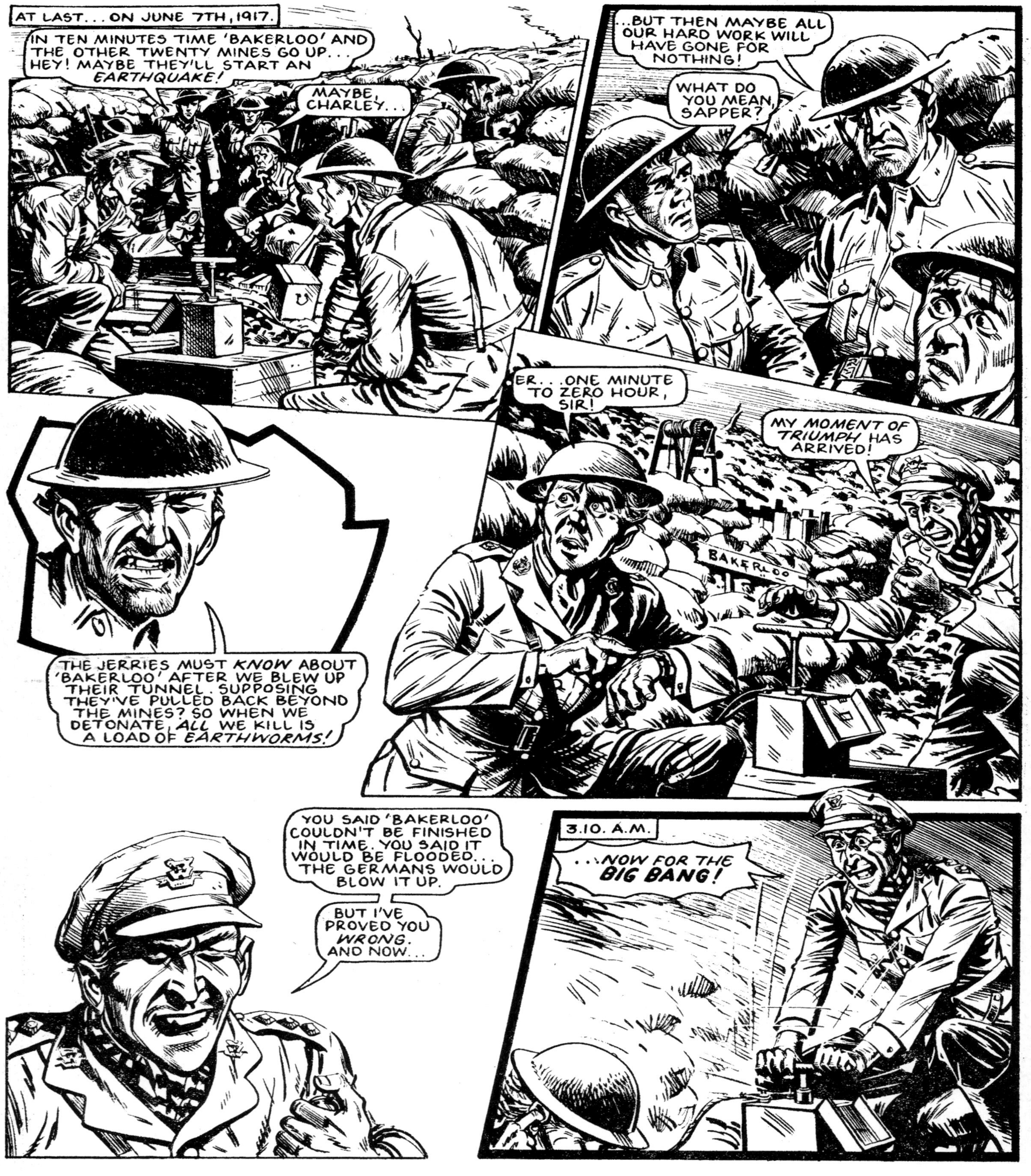

AT LAST... ON JUNE 7TH, 1917.
IN TEN MINUTES TIME 'BAKERLOO' AND THE OTHER TWENTY MINES GO UP... HEY! MAYBE THEY'LL START AN EARTHQUAKE!
MAYBE, CHARLEY...
...BUT THEN MAYBE ALL OUR HARD WORK WILL HAVE GONE FOR NOTHING!
WHAT DO YOU MEAN, SAPPER?
THE JERRIES MUST KNOW ABOUT 'BAKERLOO' AFTER WE BLEW UP THEIR TUNNEL. SUPPOSING THEY'VE PULLED BACK BEYOND THE MINES? SO WHEN WE DETONATE, ALL WE KILL IS A LOAD OF EARTHWORMS!
ER...ONE MINUTE TO ZERO HOUR, SIR!
MY MOMENT OF TRIUMPH HAS ARRIVED!
BAKERLOO
YOU SAID 'BAKERLOO' COULDN'T BE FINISHED IN TIME. YOU SAID IT WOULD BE FLOODED... THE GERMANS WOULD BLOW IT UP.
BUT I'VE PROVED YOU WRONG. AND NOW...
3.10. A.M.
...NOW FOR THE BIG BANG!

CHARLEY'S WAR

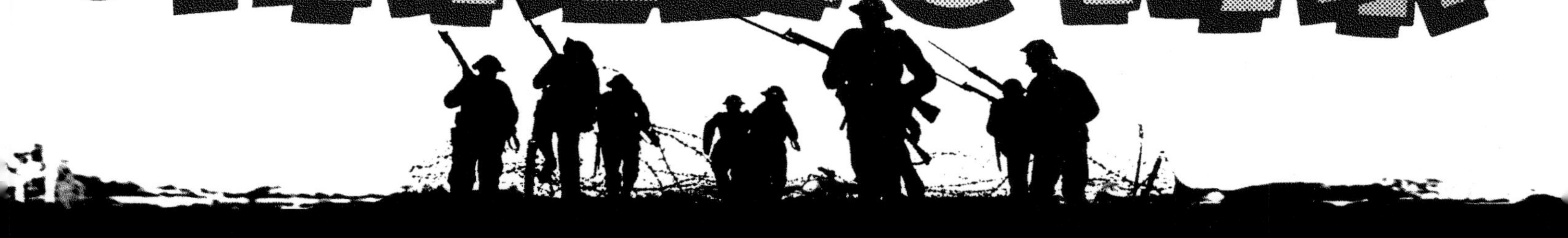

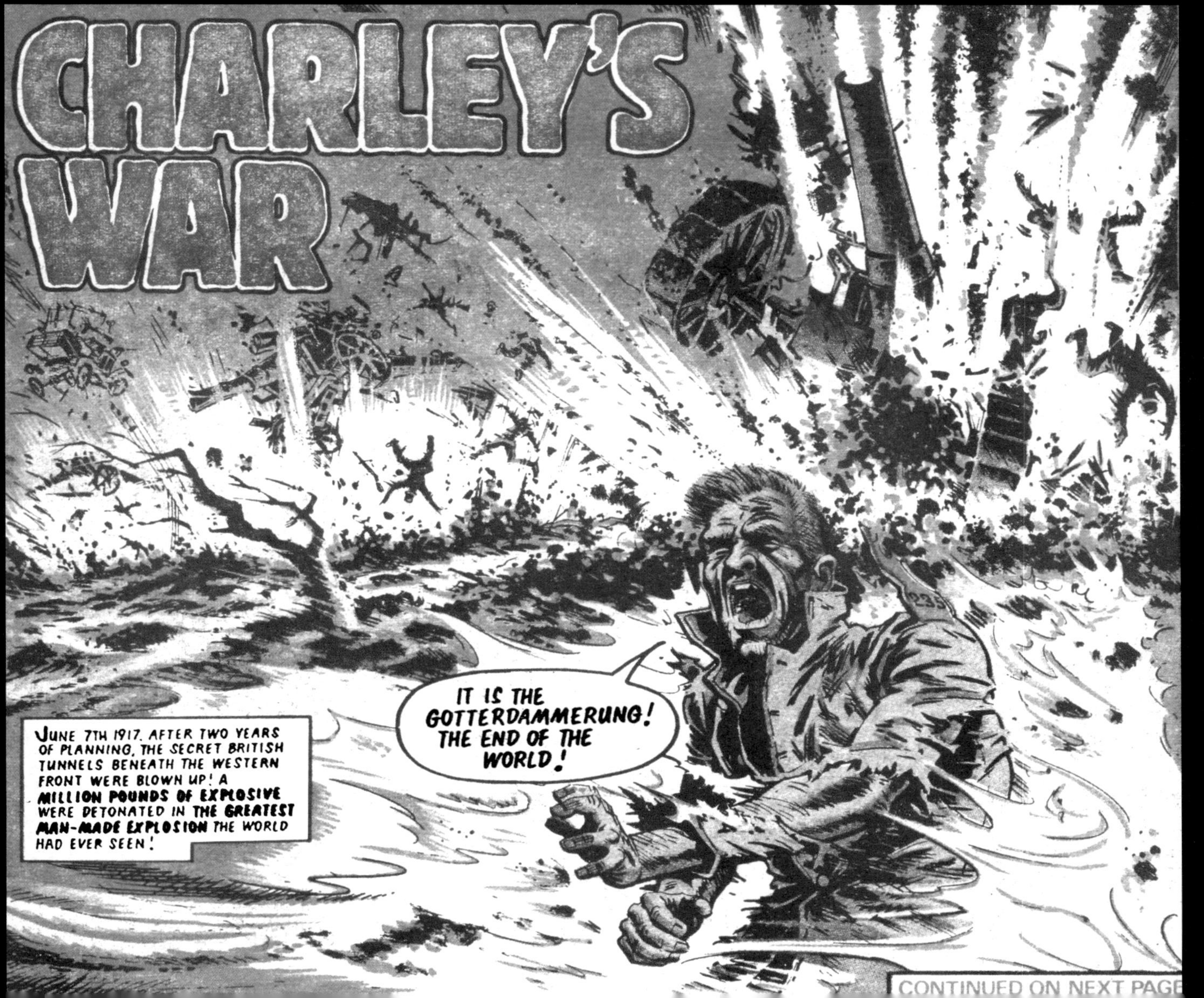
CHARLEY'S WAR
JUNE 7TH 1917. AFTER TWO YEARS OF PLANNING, THE SECRET BRITISH TUNNELS BENEATH THE WESTERN FRONT WERE BLOWN UP! A MILLION POUNDS OF EXPLOSIVE WERE DETONATED IN THE GREATEST MAN-MADE EXPLOSION THE WORLD HAD EVER SEEN!
IT IS THE GOTTERDAMMERUNG! THE END OF THE WORLD!
CONTINUED ON NEXT PAGE

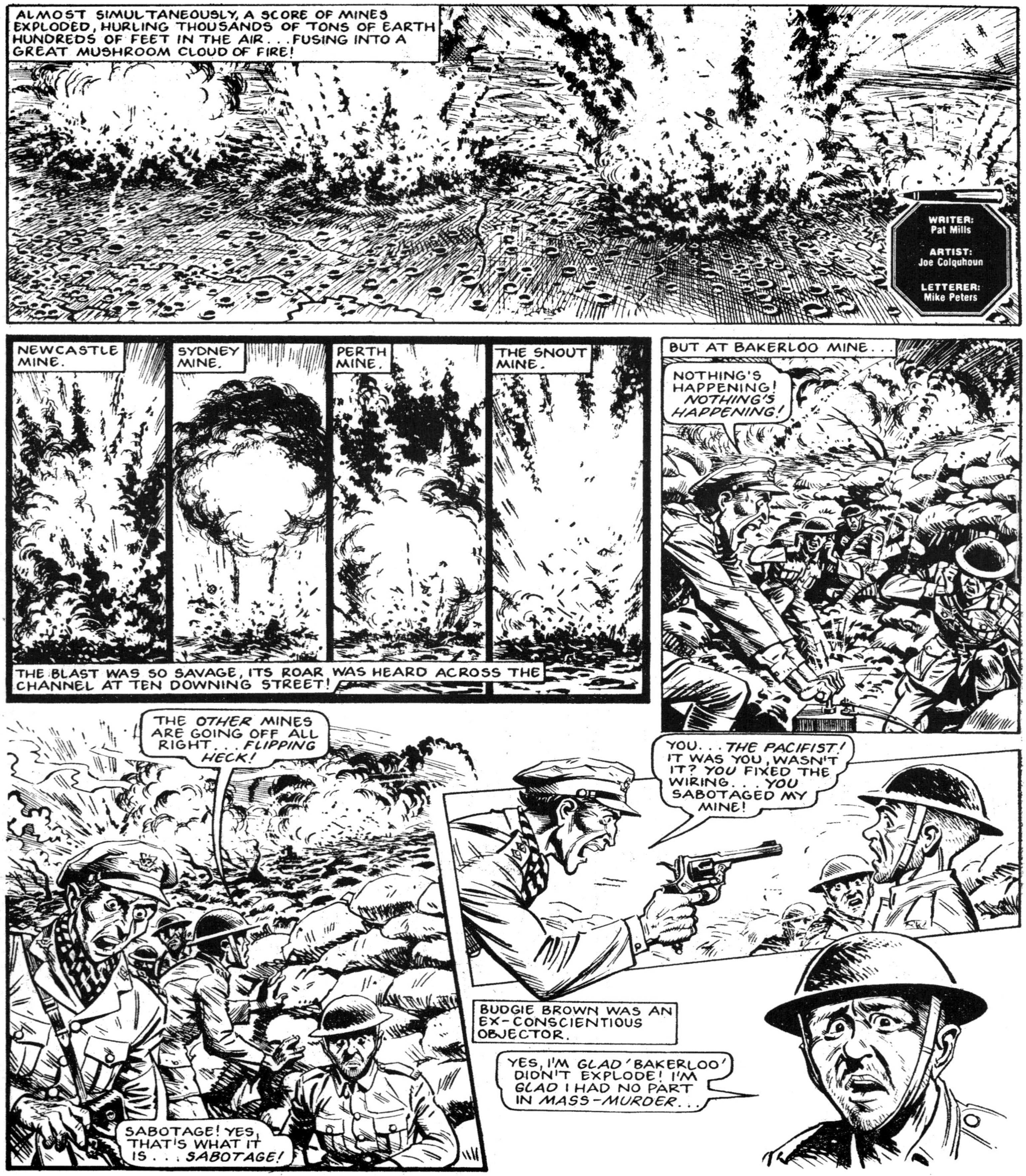
ALMOST SIMULTANEOUSLY, A SCORE OF MINES EXPLODED, HURLING THOUSANDS OF TONS OF EARTH HUNDREDS OF FEET IN THE AIR... FUSING INTO A GREAT MUSHROOM CLOUD OF FIRE!
WRITER: Pat Mills
ARTIST: Joe Colquhoun
LETTERER: Mike Peters
NEWCASTLE MINE.
SYDNEY MINE.
PERTH MINE.
THE SNOUT MINE.
THE BLAST WAS SO SAVAGE, ITS ROAR WAS HEARD ACROSS THE CHANNEL AT TEN DOWNING STREET!
BUT AT BAKERLOO MINE...
NOTHING'S HAPPENING! NOTHING'S HAPPENING!
THE OTHER MINES ARE GOING OFF ALL RIGHT... FLIPPING HECK!
SABOTAGE! YES, THAT'S WHAT IT IS... SABOTAGE!
YOU... THE PACIFIST! IT WAS YOU, WASN'T IT? YOU FIXED THE WIRING... YOU SABOTAGED MY MINE!
BUDGIE BROWN WAS AN EX-CONSCIENTIOUS OBJECTOR.
YES, I'M GLAD 'BAKERLOO' DIDN'T EXPLODE! I'M GLAD I HAD NO PART IN MASS-MURDER...

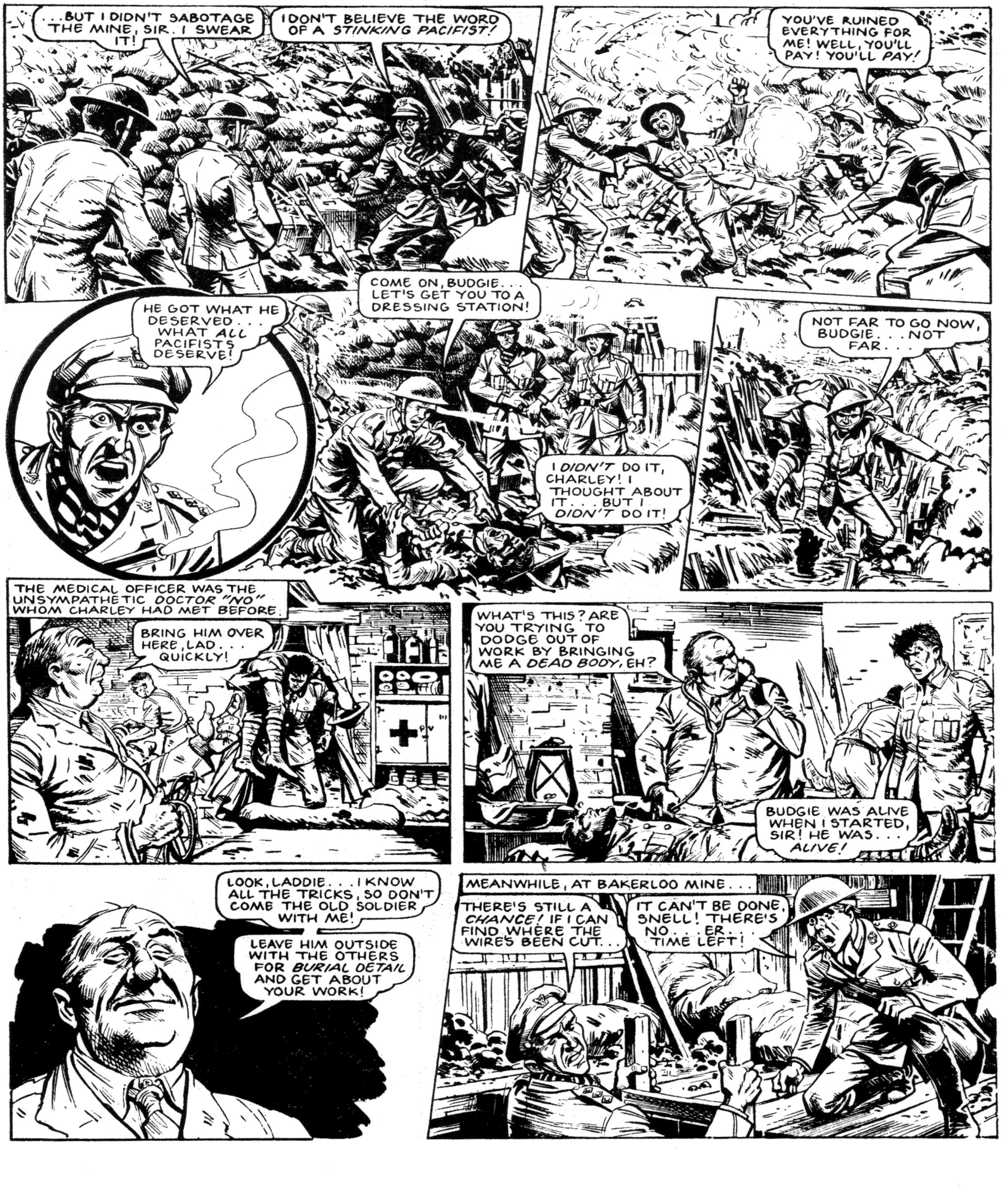

...BUT I DIDN'T SABOTAGE THE MINE, SIR. I SWEAR IT!
I DON'T BELIEVE THE WORD OF A STINKING PACIFIST!
YOU'VE RUINED EVERYTHING FOR ME! WELL, YOU'LL PAY! YOU'LL PAY!
HE GOT WHAT HE DESERVED... WHAT ALL PACIFISTS DESERVE!
COME ON, BUDGIE... LET'S GET YOU TO A DRESSING STATION!
I DIDN'T DO IT, CHARLEY! I THOUGHT ABOUT IT... BUT I DIDN'T DO IT!
NOT FAR TO GO NOW, BUDGIE... NOT FAR...
THE MEDICAL OFFICER WAS THE UNSYMPATHETIC DOCTOR "NO" WHOM CHARLEY HAD MET BEFORE.
BRING HIM OVER HERE, LAD... QUICKLY!
WHAT'S THIS? ARE YOU TRYING TO DODGE OUT OF WORK BY BRINGING ME A DEAD BODY, EH?
BUDGIE WAS ALIVE WHEN I STARTED, SIR! HE WAS... ALIVE!
LOOK, LADDIE... I KNOW ALL THE TRICKS, SO DON'T COME THE OLD SOLDIER WITH ME!
LEAVE HIM OUTSIDE WITH THE OTHERS FOR BURIAL DETAIL AND GET ABOUT YOUR WORK!
MEANWHILE, AT BAKERLOO MINE...
THERE'S STILL A CHANCE! IF I CAN FIND WHERE THE WIRE'S BEEN CUT...
IT CAN'T BE DONE, SNELL! THERE'S NO... ER... TIME LEFT!

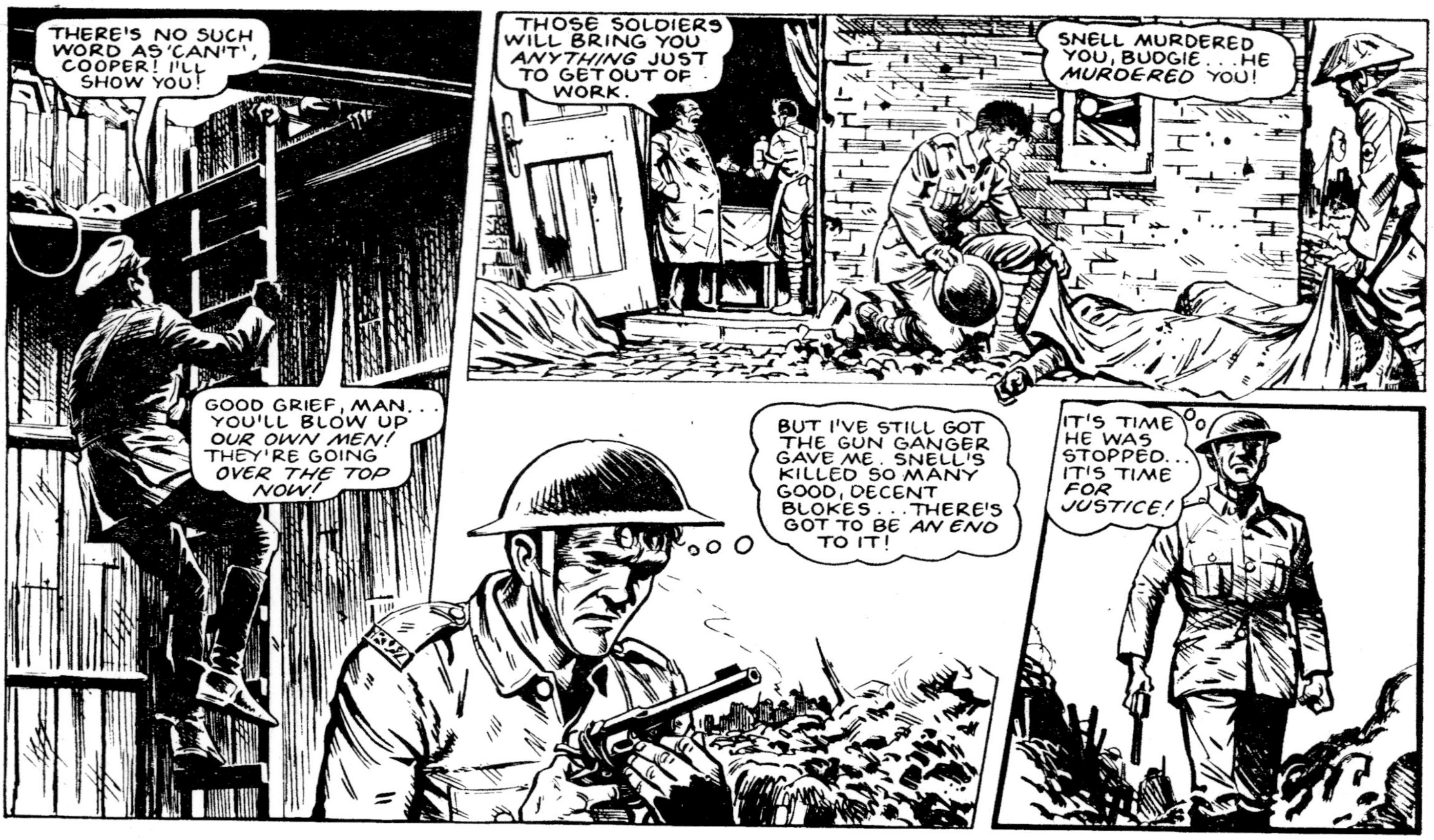
THERE'S NO SUCH WORD AS 'CAN'T', COOPER! I'LL SHOW YOU!
GOOD GRIEF, MAN... YOU'LL BLOW UP *OUR OWN MEN!* THEY'RE GOING *OVER THE TOP NOW!*
THOSE SOLDIERS WILL BRING YOU *ANYTHING* JUST TO GET OUT OF WORK.
SNELL MURDERED YOU, BUDGIE... HE *MURDERED* YOU!
BUT I'VE STILL GOT THE GUN GANGER GAVE ME. SNELL'S KILLED SO MANY GOOD, DECENT BLOKES... THERE'S GOT TO BE *AN END* TO IT!
IT'S TIME HE WAS STOPPED... IT'S TIME *FOR JUSTICE!*

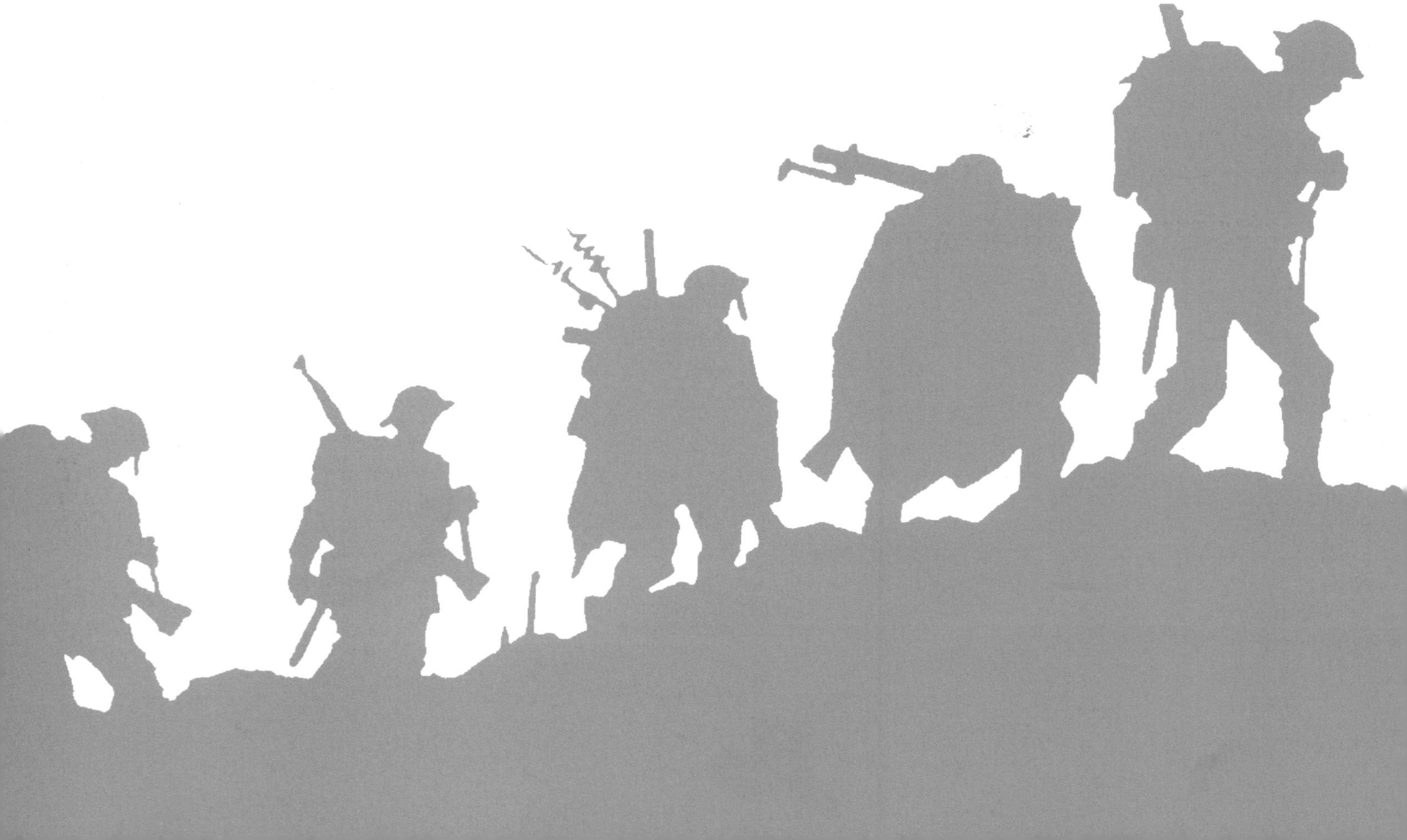

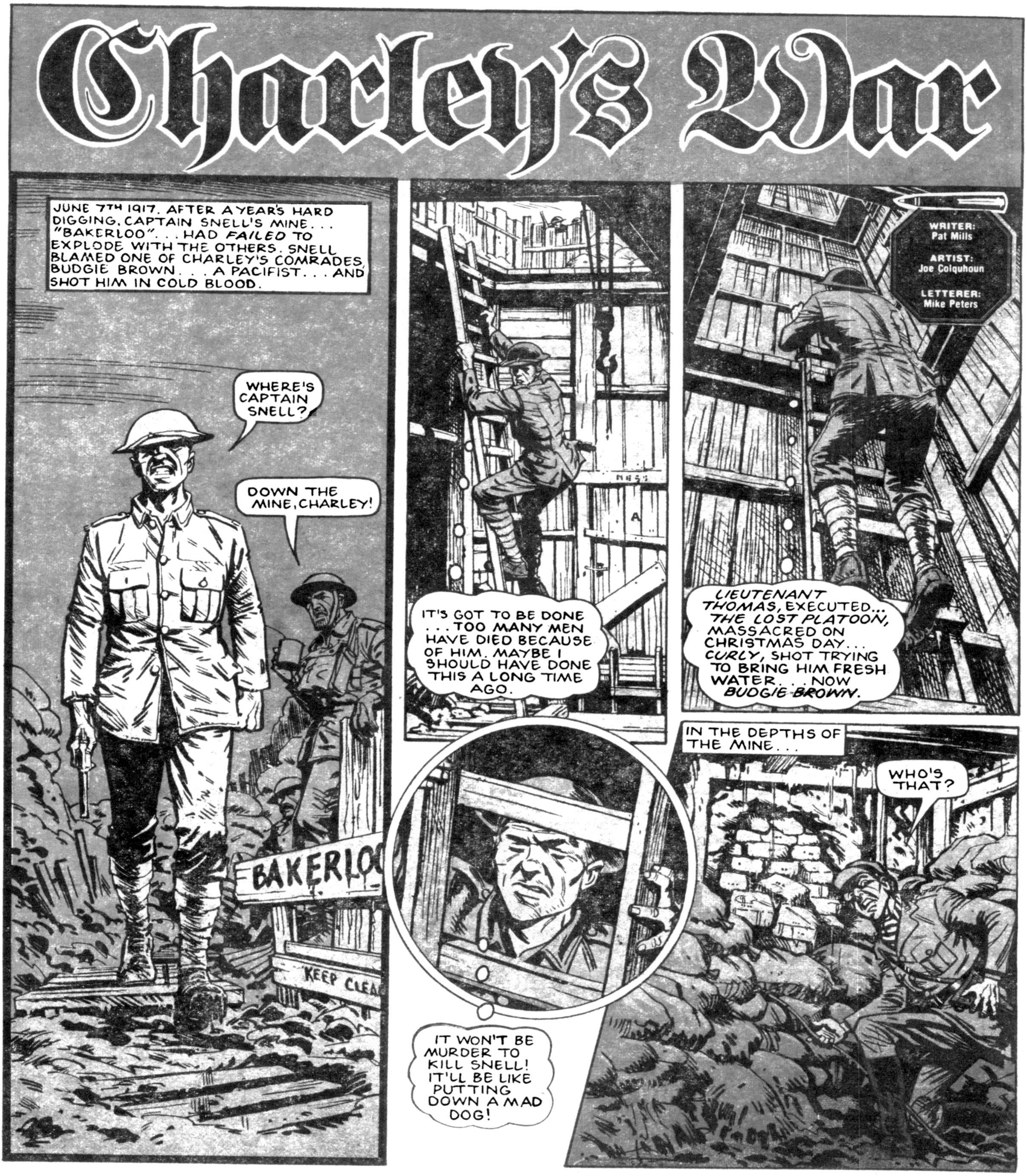
Charley's War
JUNE 7TH 1917. AFTER A YEAR'S HARD DIGGING, CAPTAIN SNELL'S MINE... "BAKERLOO"... HAD FAILED TO EXPLODE WITH THE OTHERS. SNELL BLAMED ONE OF CHARLEY'S COMRADES, BUDGIE BROWN... A PACIFIST... AND SHOT HIM IN COLD BLOOD.
WHERE'S CAPTAIN SNELL?
DOWN THE MINE, CHARLEY!
BAKERLOO
KEEP CLEA
IT'S GOT TO BE DONE ... TOO MANY MEN HAVE DIED BECAUSE OF HIM. MAYBE I SHOULD HAVE DONE THIS A LONG TIME AGO.
WRITER: Pat Mills
ARTIST: Joe Colquhoun
LETTERER: Mike Peters
LIEUTENANT THOMAS, EXECUTED... THE LOST PLATOON, MASSACRED ON CHRISTMAS DAY... CURLY, SHOT TRYING TO BRING HIM FRESH WATER... NOW BUDGIE BROWN.
IT WON'T BE MURDER TO KILL SNELL! IT'LL BE LIKE PUTTING DOWN A MAD DOG!
IN THE DEPTHS OF THE MINE...
WHO'S THAT?

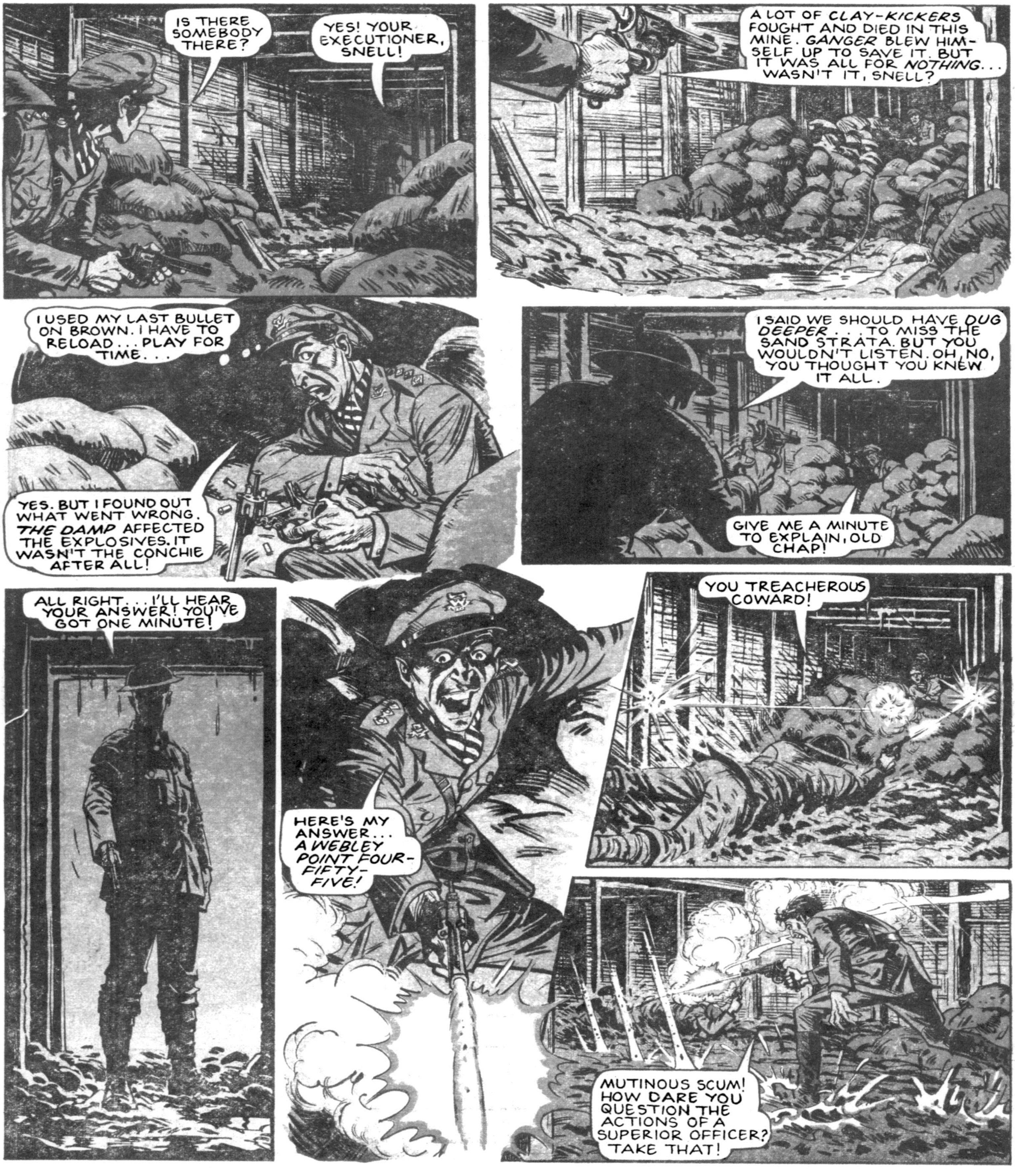
IS THERE SOMEBODY THERE?
YES! YOUR EXECUTIONER, SNELL!
A LOT OF CLAY-KICKERS FOUGHT AND DIED IN THIS MINE. GANGER BLEW HIMSELF UP TO SAVE IT. BUT IT WAS ALL FOR NOTHING... WASN'T IT, SNELL?
I USED MY LAST BULLET ON BROWN. I HAVE TO RELOAD... PLAY FOR TIME...
YES. BUT I FOUND OUT WHAT WENT WRONG. THE DAMP AFFECTED THE EXPLOSIVES. IT WASN'T THE CONCHIE AFTER ALL!
I SAID WE SHOULD HAVE DUG DEEPER... TO MISS THE SAND STRATA. BUT YOU WOULDN'T LISTEN. OH, NO, YOU THOUGHT YOU KNEW IT ALL.
GIVE ME A MINUTE TO EXPLAIN, OLD CHAP!
ALL RIGHT... I'LL HEAR YOUR ANSWER! YOU'VE GOT ONE MINUTE!
HERE'S MY ANSWER... A WEBLEY POINT FOUR-FIFTY-FIVE!
YOU TREACHEROUS COWARD!
MUTINOUS SCUM! HOW DARE YOU QUESTION THE ACTIONS OF A SUPERIOR OFFICER? TAKE THAT!

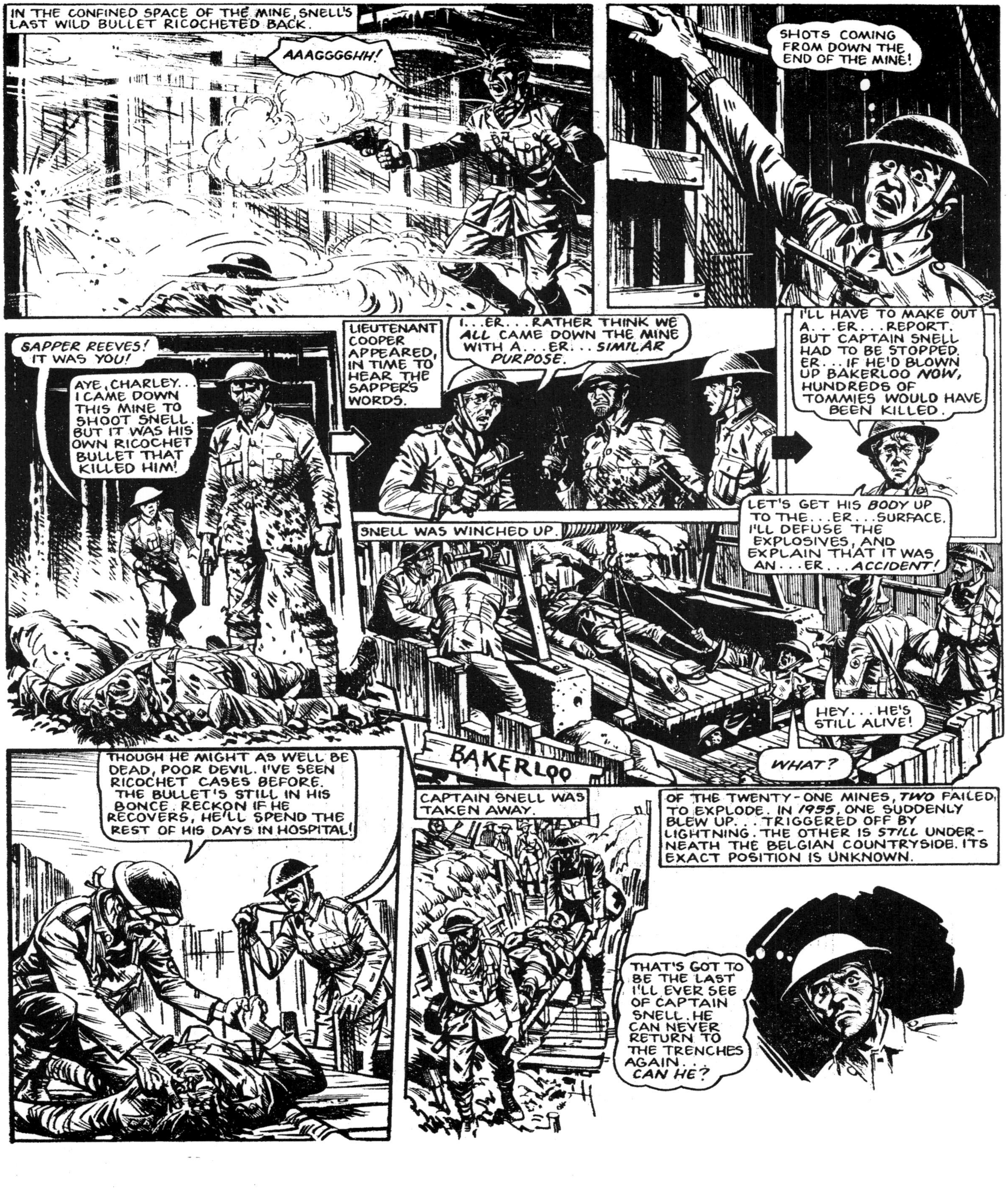

IN THE CONFINED SPACE OF THE MINE, SNELL'S LAST WILD BULLET RICOCHETED BACK.
AAAGGGGHH!
SHOTS COMING FROM DOWN THE END OF THE MINE!
SAPPER REEVES! IT WAS YOU!
AYE, CHARLEY... I CAME DOWN THIS MINE TO SHOOT SNELL. BUT IT WAS HIS OWN RICOCHET BULLET THAT KILLED HIM!
LIEUTENANT COOPER APPEARED, IN TIME TO HEAR THE SAPPER'S WORDS.
I...ER...RATHER THINK WE ALL CAME DOWN THE MINE WITH A...ER...SIMILAR PURPOSE.
I'LL HAVE TO MAKE OUT A...ER...REPORT. BUT CAPTAIN SNELL HAD TO BE STOPPED. ER...IF HE'D BLOWN UP BAKERLOO NOW, HUNDREDS OF TOMMIES WOULD HAVE BEEN KILLED.
SNELL WAS WINCHED UP.
LET'S GET HIS BODY UP TO THE...ER...SURFACE. I'LL DEFUSE THE EXPLOSIVES, AND EXPLAIN THAT IT WAS AN...ER...ACCIDENT!
BAKERLOO
HEY... HE'S STILL ALIVE!
WHAT?
THOUGH HE MIGHT AS WELL BE DEAD, POOR DEVIL. I'VE SEEN RICOCHET CASES BEFORE. THE BULLET'S STILL IN HIS BONCE. RECKON IF HE RECOVERS, HE'LL SPEND THE REST OF HIS DAYS IN HOSPITAL!
CAPTAIN SNELL WAS TAKEN AWAY.
OF THE TWENTY-ONE MINES, TWO FAILED TO EXPLODE. IN 1955, ONE SUDDENLY BLEW UP... TRIGGERED OFF BY LIGHTNING. THE OTHER IS STILL UNDERNEATH THE BELGIAN COUNTRYSIDE. ITS EXACT POSITION IS UNKNOWN.
THAT'S GOT TO BE THE LAST I'LL EVER SEE OF CAPTAIN SNELL. HE CAN NEVER RETURN TO THE TRENCHES AGAIN... CAN HE?

CHARLEY'S WAR

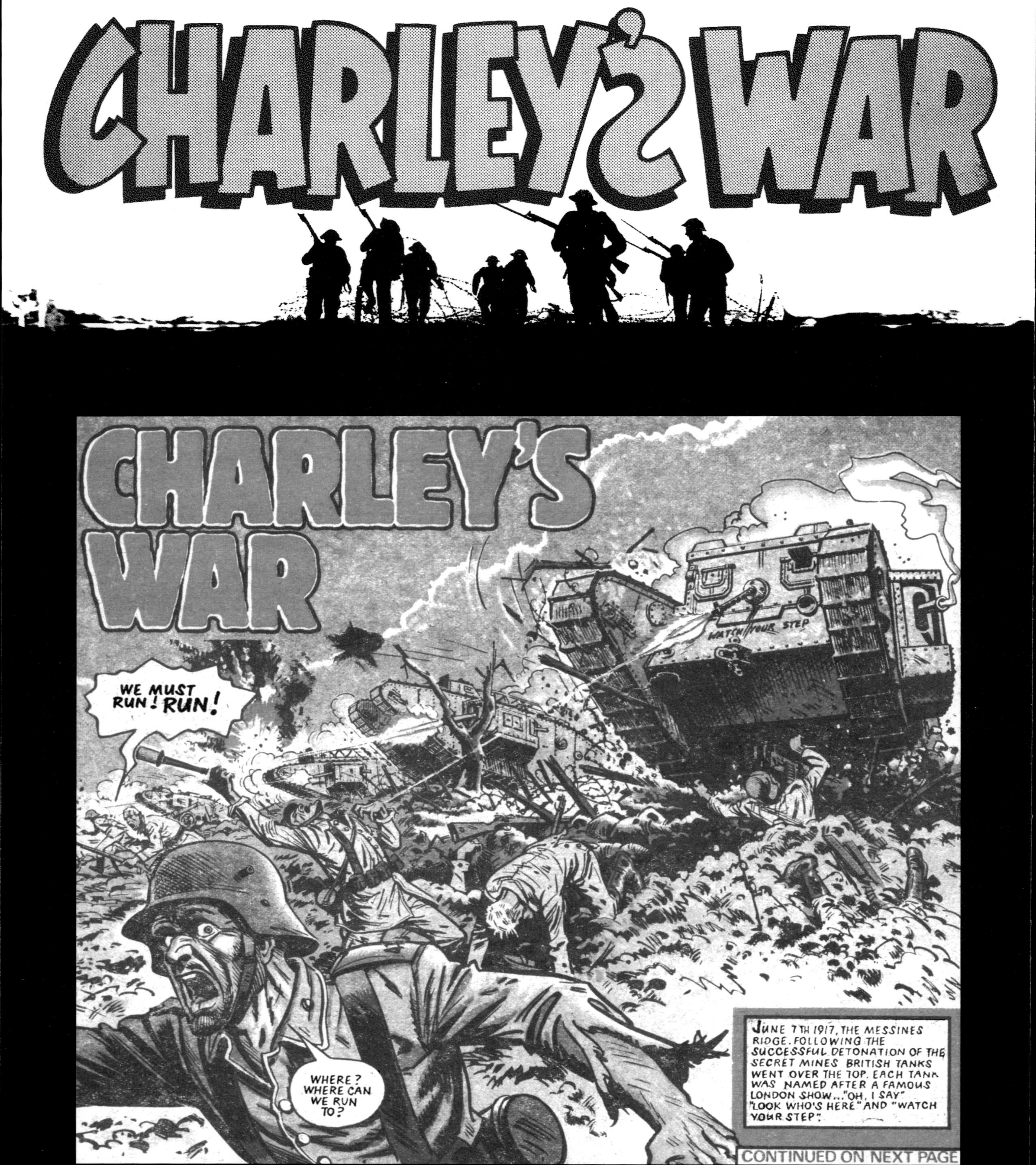
CHARLEY'S WAR
WE MUST RUN! RUN!
WATCH YOUR STEP
JUNE 7TH 1917, THE MESSINES RIDGE. FOLLOWING THE SUCCESSFUL DETONATION OF THE SECRET MINES BRITISH TANKS WENT OVER THE TOP. EACH TANK WAS NAMED AFTER A FAMOUS LONDON SHOW..."OH, I SAY" "LOOK WHO'S HERE" AND "WATCH YOUR STEP".
WHERE? WHERE CAN WE RUN TO?
CONTINUED ON NEXT PAGE

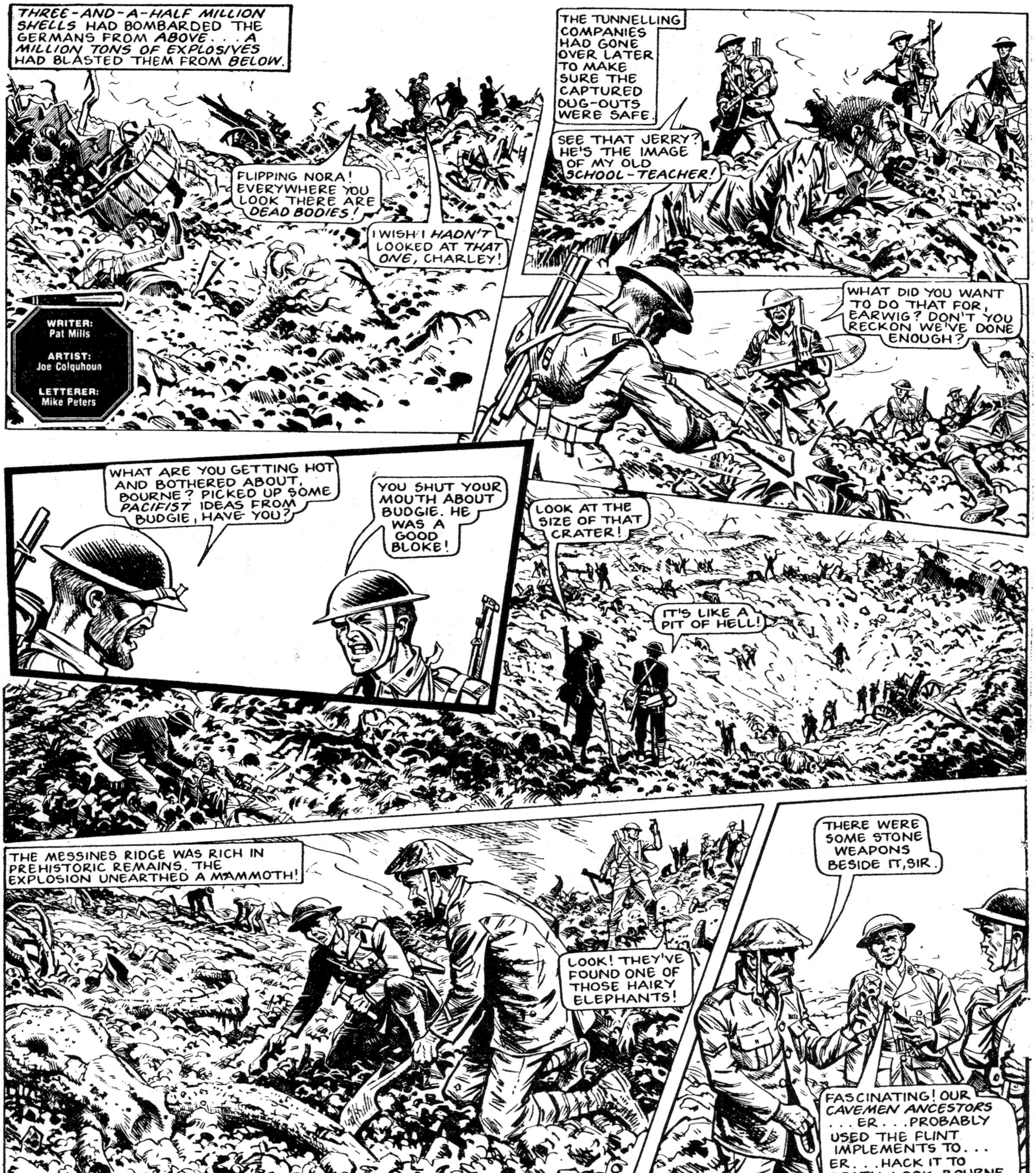

THREE-AND-A-HALF MILLION SHELLS HAD BOMBARDED THE GERMANS FROM ABOVE . . . A MILLION TONS OF EXPLOSIVES HAD BLASTED THEM FROM BELOW.
FLIPPING NORA! EVERYWHERE YOU LOOK THERE ARE DEAD BODIES!
I WISH I HADN'T LOOKED AT THAT ONE, CHARLEY!
WRITER: Pat Mills
ARTIST: Joe Colquhoun
LETTERER: Mike Peters
THE TUNNELLING COMPANIES HAD GONE OVER LATER TO MAKE SURE THE CAPTURED DUG-OUTS WERE SAFE.
SEE THAT JERRY? HE'S THE IMAGE OF MY OLD SCHOOL-TEACHER!
WHAT DID YOU WANT TO DO THAT FOR, EARWIG? DON'T YOU RECKON WE'VE DONE ENOUGH?
WHAT ARE YOU GETTING HOT AND BOTHERED ABOUT, BOURNE? PICKED UP SOME PACIFIST IDEAS FROM BUDGIE, HAVE YOU?
YOU SHUT YOUR MOUTH ABOUT BUDGIE. HE WAS A GOOD BLOKE!
LOOK AT THE SIZE OF THAT CRATER!
IT'S LIKE A PIT OF HELL!
THE MESSINES RIDGE WAS RICH IN PREHISTORIC REMAINS. THE EXPLOSION UNEARTHED A MAMMOTH!
LOOK! THEY'VE FOUND ONE OF THOSE HAIRY ELEPHANTS!
THERE WERE SOME STONE WEAPONS BESIDE IT, SIR.
FASCINATING! OUR CAVEMEN ANCESTORS . . . ER . . . PROBABLY USED THE FLINT IMPLEMENTS TO . . . ER . . . HACK IT TO DEATH. LOOK, BOURNE.

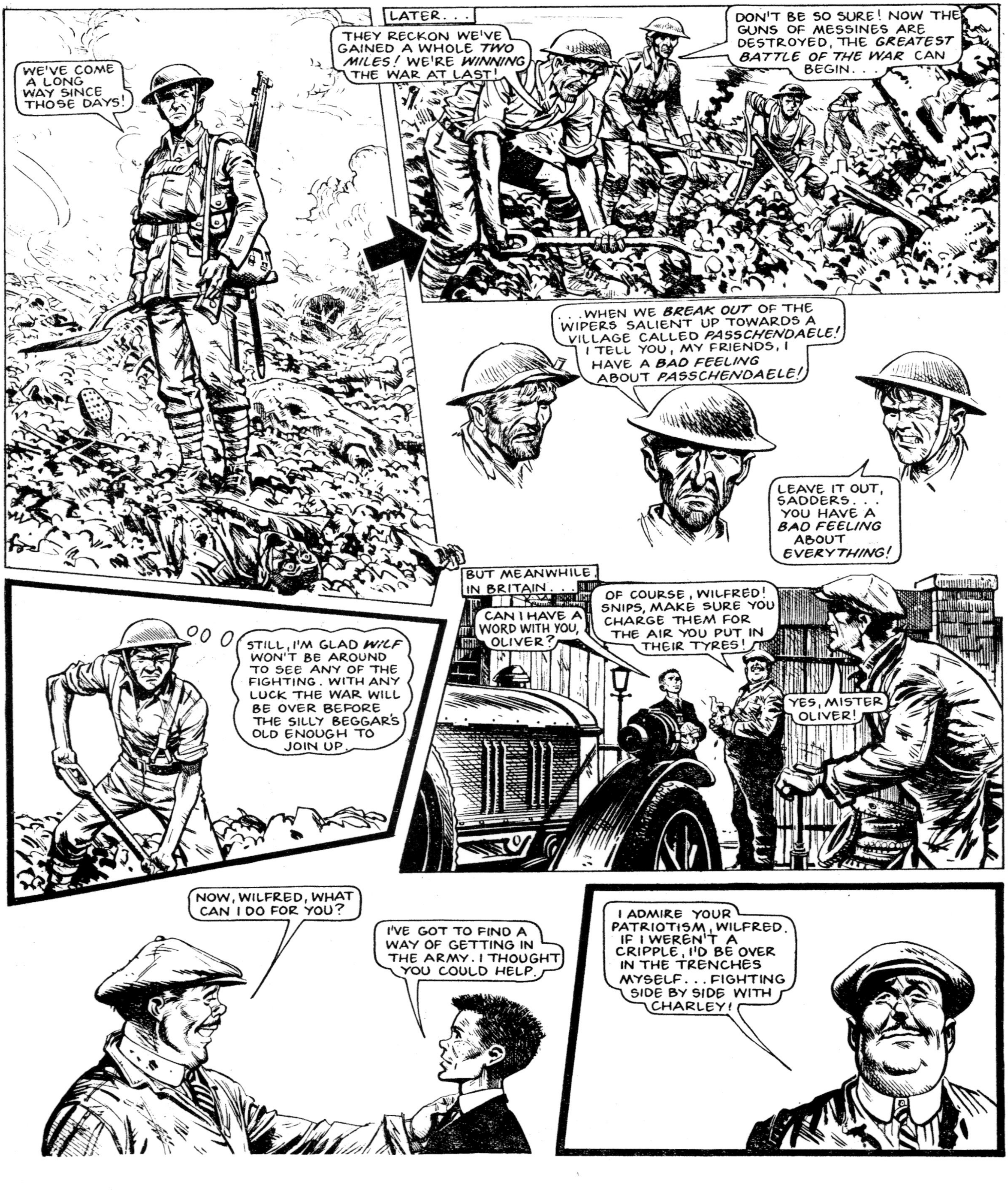

WE'VE COME A LONG WAY SINCE THOSE DAYS!
LATER. . .
THEY RECKON WE'VE GAINED A WHOLE TWO MILES! WE'RE WINNING THE WAR AT LAST!
DON'T BE SO SURE! NOW THE GUNS OF MESSINES ARE DESTROYED, THE GREATEST BATTLE OF THE WAR CAN BEGIN. . .
. . .WHEN WE BREAK OUT OF THE WIPERS SALIENT UP TOWARDS A VILLAGE CALLED PASSCHENDAELE! I TELL YOU, MY FRIENDS, I HAVE A BAD FEELING ABOUT PASSCHENDAELE!
LEAVE IT OUT, SADDERS. . . YOU HAVE A BAD FEELING ABOUT EVERYTHING!
STILL, I'M GLAD WILF WON'T BE AROUND TO SEE ANY OF THE FIGHTING. WITH ANY LUCK THE WAR WILL BE OVER BEFORE THE SILLY BEGGAR'S OLD ENOUGH TO JOIN UP.
BUT MEANWHILE IN BRITAIN. . .
CAN I HAVE A WORD WITH YOU, OLIVER?
OF COURSE, WILFRED! SNIPS, MAKE SURE YOU CHARGE THEM FOR THE AIR YOU PUT IN THEIR TYRES!
YES, MISTER OLIVER!
NOW, WILFRED, WHAT CAN I DO FOR YOU?
I'VE GOT TO FIND A WAY OF GETTING IN THE ARMY. I THOUGHT YOU COULD HELP.
I ADMIRE YOUR PATRIOTISM, WILFRED. IF I WEREN'T A CRIPPLE, I'D BE OVER IN THE TRENCHES MYSELF. . . FIGHTING SIDE BY SIDE WITH CHARLEY!

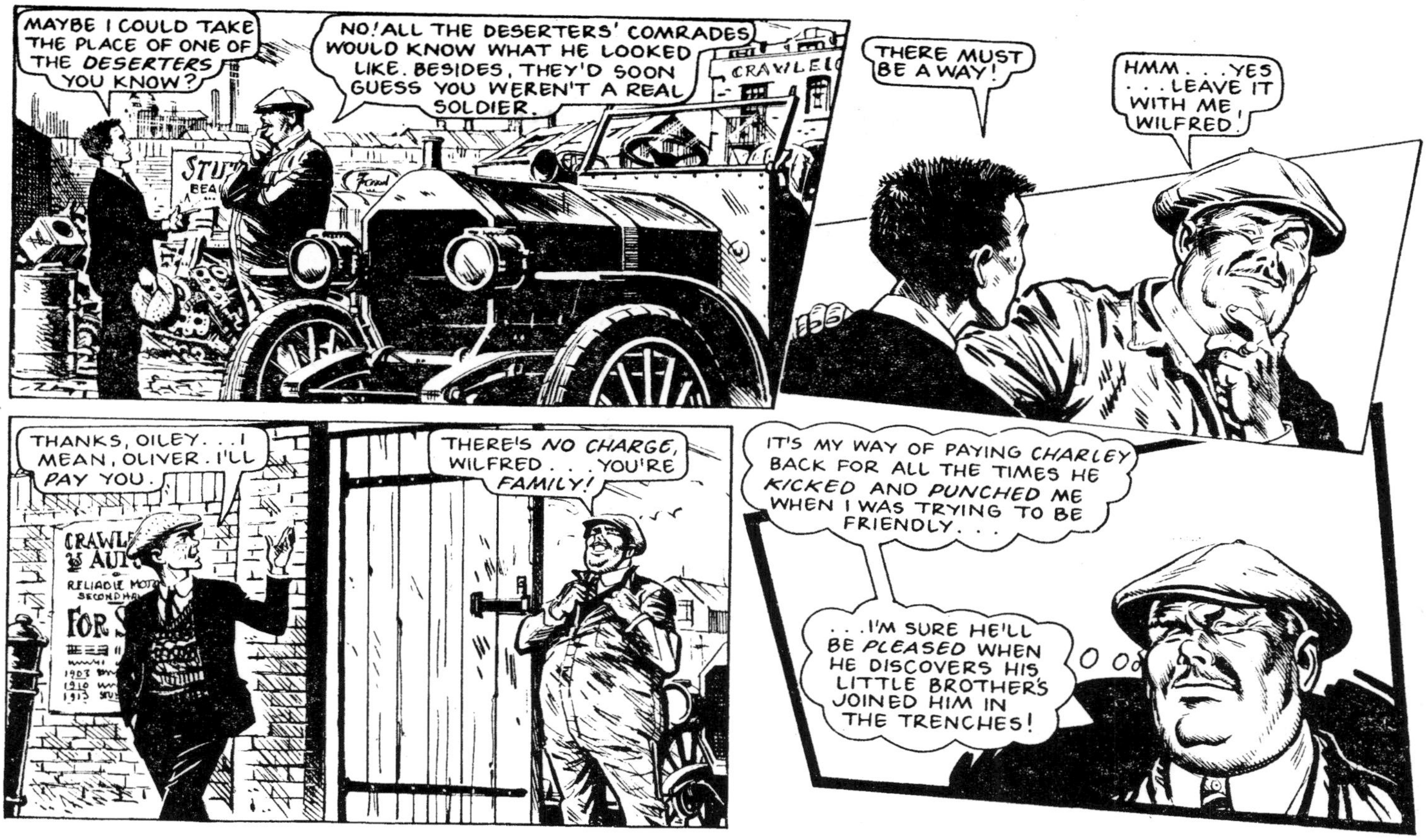
MAYBE I COULD TAKE THE PLACE OF ONE OF THE *DESERTERS* YOU KNOW?
NO! ALL THE DESERTERS' COMRADES WOULD KNOW WHAT HE LOOKED LIKE. BESIDES, THEY'D SOON GUESS YOU WEREN'T A REAL SOLDIER.
CRAWLE
THERE MUST BE A WAY!
HMM. . . YES . . . LEAVE IT WITH ME, WILFRED!
THANKS, OILEY. . . I MEAN, OLIVER. I'LL *PAY* YOU.
CRAWL AUT
RELIABLE MOTO
FOR S
THERE'S *NO CHARGE*, WILFRED . . . YOU'RE *FAMILY!*
IT'S MY WAY OF PAYING *CHARLEY* BACK FOR ALL THE TIMES HE *KICKED* AND *PUNCHED* ME WHEN I WAS TRYING TO BE FRIENDLY. . .
. . . I'M SURE HE'LL BE *PLEASED* WHEN HE DISCOVERS HIS LITTLE BROTHER'S JOINED HIM IN THE TRENCHES!

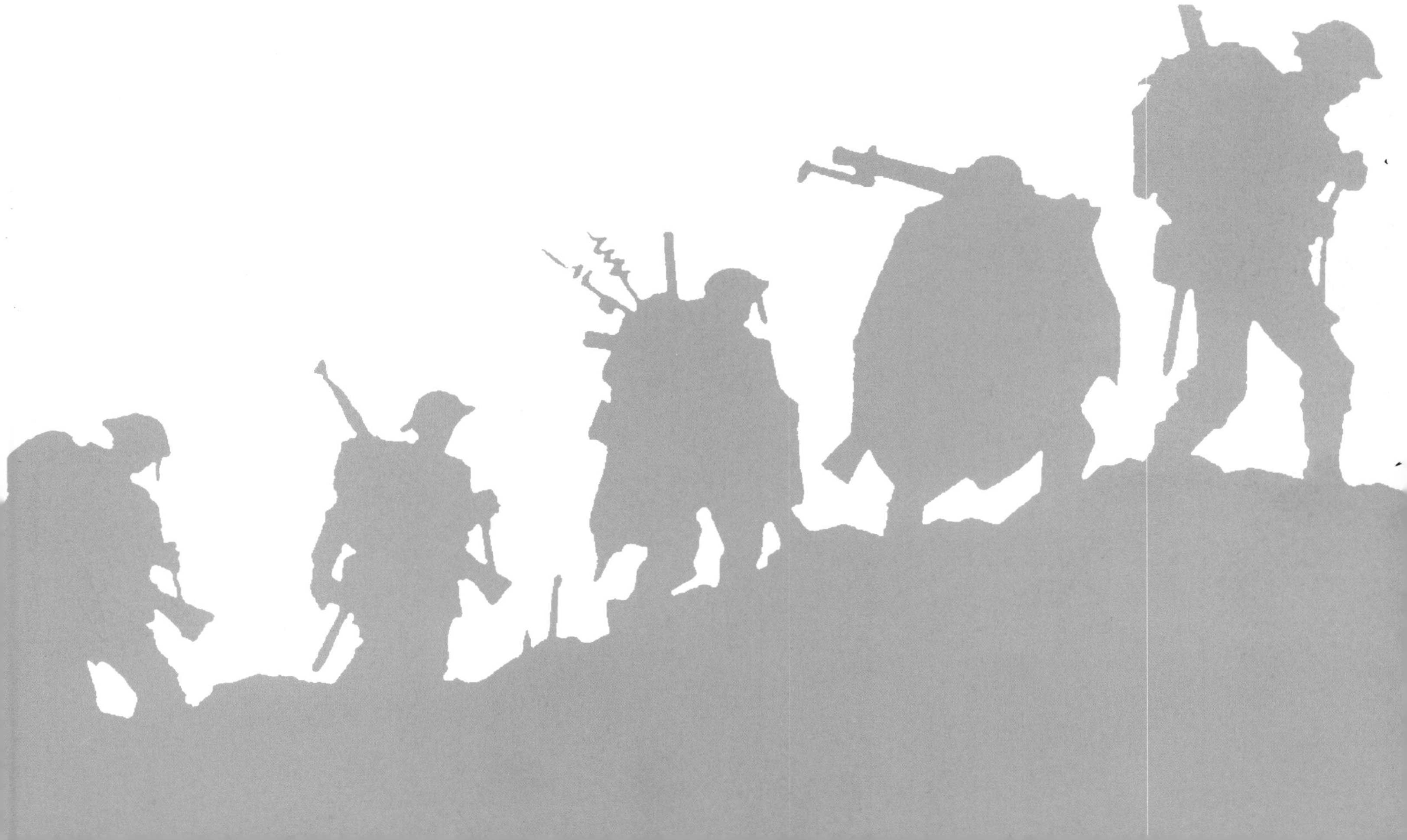

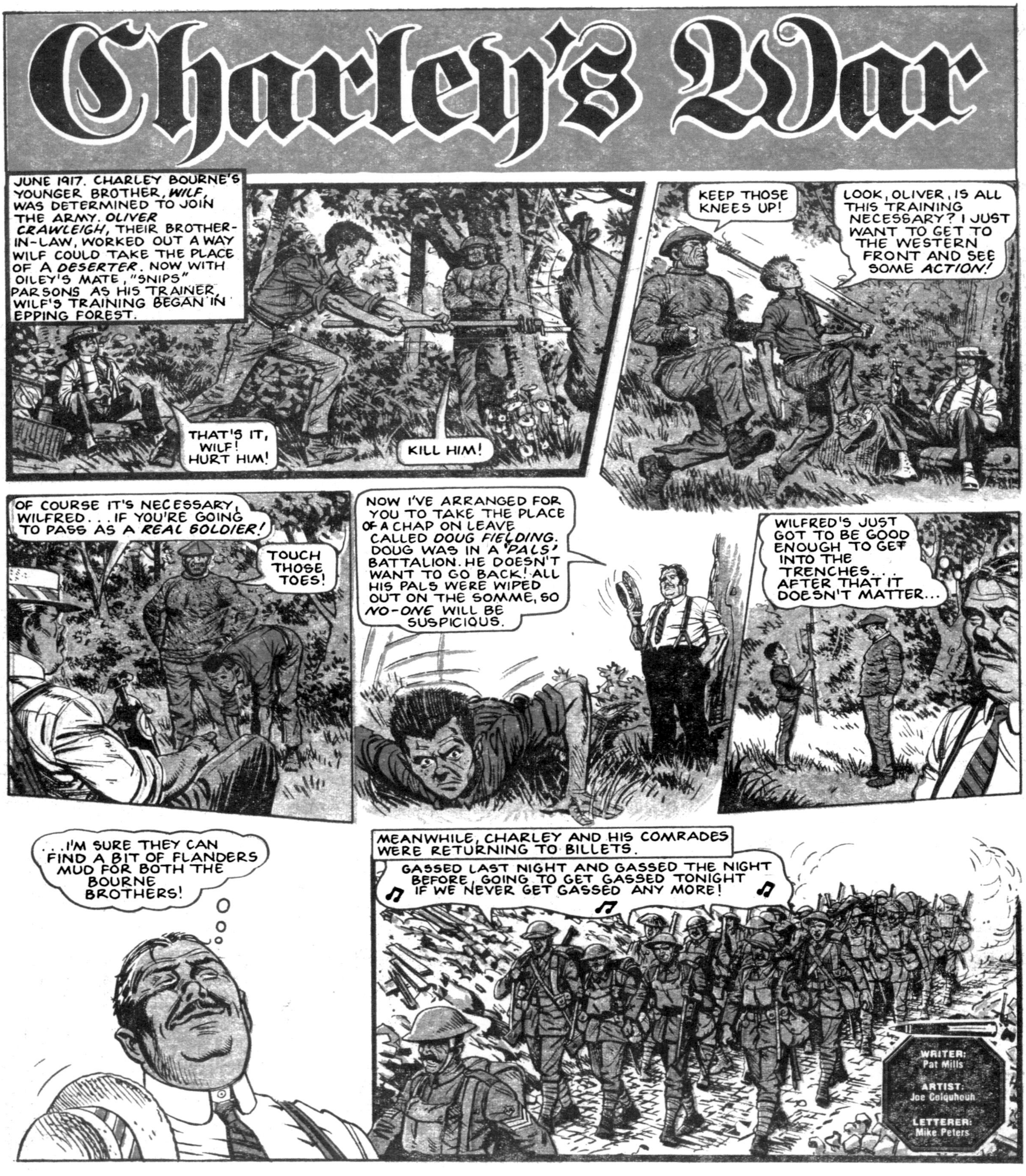
Charley's War
JUNE 1917. CHARLEY BOURNE'S YOUNGER BROTHER, WILF, WAS DETERMINED TO JOIN THE ARMY. OLIVER CRAWLEIGH, THEIR BROTHER-IN-LAW, WORKED OUT A WAY WILF COULD TAKE THE PLACE OF A DESERTER. NOW WITH OILEY'S MATE, "SNIPS" PARSONS AS HIS TRAINER, WILF'S TRAINING BEGAN IN EPPING FOREST.
THAT'S IT, WILF! HURT HIM!
KILL HIM!
KEEP THOSE KNEES UP!
LOOK, OLIVER, IS ALL THIS TRAINING NECESSARY? I JUST WANT TO GET TO THE WESTERN FRONT AND SEE SOME ACTION!
OF COURSE IT'S NECESSARY, WILFRED... IF YOU'RE GOING TO PASS AS A REAL SOLDIER!
TOUCH THOSE TOES!
NOW I'VE ARRANGED FOR YOU TO TAKE THE PLACE OF A CHAP ON LEAVE CALLED DOUG FIELDING. DOUG WAS IN A 'PALS' BATTALION. HE DOESN'T WANT TO GO BACK! ALL HIS PALS WERE WIPED OUT ON THE SOMME, SO NO-ONE WILL BE SUSPICIOUS.
WILFRED'S JUST GOT TO BE GOOD ENOUGH TO GET INTO THE TRENCHES... AFTER THAT IT DOESN'T MATTER...
...I'M SURE THEY CAN FIND A BIT OF FLANDERS MUD FOR BOTH THE BOURNE BROTHERS!
MEANWHILE, CHARLEY AND HIS COMRADES WERE RETURNING TO BILLETS.
GASSED LAST NIGHT AND GASSED THE NIGHT BEFORE, GOING TO GET GASSED TONIGHT IF WE NEVER GET GASSED ANY MORE!
WRITER: Pat Mills
ARTIST: Joe Colquhoun
LETTERER: Mike Peters

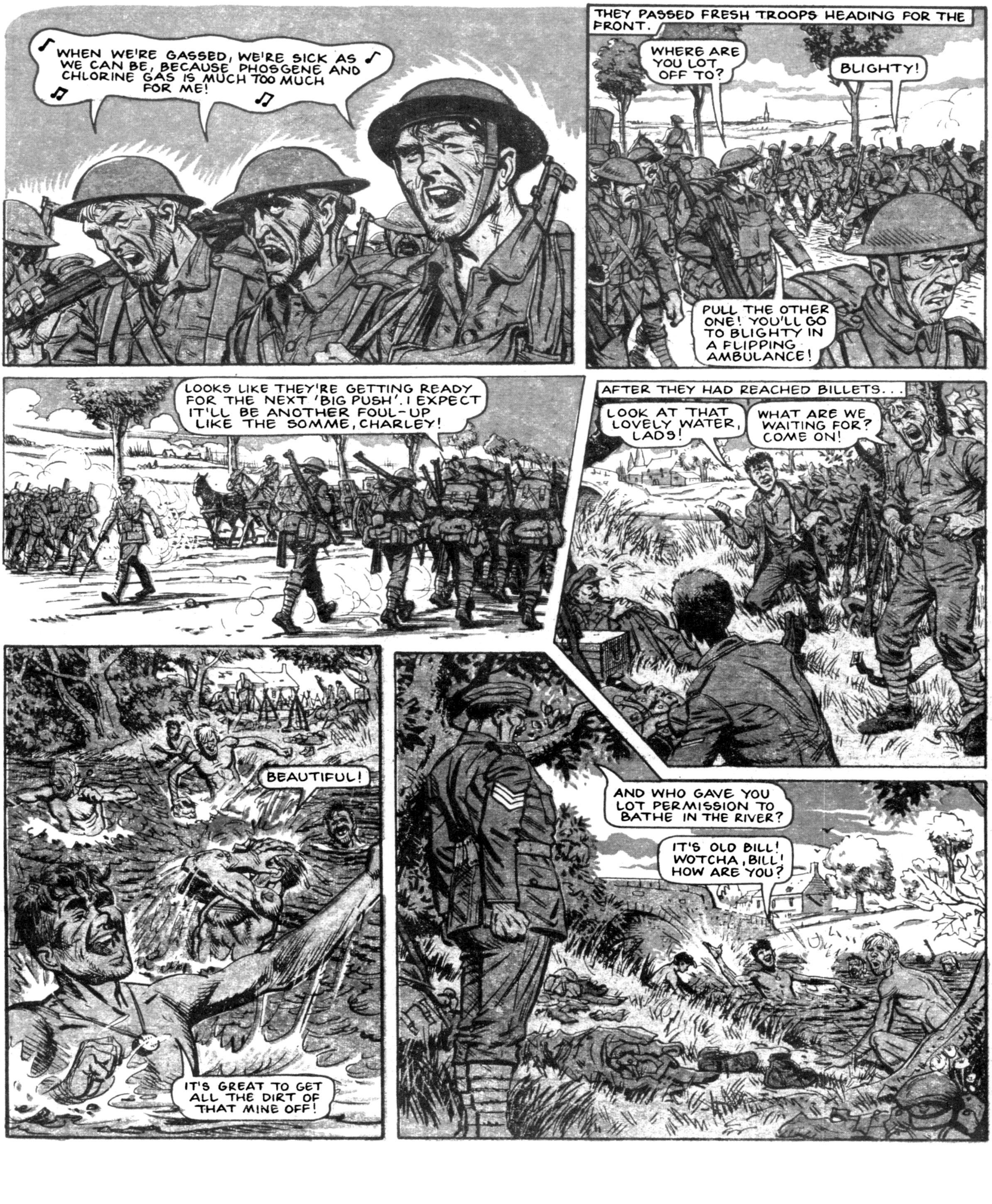

WHEN WE'RE GASSED, WE'RE SICK AS WE CAN BE, BECAUSE PHOSGENE AND CHLORINE GAS IS MUCH TOO MUCH FOR ME!
THEY PASSED FRESH TROOPS HEADING FOR THE FRONT.
WHERE ARE YOU LOT OFF TO?
BLIGHTY!
PULL THE OTHER ONE! YOU'LL GO TO BLIGHTY IN A FLIPPING AMBULANCE!
LOOKS LIKE THEY'RE GETTING READY FOR THE NEXT 'BIG PUSH'. I EXPECT IT'LL BE ANOTHER FOUL-UP LIKE THE SOMME, CHARLEY!
AFTER THEY HAD REACHED BILLETS...
LOOK AT THAT LOVELY WATER, LADS!
WHAT ARE WE WAITING FOR? COME ON!
BEAUTIFUL!
IT'S GREAT TO GET ALL THE DIRT OF THAT MINE OFF!
AND WHO GAVE YOU LOT PERMISSION TO BATHE IN THE RIVER?
IT'S OLD BILL! WOTCHA, BILL! HOW ARE YOU?

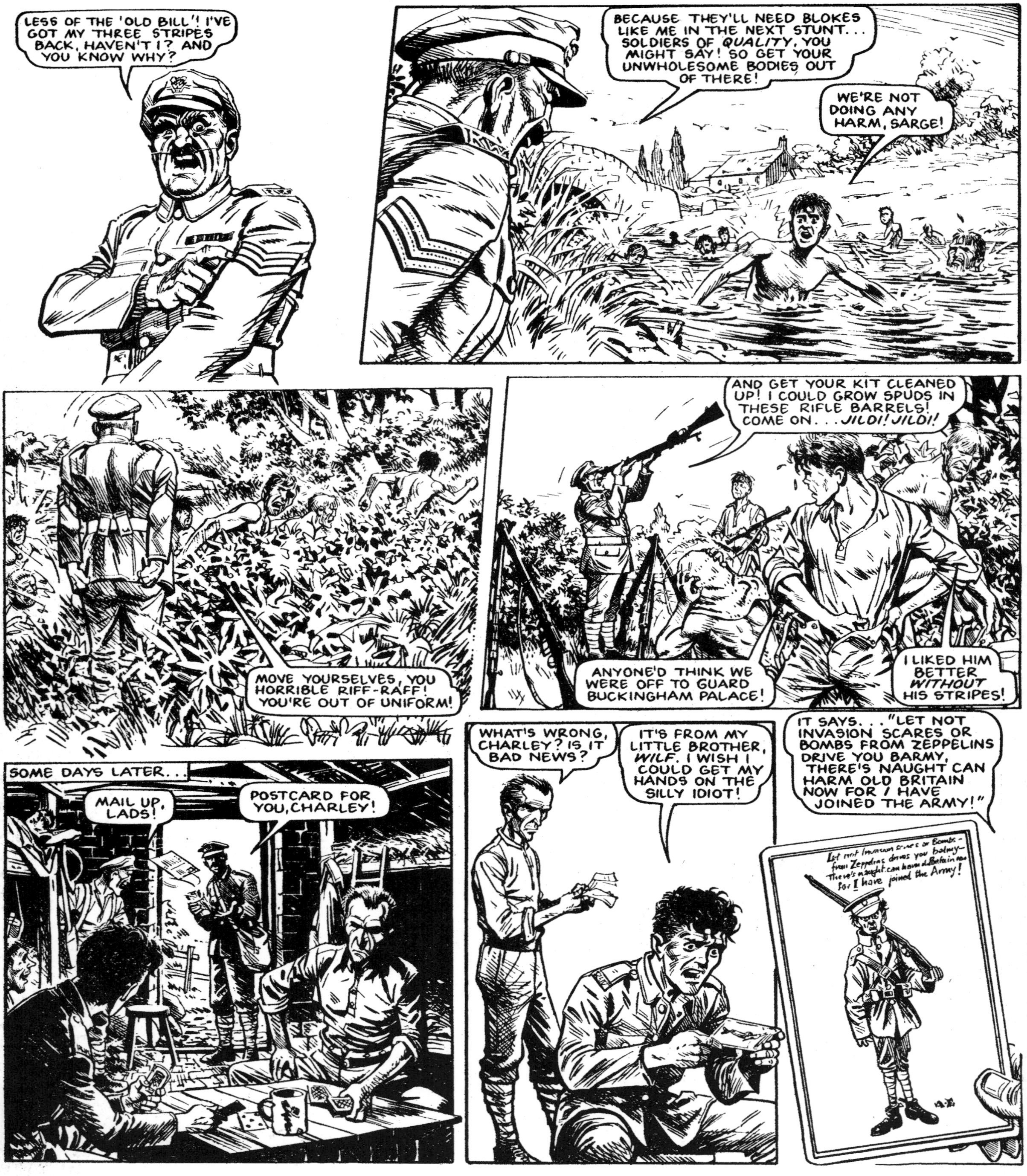

LESS OF THE 'OLD BILL'! I'VE GOT MY THREE STRIPES BACK, HAVEN'T I? AND YOU KNOW WHY?
BECAUSE THEY'LL NEED BLOKES LIKE ME IN THE NEXT STUNT... SOLDIERS OF QUALITY, YOU MIGHT SAY! SO GET YOUR UNWHOLESOME BODIES OUT OF THERE!
WE'RE NOT DOING ANY HARM, SARGE!
MOVE YOURSELVES, YOU HORRIBLE RIFF-RAFF! YOU'RE OUT OF UNIFORM!
AND GET YOUR KIT CLEANED UP! I COULD GROW SPUDS IN THESE RIFLE BARRELS! COME ON... JILDI! JILDI!
ANYONE'D THINK WE WERE OFF TO GUARD BUCKINGHAM PALACE!
I LIKED HIM BETTER WITHOUT HIS STRIPES!
SOME DAYS LATER...
MAIL UP, LADS!
POSTCARD FOR YOU, CHARLEY!
WHAT'S WRONG, CHARLEY? IS IT BAD NEWS?
IT'S FROM MY LITTLE BROTHER, WILF. I WISH I COULD GET MY HANDS ON THE SILLY IDIOT!
IT SAYS..."LET NOT INVASION SCARES OR BOMBS FROM ZEPPELINS DRIVE YOU BARMY, THERE'S NAUGHT CAN HARM OLD BRITAIN NOW FOR I HAVE JOINED THE ARMY!"

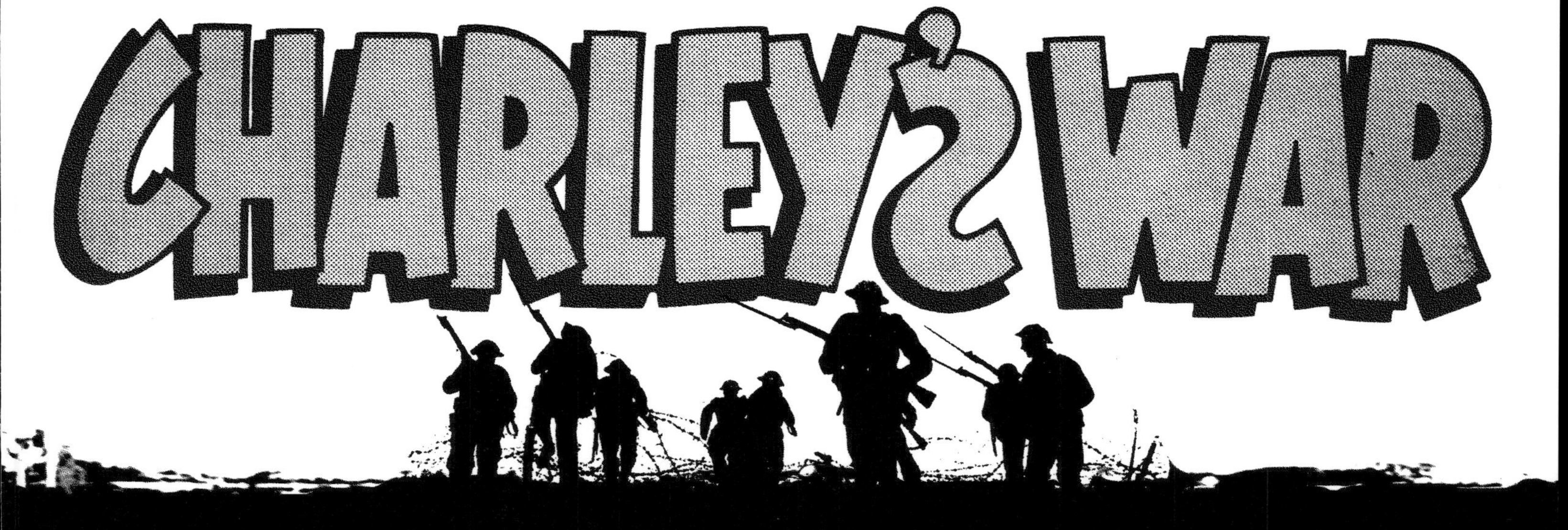
CHARLEY'S WAR

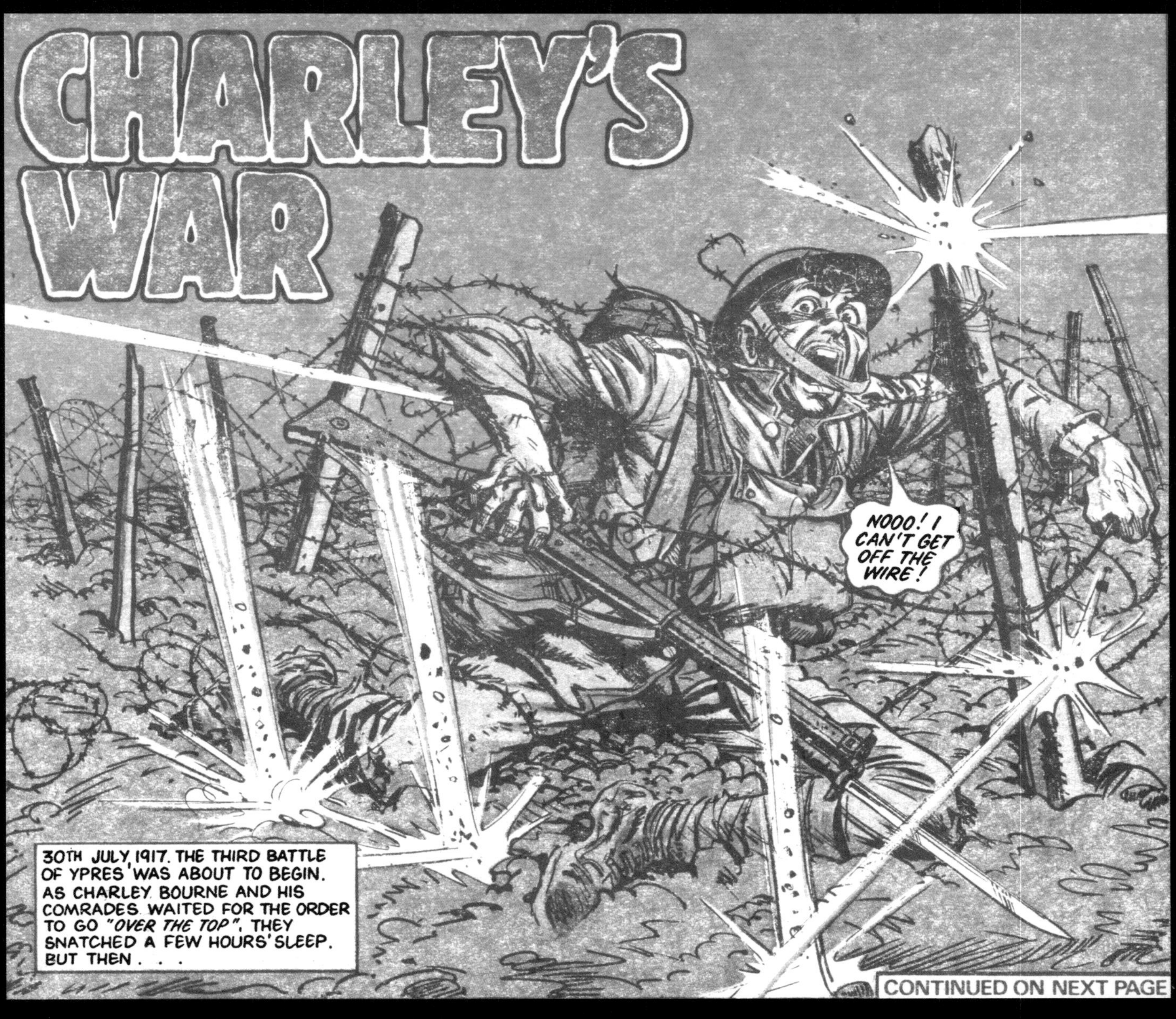
CHARLEY'S WAR
NOOO! I CAN'T GET OFF THE WIRE!
30TH JULY, 1917. THE THIRD BATTLE OF YPRES WAS ABOUT TO BEGIN. AS CHARLEY BOURNE AND HIS COMRADES WAITED FOR THE ORDER TO GO "OVER THE TOP", THEY SNATCHED A FEW HOURS' SLEEP. BUT THEN . . .

CONTINUED ON NEXT PAGE

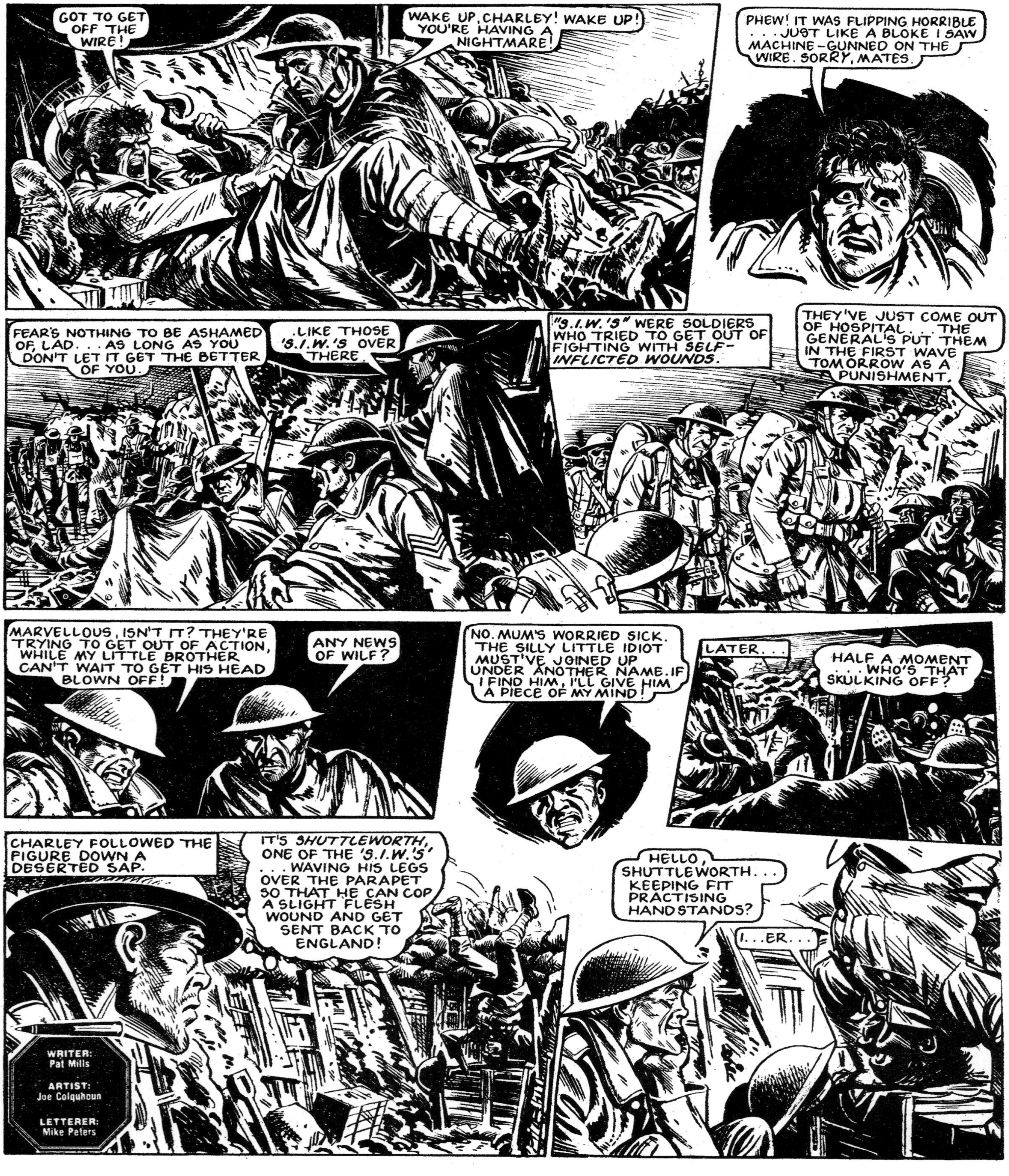
GOT TO GET OFF THE WIRE!
WAKE UP, CHARLEY! WAKE UP! YOU'RE HAVING A NIGHTMARE!
PHEW! IT WAS FLIPPING HORRIBLE . . . JUST LIKE A BLOKE I SAW MACHINE-GUNNED ON THE WIRE. SORRY, MATES.
FEAR'S NOTHING TO BE ASHAMED OF, LAD . . . AS LONG AS YOU DON'T LET IT GET THE BETTER OF YOU.
. . . LIKE THOSE 'S.I.W.'S' OVER THERE.
"S.I.W.'S" WERE SOLDIERS WHO TRIED TO GET OUT OF FIGHTING WITH SELF-INFLICTED WOUNDS.
THEY'VE JUST COME OUT OF HOSPITAL . . . THE GENERAL'S PUT THEM IN THE FIRST WAVE TOMORROW AS A PUNISHMENT.
MARVELLOUS, ISN'T IT? THEY'RE TRYING TO GET OUT OF ACTION, WHILE MY LITTLE BROTHER CAN'T WAIT TO GET HIS HEAD BLOWN OFF!
ANY NEWS OF WILF?
NO. MUM'S WORRIED SICK. THE SILLY LITTLE IDIOT MUST'VE JOINED UP UNDER ANOTHER NAME. IF I FIND HIM, I'LL GIVE HIM A PIECE OF MY MIND!
LATER . . .
HALF A MOMENT . . . WHO'S THAT SKULKING OFF?
CHARLEY FOLLOWED THE FIGURE DOWN A DESERTED SAP.
IT'S SHUTTLEWORTH, ONE OF THE 'S.I.W.'S' . . . WAVING HIS LEGS OVER THE PARAPET SO THAT HE CAN COP A SLIGHT FLESH WOUND AND GET SENT BACK TO ENGLAND!
HELLO, SHUTTLEWORTH . . . KEEPING FIT PRACTISING HANDSTANDS?
I . . . ER . . .
WRITER: Pat Mills
ARTIST: Joe Colquhoun
LETTERER: Mike Peters

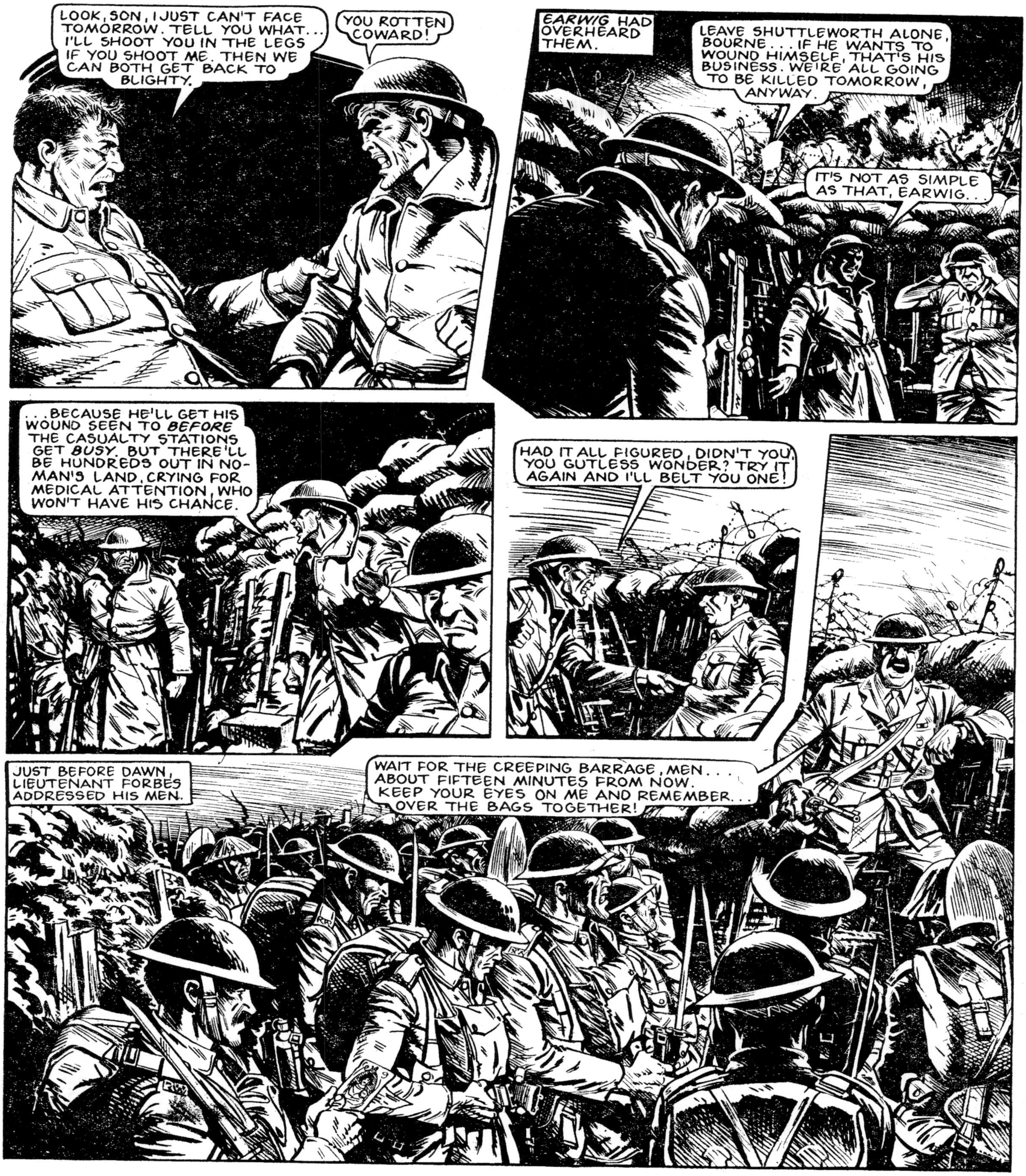
LOOK, SON, I JUST CAN'T FACE TOMORROW. TELL YOU WHAT... I'LL SHOOT YOU IN THE LEGS IF YOU SHOOT ME. THEN WE CAN BOTH GET BACK TO BLIGHTY.
YOU ROTTEN COWARD!
EARWIG HAD OVERHEARD THEM.
LEAVE SHUTTLEWORTH ALONE, BOURNE... IF HE WANTS TO WOUND HIMSELF, THAT'S HIS BUSINESS. WE'RE ALL GOING TO BE KILLED TOMORROW, ANYWAY.
IT'S NOT AS SIMPLE AS THAT, EARWIG...
...BECAUSE HE'LL GET HIS WOUND SEEN TO BEFORE THE CASUALTY STATIONS GET BUSY. BUT THERE'LL BE HUNDREDS OUT IN NO-MAN'S LAND, CRYING FOR MEDICAL ATTENTION, WHO WON'T HAVE HIS CHANCE.
HAD IT ALL FIGURED, DIDN'T YOU, YOU GUTLESS WONDER? TRY IT AGAIN AND I'LL BELT YOU ONE!
JUST BEFORE DAWN, LIEUTENANT FORBES ADDRESSED HIS MEN.
WAIT FOR THE CREEPING BARRAGE, MEN... ABOUT FIFTEEN MINUTES FROM NOW. KEEP YOUR EYES ON ME AND REMEMBER... OVER THE BAGS TOGETHER!

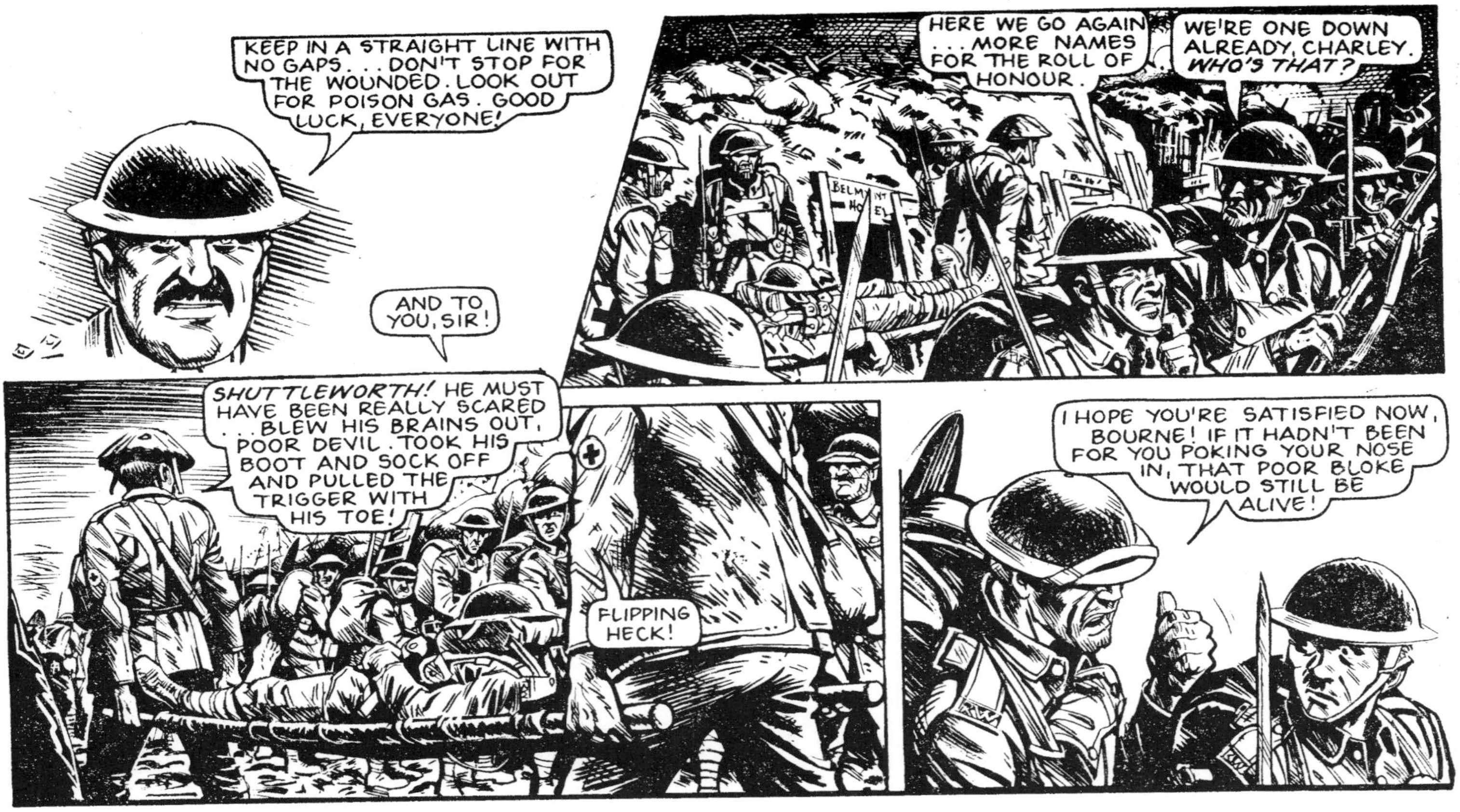
KEEP IN A STRAIGHT LINE WITH NO GAPS . . . DON'T STOP FOR THE WOUNDED. LOOK OUT FOR POISON GAS. GOOD LUCK, EVERYONE!
AND TO YOU, SIR!
HERE WE GO AGAIN . . . MORE NAMES FOR THE ROLL OF HONOUR.
WE'RE ONE DOWN ALREADY, CHARLEY. *WHO'S THAT?*
SHUTTLEWORTH! HE MUST HAVE BEEN REALLY SCARED . . BLEW HIS BRAINS OUT, POOR DEVIL. TOOK HIS BOOT AND SOCK OFF AND PULLED THE TRIGGER WITH HIS TOE!
FLIPPING HECK!
I HOPE YOU'RE SATISFIED NOW, BOURNE! IF IT HADN'T BEEN FOR YOU POKING YOUR NOSE IN, THAT POOR BLOKE WOULD STILL BE ALIVE!

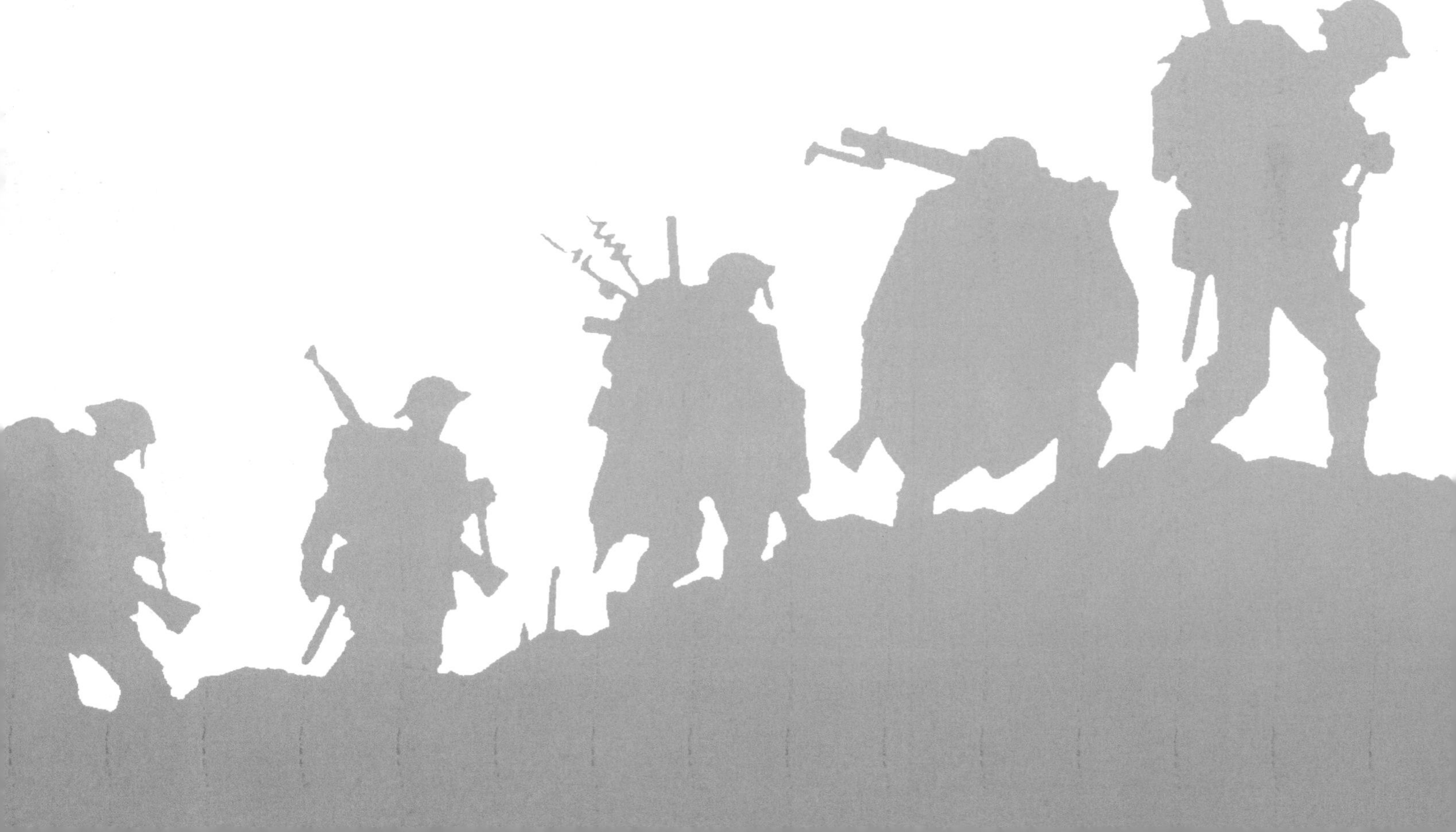

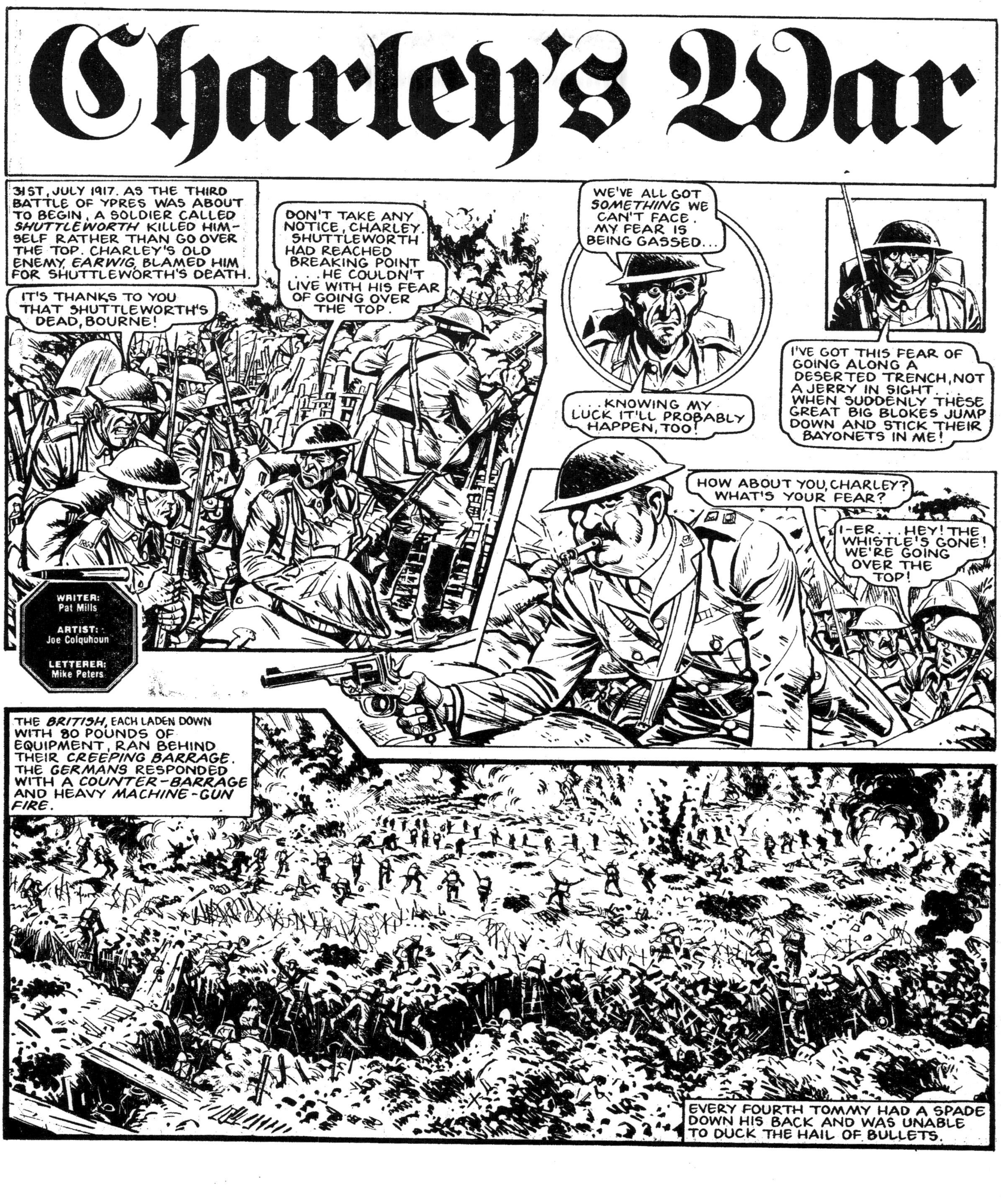

Charley's War
31ST, JULY 1917. AS THE THIRD BATTLE OF YPRES WAS ABOUT TO BEGIN, A SOLDIER CALLED *SHUTTLEWORTH* KILLED HIMSELF RATHER THAN GO OVER THE TOP. CHARLEY'S OLD ENEMY, *EARWIG*, BLAMED HIM FOR SHUTTLEWORTH'S DEATH.
IT'S THANKS TO YOU THAT SHUTTLEWORTH'S DEAD, BOURNE!
DON'T TAKE ANY NOTICE, CHARLEY. SHUTTLEWORTH HAD REACHED BREAKING POINT . . . HE COULDN'T LIVE WITH HIS FEAR OF GOING OVER THE TOP.
WRITER: Pat Mills
ARTIST: Joe Colquhoun
LETTERER: Mike Peters
WE'VE ALL GOT *SOMETHING* WE CAN'T FACE. MY FEAR IS BEING GASSED...
...KNOWING MY LUCK IT'LL PROBABLY HAPPEN, TOO!
I'VE GOT THIS FEAR OF GOING ALONG A DESERTED TRENCH, NOT A JERRY IN SIGHT. WHEN SUDDENLY THESE GREAT BIG BLOKES JUMP DOWN AND STICK THEIR BAYONETS IN ME!
HOW ABOUT YOU, CHARLEY? WHAT'S YOUR FEAR?
I-ER... HEY! THE WHISTLE'S GONE! WE'RE GOING OVER THE TOP!
THE *BRITISH*, EACH LADEN DOWN WITH 80 POUNDS OF EQUIPMENT, RAN BEHIND THEIR *CREEPING BARRAGE*. THE *GERMANS* RESPONDED WITH A *COUNTER-BARRAGE* AND HEAVY *MACHINE-GUN FIRE*.
EVERY FOURTH TOMMY HAD A SPADE DOWN HIS BACK AND WAS UNABLE TO DUCK THE HAIL OF BULLETS.

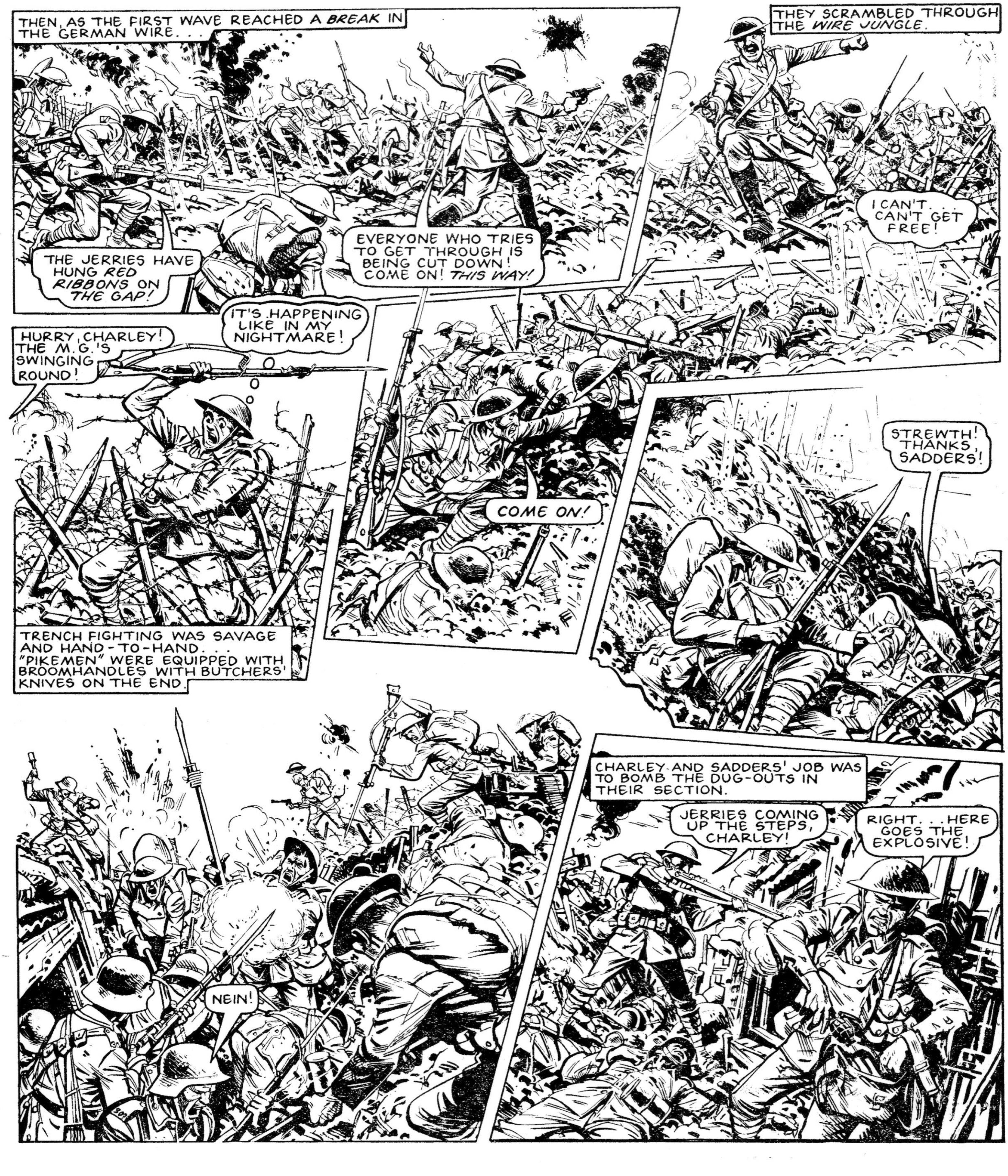

THEN, AS THE FIRST WAVE REACHED A *BREAK* IN THE GERMAN WIRE. . .
THE JERRIES HAVE HUNG *RED RIBBONS* ON *THE GAP!*
EVERYONE WHO TRIES TO GET THROUGH IS BEING CUT DOWN! COME ON! *THIS WAY!*
THEY SCRAMBLED THROUGH THE *WIRE JUNGLE*.
I CAN'T. . . CAN'T GET FREE!
HURRY, CHARLEY! THE M.G.'S SWINGING ROUND!
IT'S HAPPENING LIKE IN MY NIGHTMARE!
TRENCH FIGHTING WAS SAVAGE AND HAND-TO-HAND. . . "PIKEMEN" WERE EQUIPPED WITH BROOMHANDLES WITH BUTCHERS' KNIVES ON THE END.
COME ON!
STREWTH! THANKS, SADDERS!
NEIN!
CHARLEY AND SADDERS' JOB WAS TO BOMB THE DUG-OUTS IN THEIR SECTION.
JERRIES COMING UP THE STEPS, CHARLEY!
RIGHT. . . HERE GOES THE EXPLOSIVE!

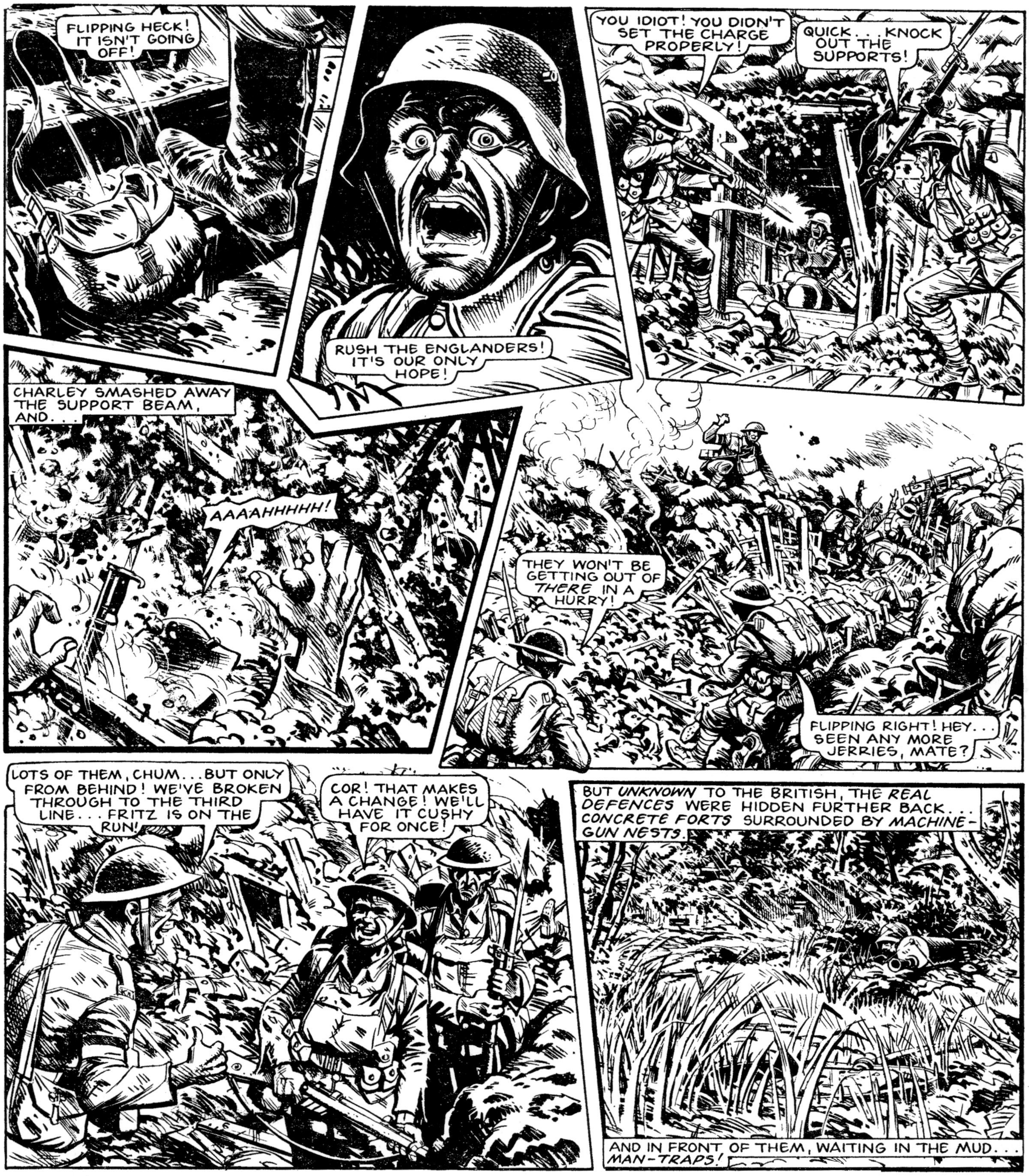
FLIPPING HECK! IT ISN'T GOING OFF!
RUSH THE ENGLANDERS! IT'S OUR ONLY HOPE!
YOU IDIOT! YOU DIDN'T SET THE CHARGE PROPERLY!
QUICK... KNOCK OUT THE SUPPORTS!
CHARLEY SMASHED AWAY THE SUPPORT BEAM, AND...
AAAAHHHHH!
THEY WON'T BE GETTING OUT OF THERE IN A HURRY!
FLIPPING RIGHT! HEY... SEEN ANY MORE JERRIES, MATE?
LOTS OF THEM, CHUM... BUT ONLY FROM BEHIND! WE'VE BROKEN THROUGH TO THE THIRD LINE... FRITZ IS ON THE RUN!
COR! THAT MAKES A CHANGE! WE'LL HAVE IT CUSHY FOR ONCE!
BUT UNKNOWN TO THE BRITISH, THE REAL DEFENCES WERE HIDDEN FURTHER BACK... CONCRETE FORTS SURROUNDED BY MACHINE-GUN NESTS.
AND IN FRONT OF THEM, WAITING IN THE MUD... MAN-TRAPS!

CHARLEY'S WAR

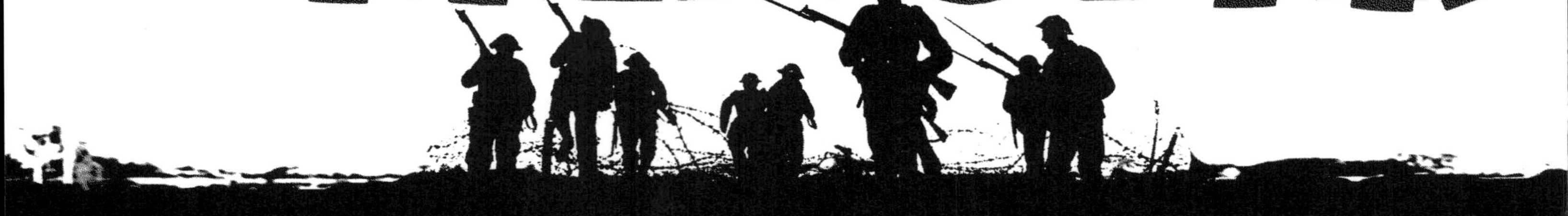

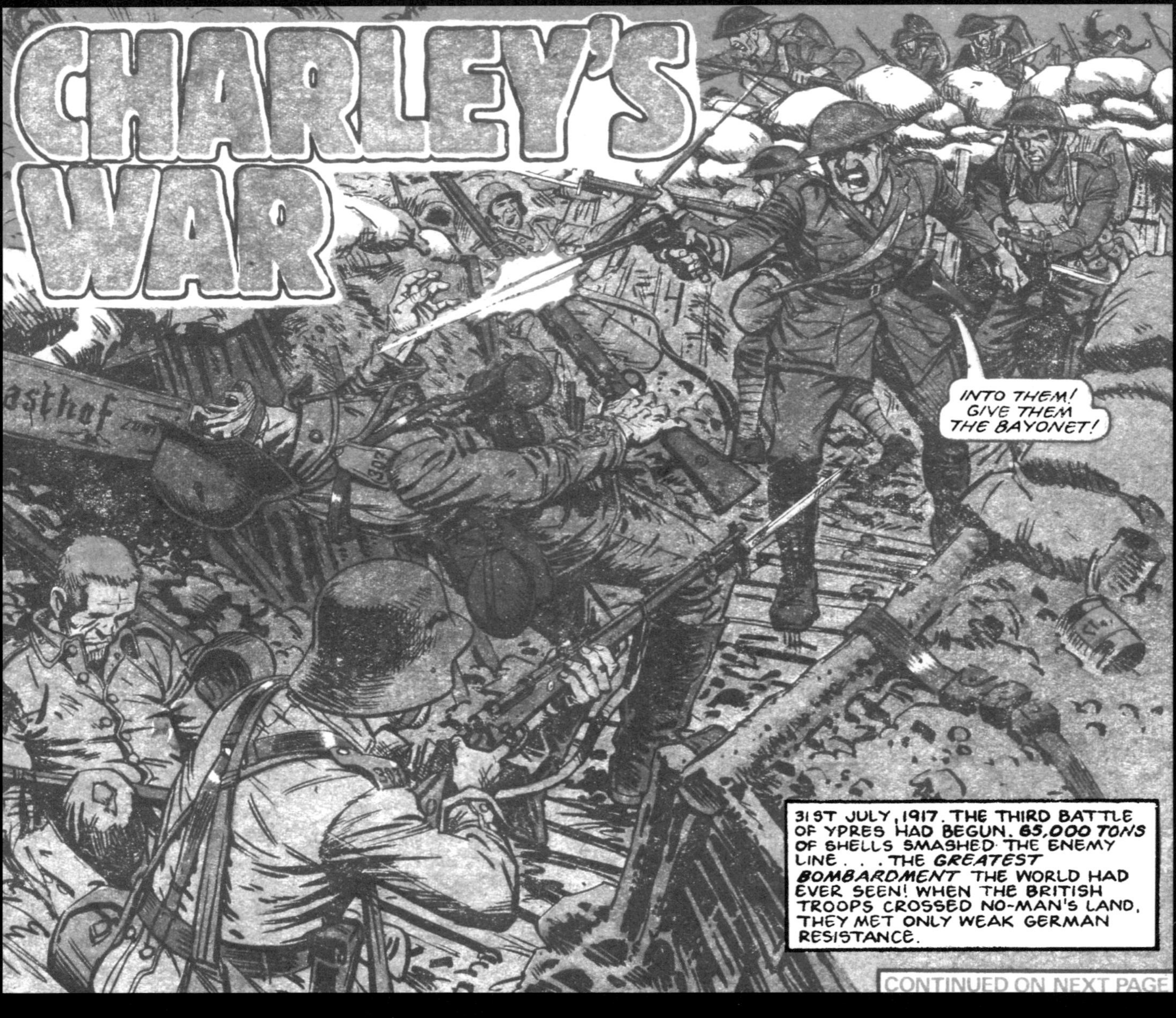
CHARLEY'S WAR
INTO THEM! GIVE THEM THE BAYONET!
31ST JULY, 1917. THE THIRD BATTLE OF YPRES HAD BEGUN. 65,000 TONS OF SHELLS SMASHED THE ENEMY LINE . . . THE GREATEST BOMBARDMENT THE WORLD HAD EVER SEEN! WHEN THE BRITISH TROOPS CROSSED NO-MAN'S LAND, THEY MET ONLY WEAK GERMAN RESISTANCE.
CONTINUED ON NEXT PAGE

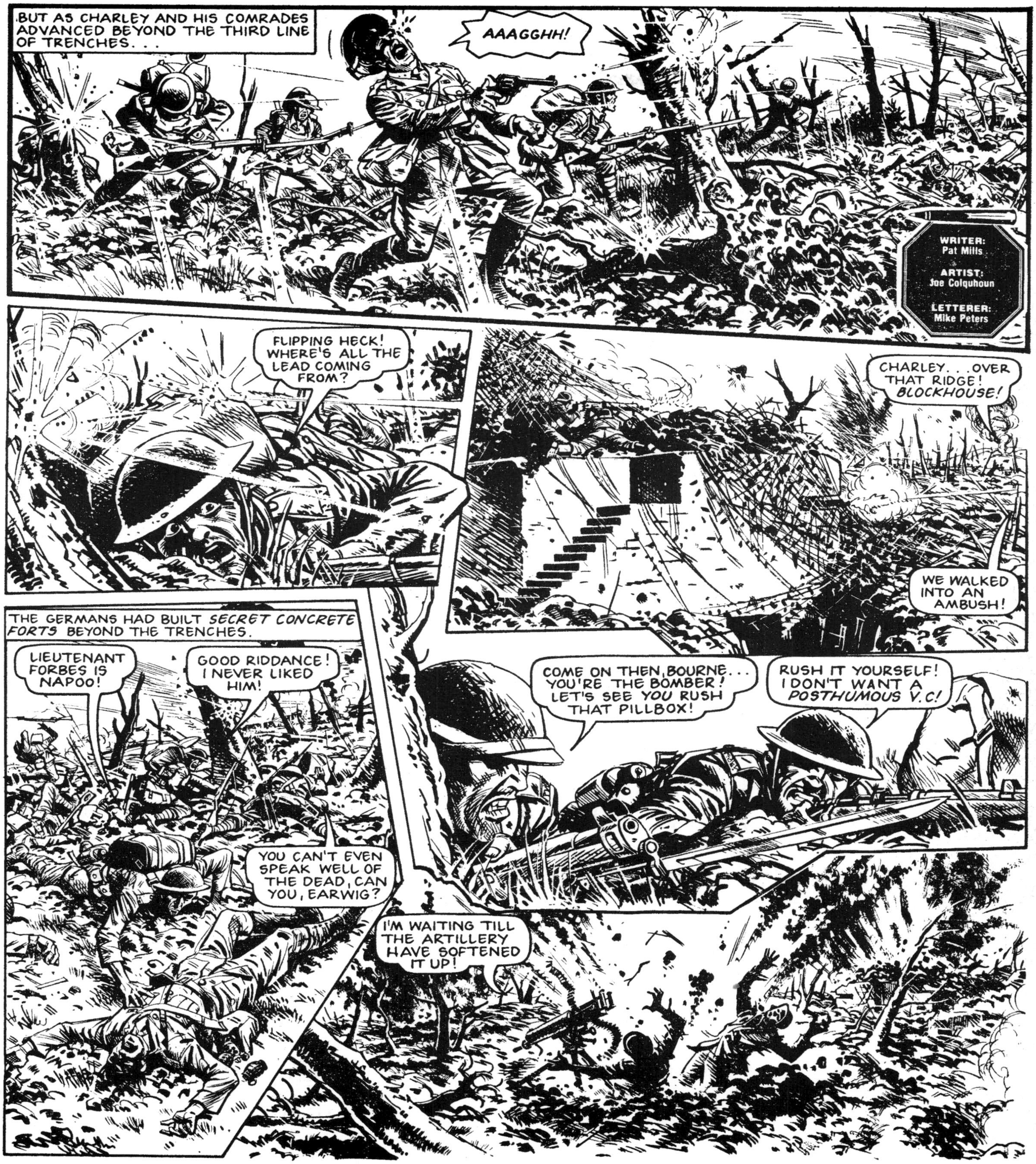
BUT AS CHARLEY AND HIS COMRADES ADVANCED BEYOND THE THIRD LINE OF TRENCHES...
AAAGGHH!
WRITER: Pat Mills
ARTIST: Joe Colquhoun
LETTERER: Mike Peters
FLIPPING HECK! WHERE'S ALL THE LEAD COMING FROM?
CHARLEY... OVER THAT RIDGE! BLOCKHOUSE!
WE WALKED INTO AN AMBUSH!
THE GERMANS HAD BUILT SECRET CONCRETE FORTS BEYOND THE TRENCHES.
LIEUTENANT FORBES IS NAPOO!
GOOD RIDDANCE! I NEVER LIKED HIM!
YOU CAN'T EVEN SPEAK WELL OF THE DEAD, CAN YOU, EARWIG?
COME ON THEN, BOURNE... YOU'RE THE BOMBER! LET'S SEE YOU RUSH THAT PILLBOX!
RUSH IT YOURSELF! I DON'T WANT A POSTHUMOUS V.C!
I'M WAITING TILL THE ARTILLERY HAVE SOFTENED IT UP!

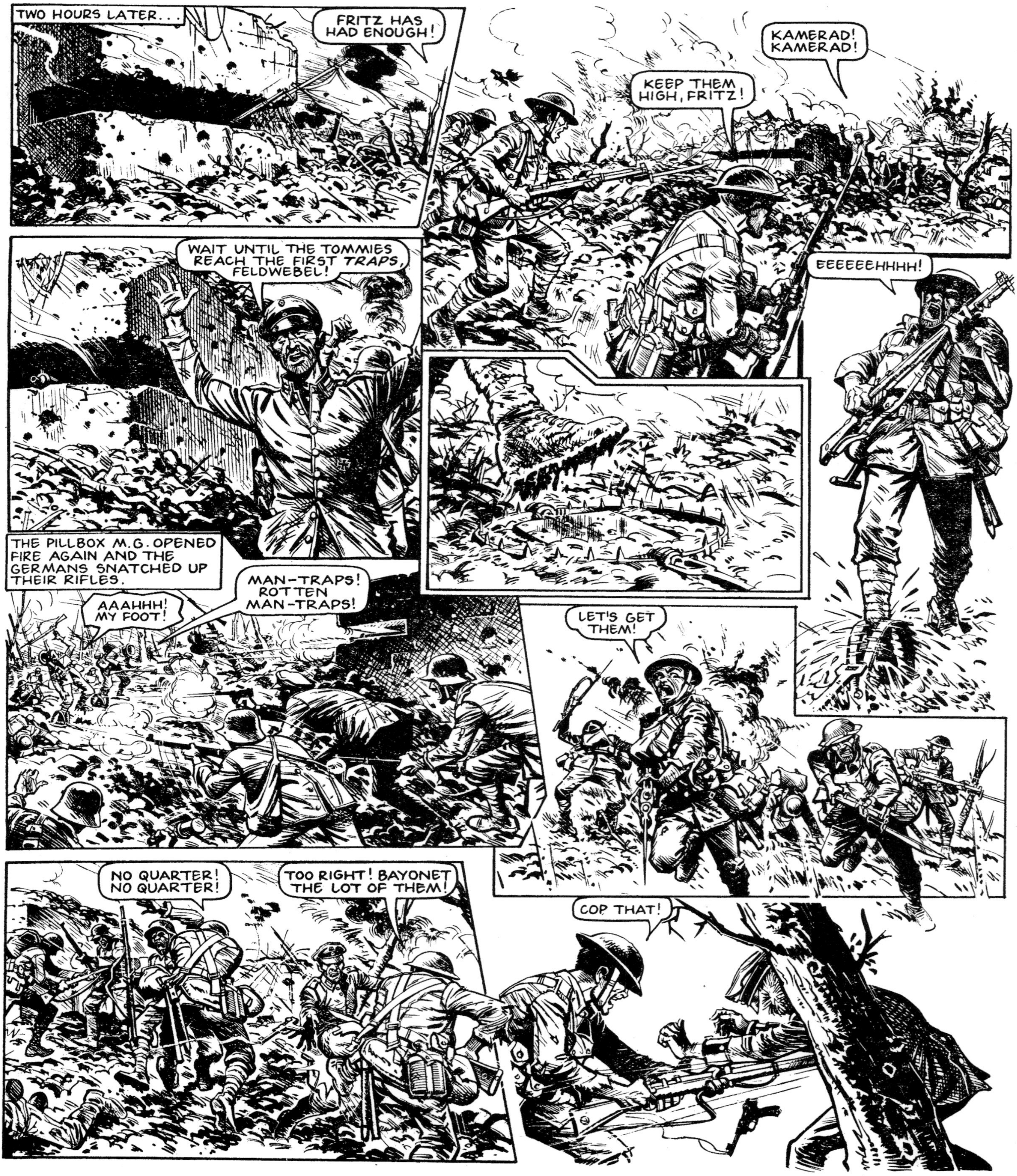

TWO HOURS LATER...
FRITZ HAS HAD ENOUGH!
KEEP THEM HIGH, FRITZ!
KAMERAD! KAMERAD!
WAIT UNTIL THE TOMMIES REACH THE FIRST TRAPS, FELDWEBEL!
EEEEEEHHHH!
THE PILLBOX M.G. OPENED FIRE AGAIN AND THE GERMANS SNATCHED UP THEIR RIFLES.
AAAHHH! MY FOOT!
MAN-TRAPS! ROTTEN MAN-TRAPS!
LET'S GET THEM!
NO QUARTER! NO QUARTER!
TOO RIGHT! BAYONET THE LOT OF THEM!
COP THAT!

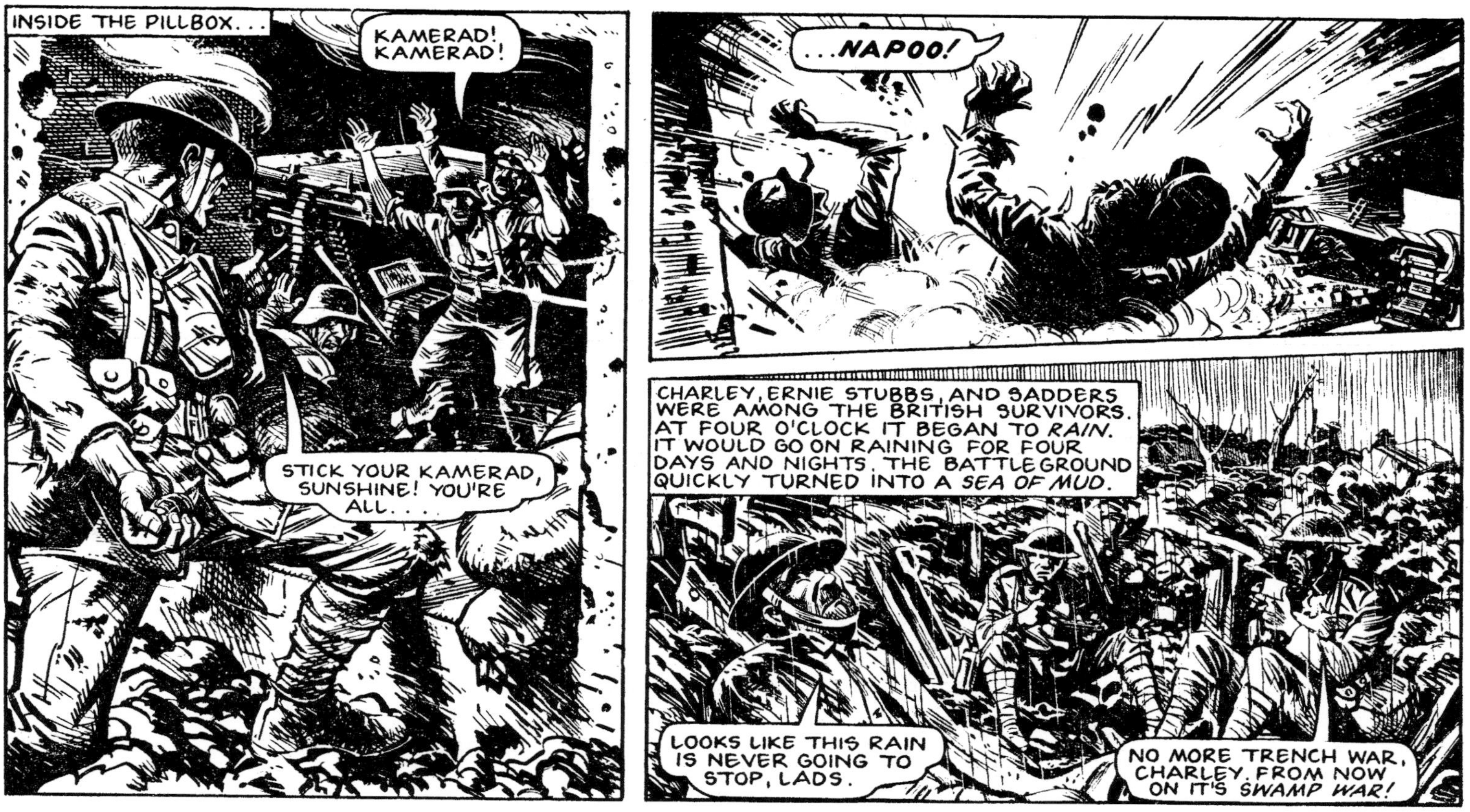
INSIDE THE PILLBOX...
KAMERAD! KAMERAD!
STICK YOUR KAMERAD, SUNSHINE! YOU'RE ALL...
...NAPOO!
CHARLEY, ERNIE STUBBS, AND SADDERS WERE AMONG THE BRITISH SURVIVORS. AT FOUR O'CLOCK IT BEGAN TO RAIN. IT WOULD GO ON RAINING FOR FOUR DAYS AND NIGHTS. THE BATTLEGROUND QUICKLY TURNED INTO A SEA OF MUD.
LOOKS LIKE THIS RAIN IS NEVER GOING TO STOP, LADS.
NO MORE TRENCH WAR, CHARLEY. FROM NOW ON IT'S SWAMP WAR!

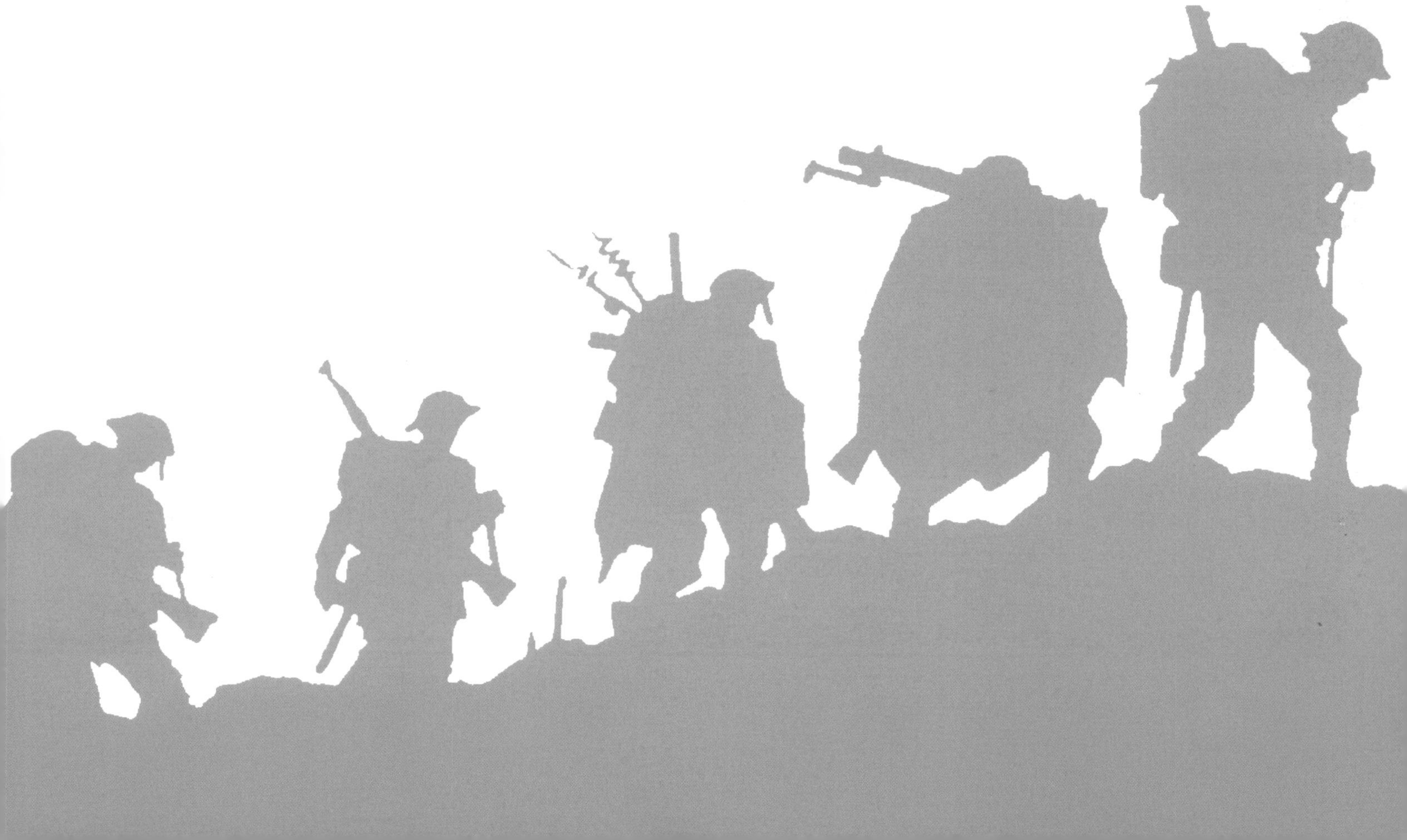

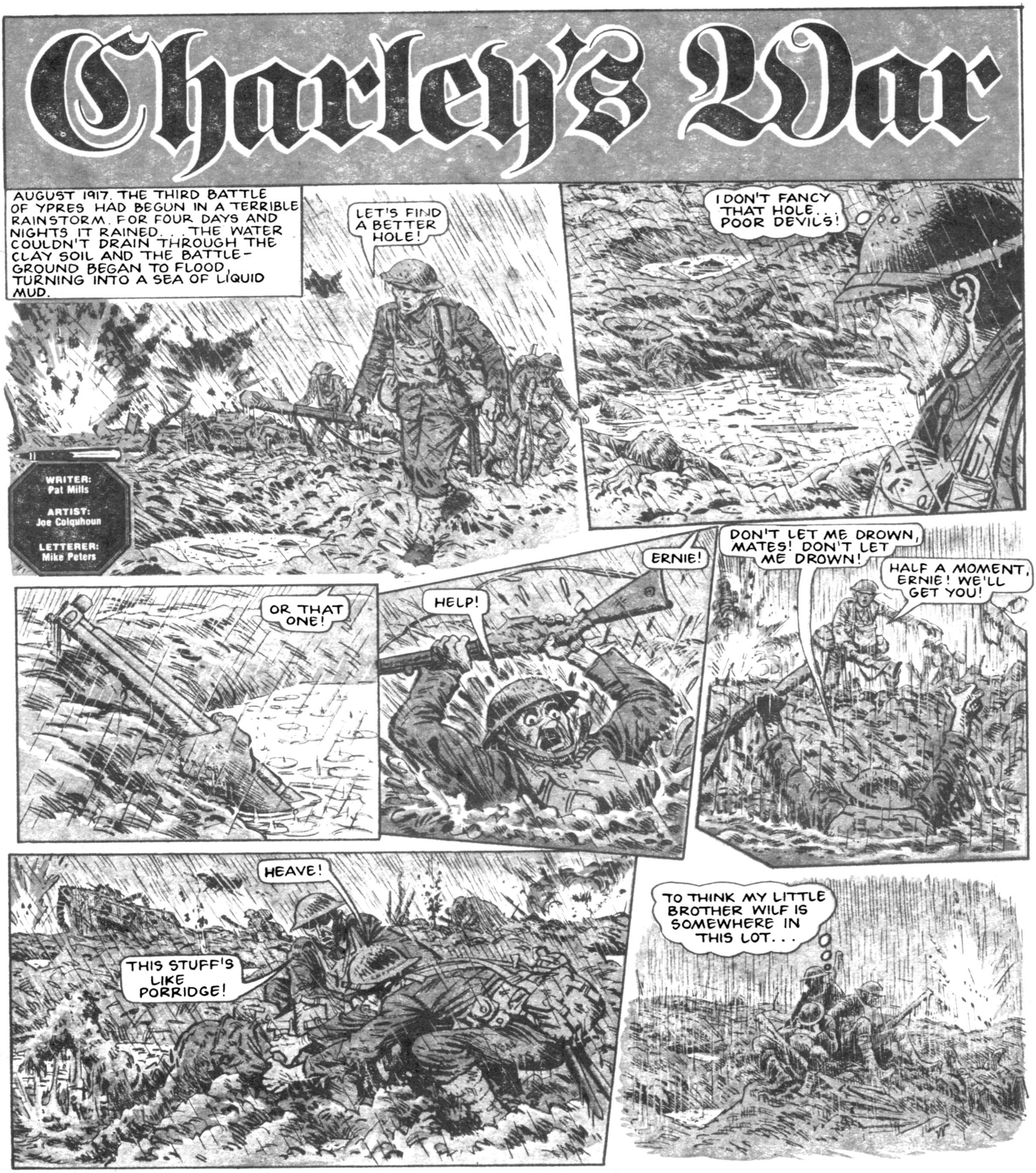

Charley's War
AUGUST 1917. THE THIRD BATTLE OF YPRES HAD BEGUN IN A TERRIBLE RAINSTORM. FOR FOUR DAYS AND NIGHTS IT RAINED. . . THE WATER COULDN'T DRAIN THROUGH THE CLAY SOIL AND THE BATTLE-GROUND BEGAN TO FLOOD, TURNING INTO A SEA OF LIQUID MUD.
LET'S FIND A BETTER HOLE!
WRITER: Pat Mills
ARTIST: Joe Colquhoun
LETTERER: Mike Peters
I DON'T FANCY THAT HOLE.. POOR DEVILS!
OR THAT ONE!
ERNIE!
HELP!
DON'T LET ME DROWN, MATES! DON'T LET ME DROWN!
HALF A MOMENT, ERNIE! WE'LL GET YOU!
HEAVE!
THIS STUFF'S LIKE PORRIDGE!
TO THINK MY LITTLE BROTHER WILF IS SOMEWHERE IN THIS LOT...

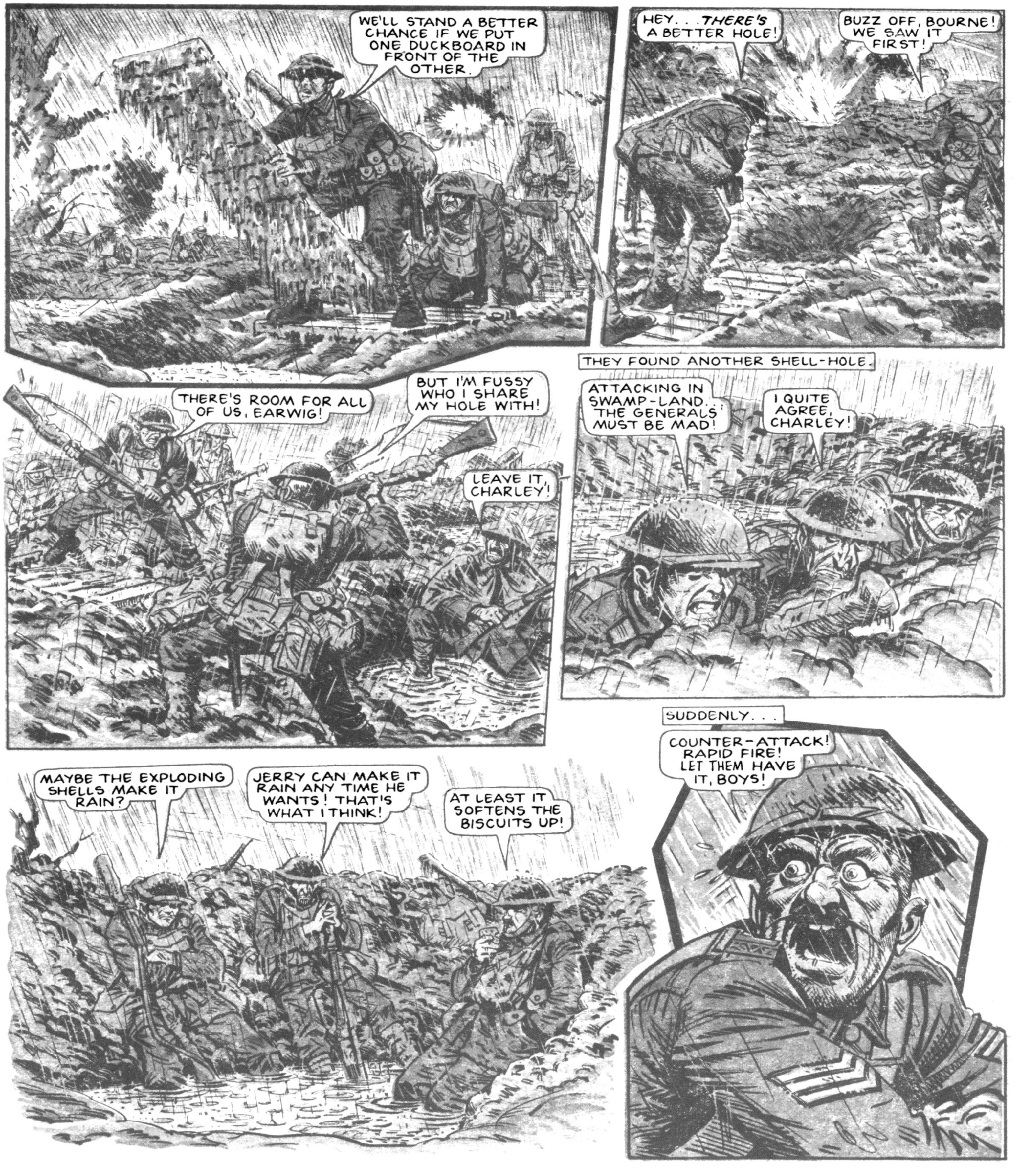
WE'LL STAND A BETTER CHANCE IF WE PUT ONE DUCKBOARD IN FRONT OF THE OTHER.
HEY. . . THERE'S A BETTER HOLE!
BUZZ OFF, BOURNE! WE SAW IT FIRST!
THERE'S ROOM FOR ALL OF US, EARWIG!
BUT I'M FUSSY WHO I SHARE MY HOLE WITH!
LEAVE IT, CHARLEY!
THEY FOUND ANOTHER SHELL-HOLE.
ATTACKING IN SWAMP-LAND. . THE GENERALS MUST BE MAD!
I QUITE AGREE, CHARLEY!
MAYBE THE EXPLODING SHELLS MAKE IT RAIN?
JERRY CAN MAKE IT RAIN ANY TIME HE WANTS! THAT'S WHAT I THINK!
AT LEAST IT SOFTENS THE BISCUITS UP!
SUDDENLY. . .
COUNTER-ATTACK! RAPID FIRE! LET THEM HAVE IT, BOYS!

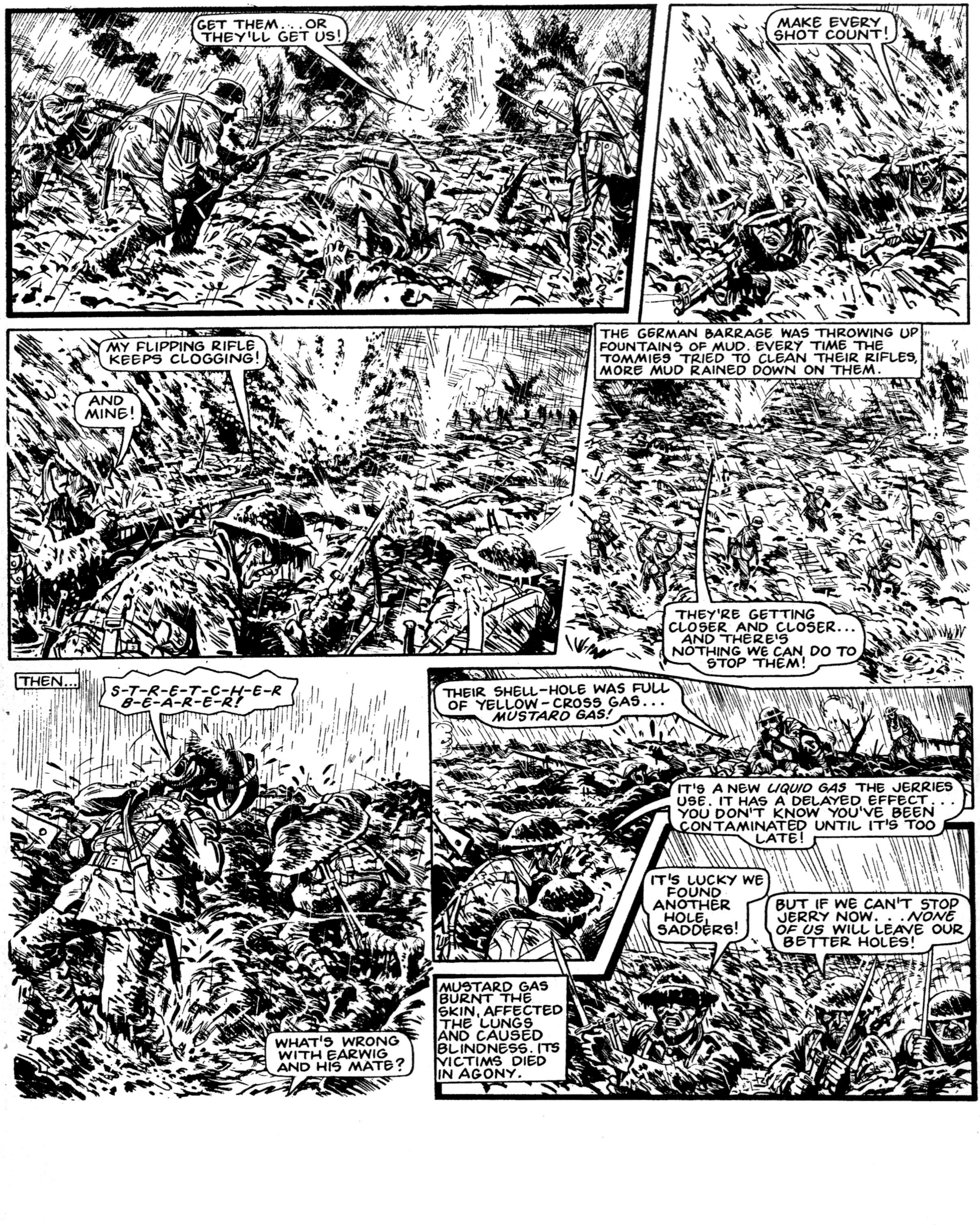

GET THEM . . . OR THEY'LL GET US!
MAKE EVERY SHOT COUNT!
MY FLIPPING RIFLE KEEPS CLOGGING!
AND MINE!
THE GERMAN BARRAGE WAS THROWING UP FOUNTAINS OF MUD. EVERY TIME THE TOMMIES TRIED TO CLEAN THEIR RIFLES, MORE MUD RAINED DOWN ON THEM.
THEY'RE GETTING CLOSER AND CLOSER... AND THERE'S NOTHING WE CAN DO TO STOP THEM!
THEN...
S-T-R-E-T-C-H-E-R B-E-A-R-E-R!
WHAT'S WRONG WITH EARWIG AND HIS MATE?
THEIR SHELL-HOLE WAS FULL OF YELLOW-CROSS GAS . . . MUSTARD GAS!
IT'S A NEW LIQUID GAS THE JERRIES USE. IT HAS A DELAYED EFFECT . . . YOU DON'T KNOW YOU'VE BEEN CONTAMINATED UNTIL IT'S TOO LATE!
MUSTARD GAS BURNT THE SKIN, AFFECTED THE LUNGS AND CAUSED BLINDNESS. ITS VICTIMS DIED IN AGONY.
IT'S LUCKY WE FOUND ANOTHER HOLE, SADDERS!
BUT IF WE CAN'T STOP JERRY NOW. . . NONE OF US WILL LEAVE OUR BETTER HOLES!

CHARLEY'S WAR

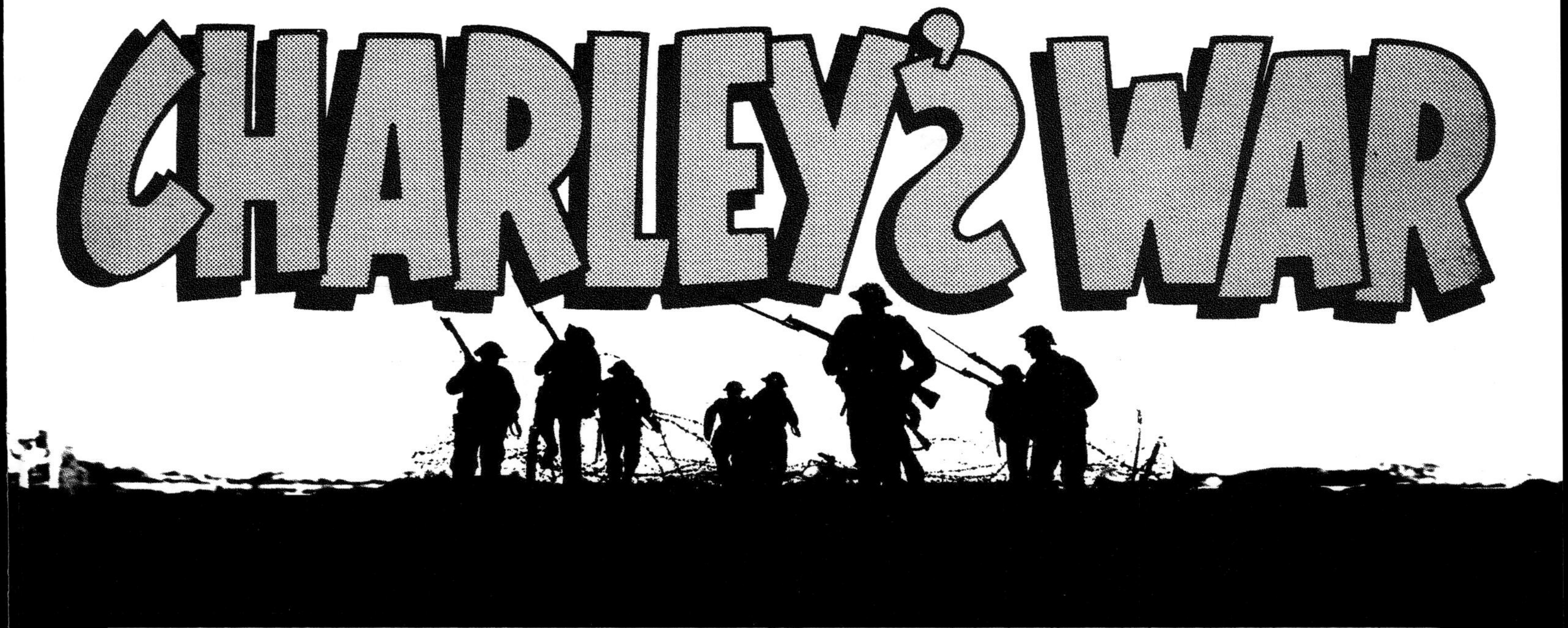

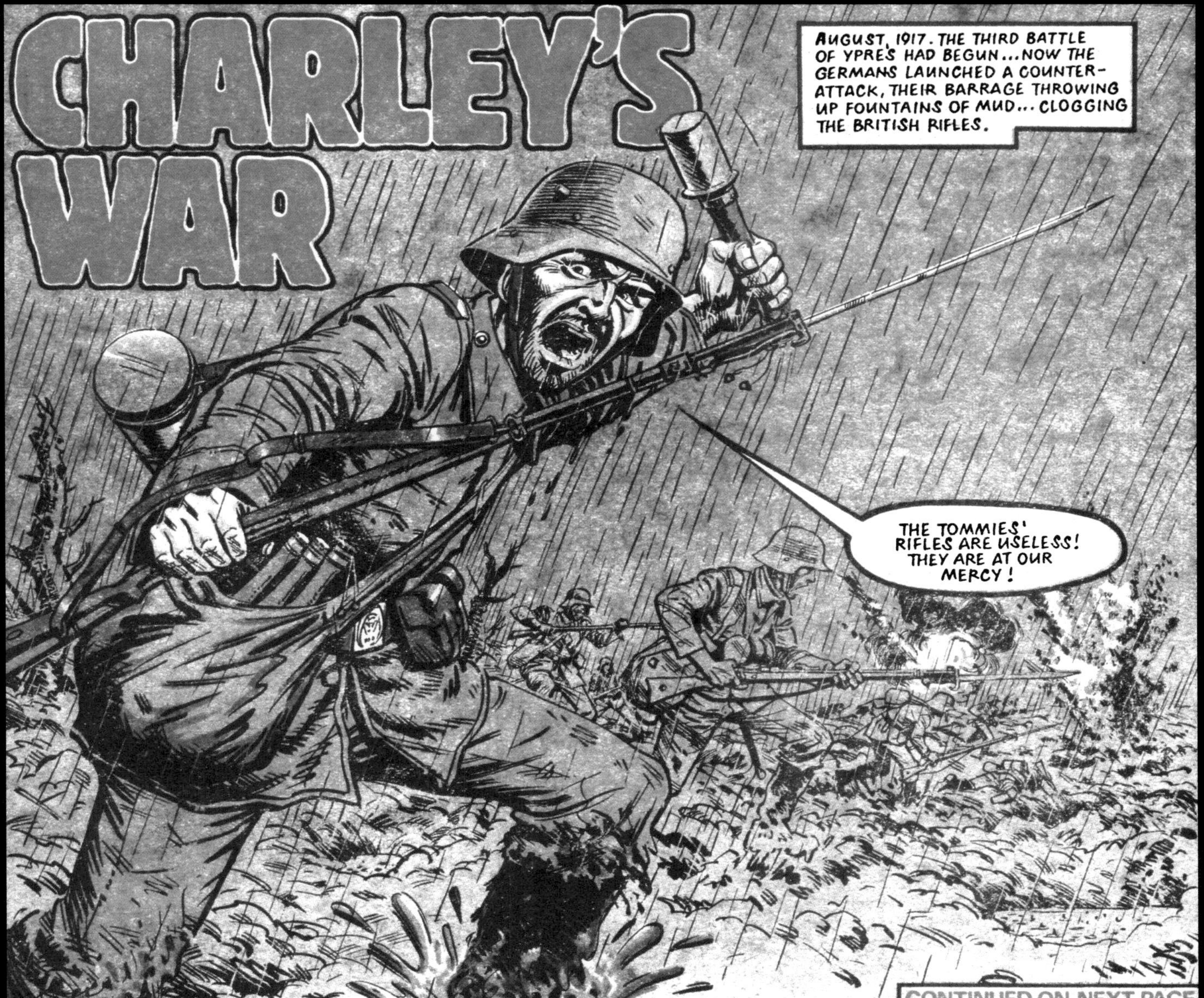
CHARLEY'S WAR
AUGUST, 1917. THE THIRD BATTLE OF YPRES HAD BEGUN... NOW THE GERMANS LAUNCHED A COUNTER-ATTACK, THEIR BARRAGE THROWING UP FOUNTAINS OF MUD... CLOGGING THE BRITISH RIFLES.
THE TOMMIES' RIFLES ARE USELESS! THEY ARE AT OUR MERCY!

CONTINUED ON NEXT PAGE

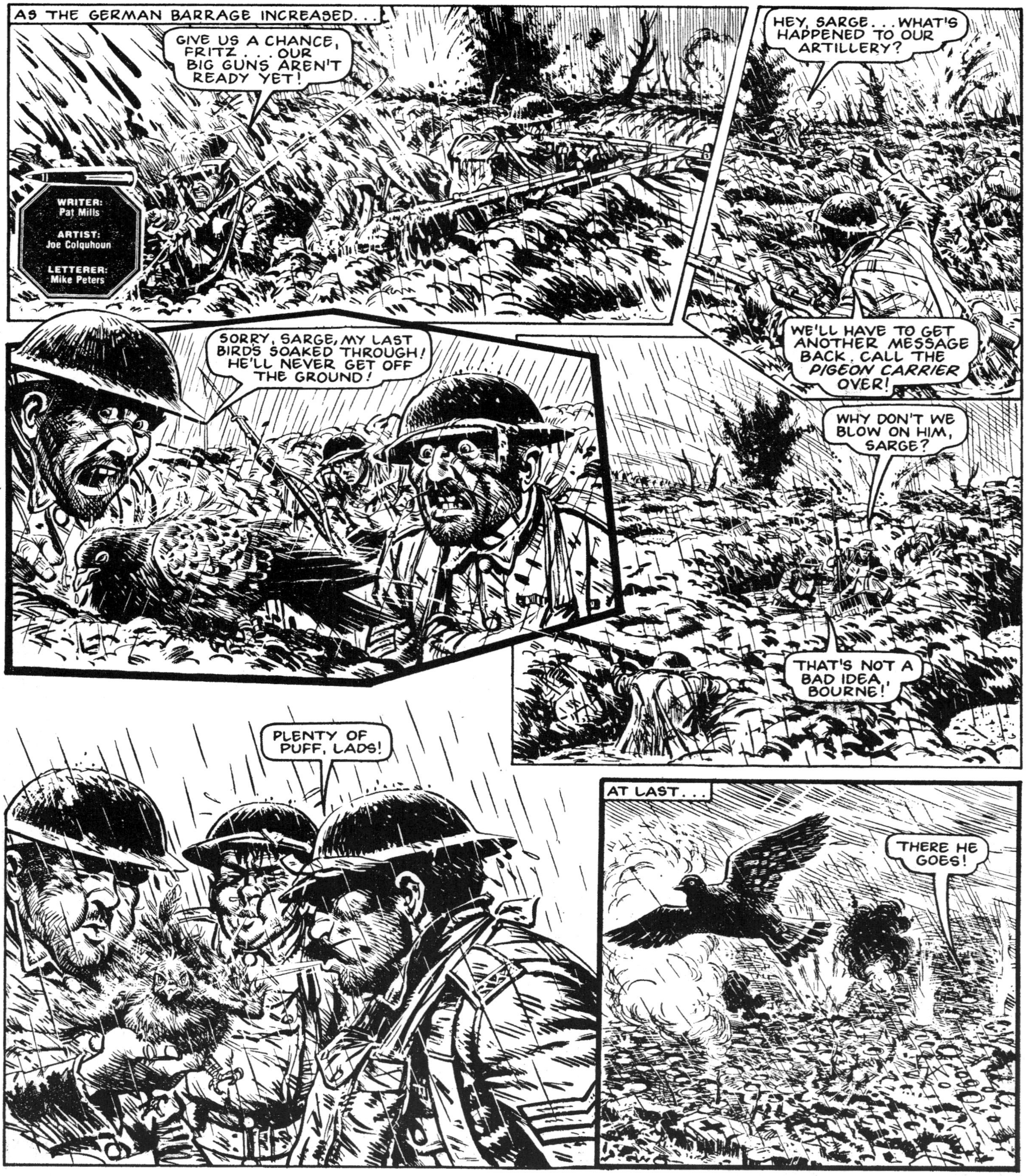
AS THE GERMAN BARRAGE INCREASED...
GIVE US A CHANCE, FRITZ... OUR BIG GUNS AREN'T READY YET!
WRITER: Pat Mills
ARTIST: Joe Colquhoun
LETTERER: Mike Peters
HEY, SARGE... WHAT'S HAPPENED TO OUR ARTILLERY?
WE'LL HAVE TO GET ANOTHER MESSAGE BACK. CALL THE PIGEON CARRIER OVER!
SORRY, SARGE, MY LAST BIRDS SOAKED THROUGH! HE'LL NEVER GET OFF THE GROUND!
WHY DON'T WE BLOW ON HIM, SARGE?
THAT'S NOT A BAD IDEA, BOURNE!
PLENTY OF PUFF, LADS!
AT LAST...
THERE HE GOES!

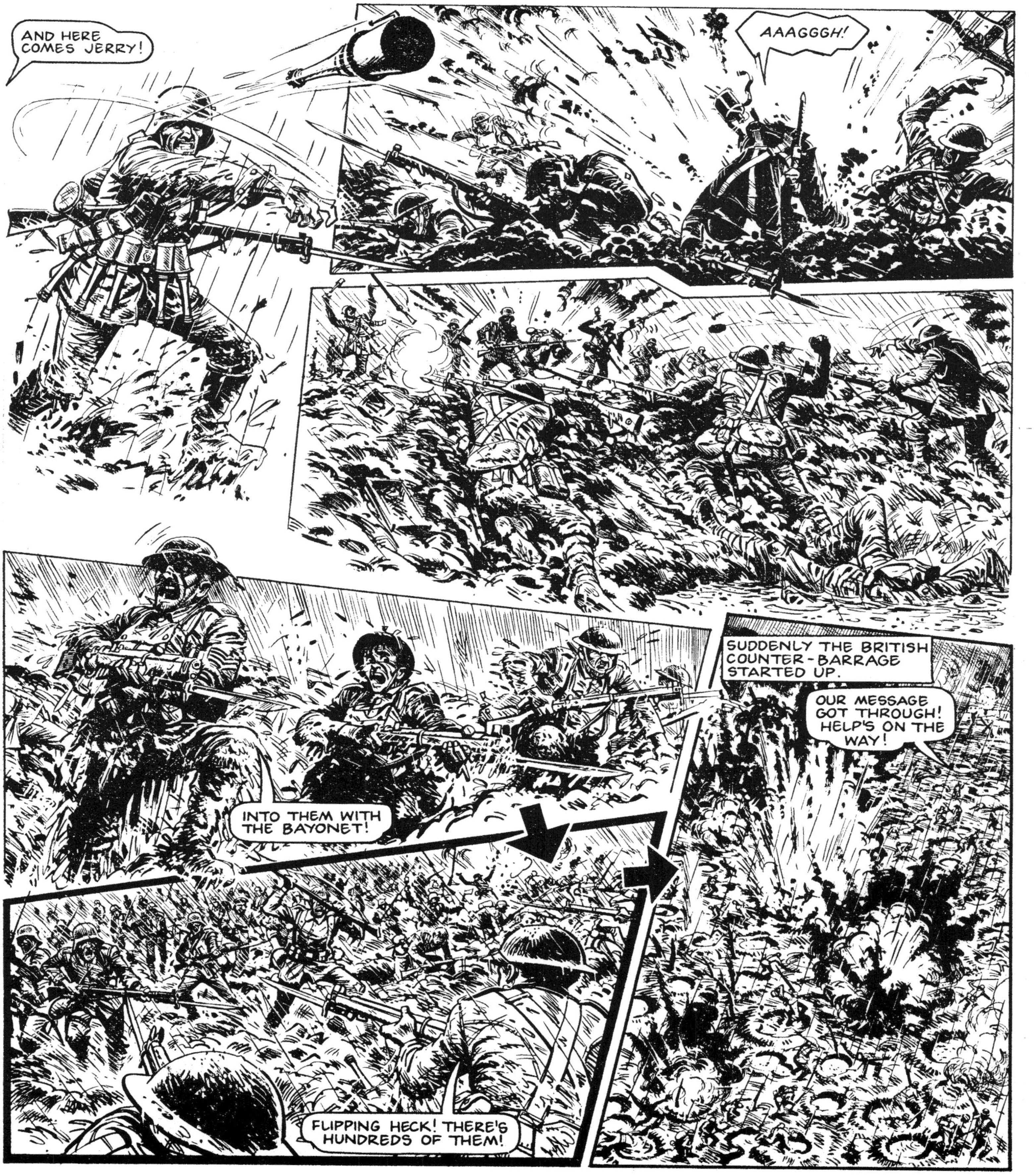
AND HERE COMES JERRY!
AAAGGGH!
INTO THEM WITH THE BAYONET!
FLIPPING HECK! THERE'S HUNDREDS OF THEM!
SUDDENLY THE BRITISH COUNTER-BARRAGE STARTED UP.
OUR MESSAGE GOT THROUGH! HELP'S ON THE WAY!

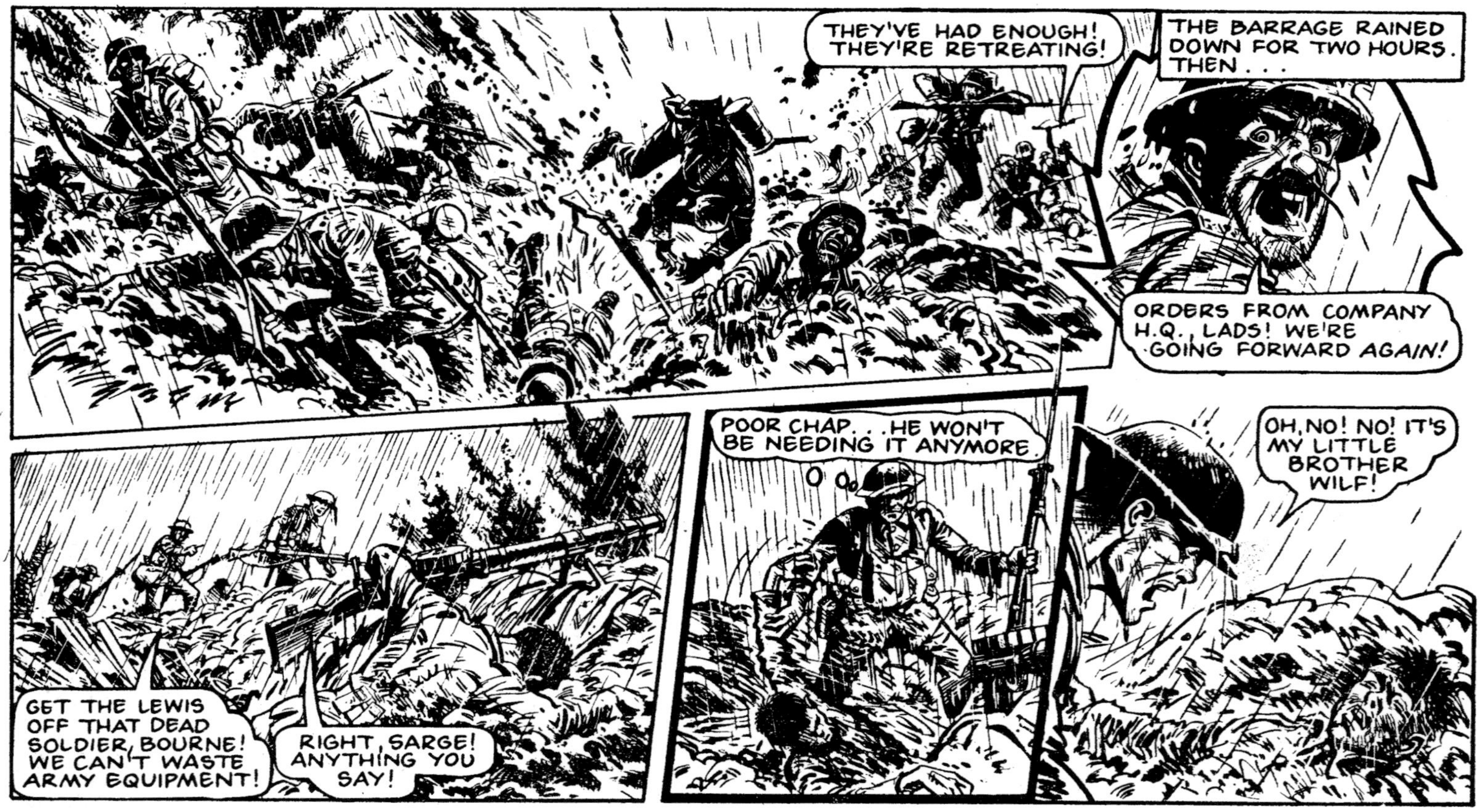
THEY'VE HAD ENOUGH! THEY'RE RETREATING!
THE BARRAGE RAINED DOWN FOR TWO HOURS. THEN . . .
ORDERS FROM COMPANY H.Q., LADS! WE'RE GOING FORWARD AGAIN!
GET THE LEWIS OFF THAT DEAD SOLDIER, BOURNE! WE CAN'T WASTE ARMY EQUIPMENT!
RIGHT, SARGE! ANYTHING YOU SAY!
POOR CHAP. . .HE WON'T BE NEEDING IT ANYMORE.
OH, NO! NO! IT'S MY LITTLE BROTHER WILF!

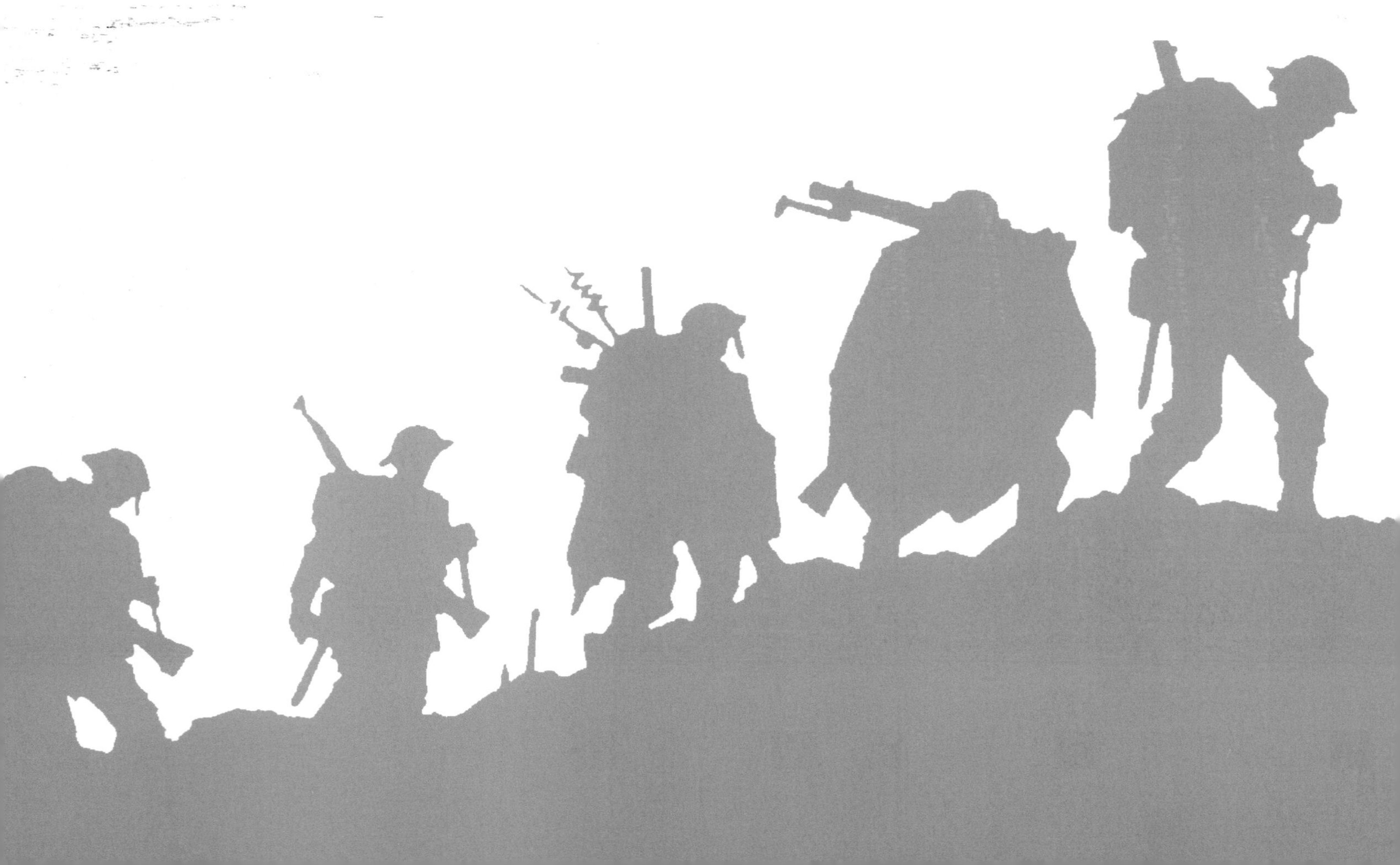

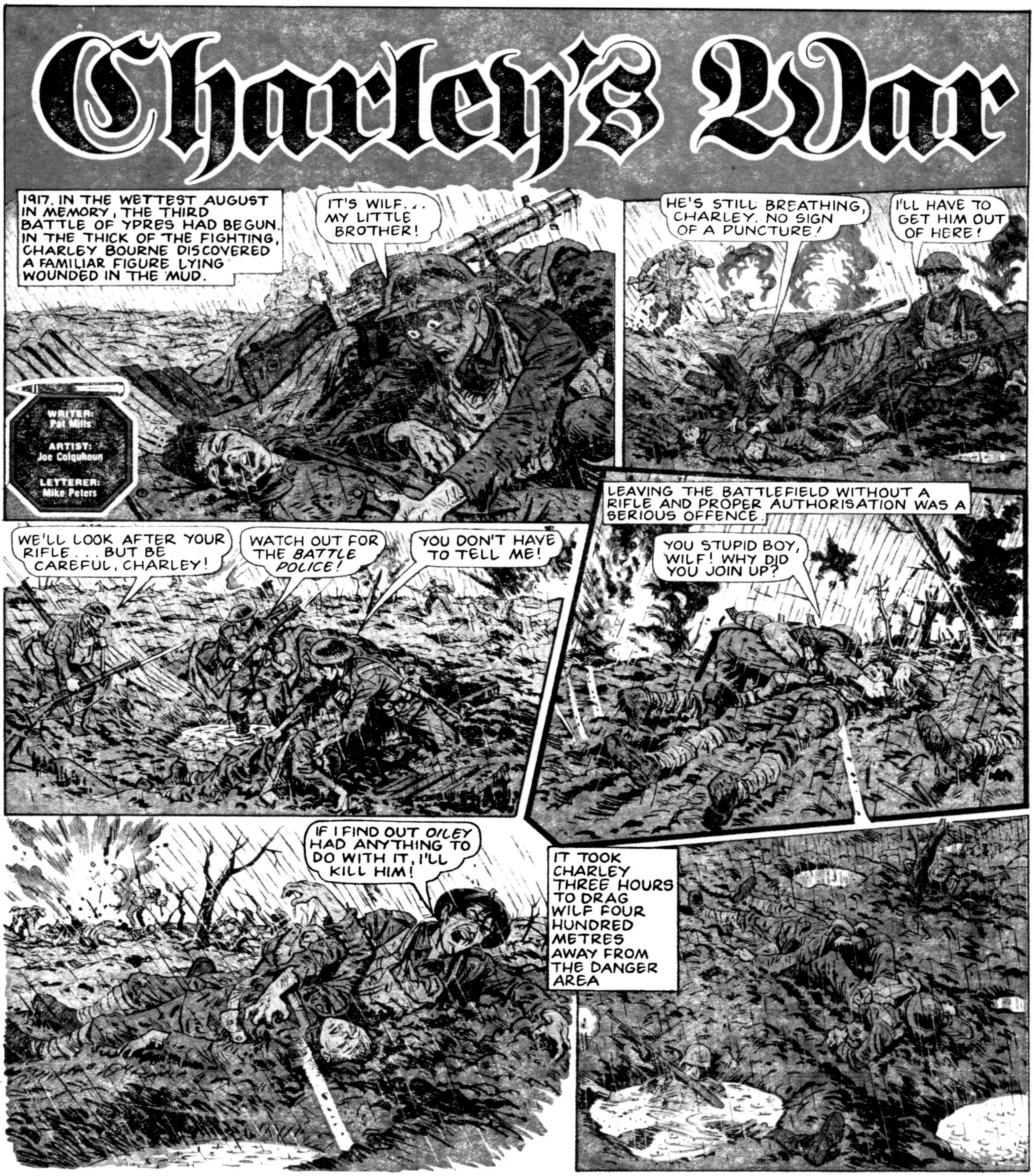
Charley's War
1917. IN THE WETTEST AUGUST IN MEMORY, THE THIRD BATTLE OF YPRES HAD BEGUN. IN THE THICK OF THE FIGHTING, CHARLEY BOURNE DISCOVERED A FAMILIAR FIGURE LYING WOUNDED IN THE MUD.
IT'S WILF... MY LITTLE BROTHER!
WRITER: Pat Mills
ARTIST: Joe Colquhoun
LETTERER: Mike Peters
HE'S STILL BREATHING, CHARLEY. NO SIGN OF A PUNCTURE!
I'LL HAVE TO GET HIM OUT OF HERE!
WE'LL LOOK AFTER YOUR RIFLE . . . BUT BE CAREFUL, CHARLEY!
WATCH OUT FOR THE BATTLE POLICE!
YOU DON'T HAVE TO TELL ME!
LEAVING THE BATTLEFIELD WITHOUT A RIFLE AND PROPER AUTHORISATION WAS A SERIOUS OFFENCE.
YOU STUPID BOY, WILF! WHY DID YOU JOIN UP?
IF I FIND OUT OILEY HAD ANYTHING TO DO WITH IT, I'LL KILL HIM!
IT TOOK CHARLEY THREE HOURS TO DRAG WILF FOUR HUNDRED METRES AWAY FROM THE DANGER AREA

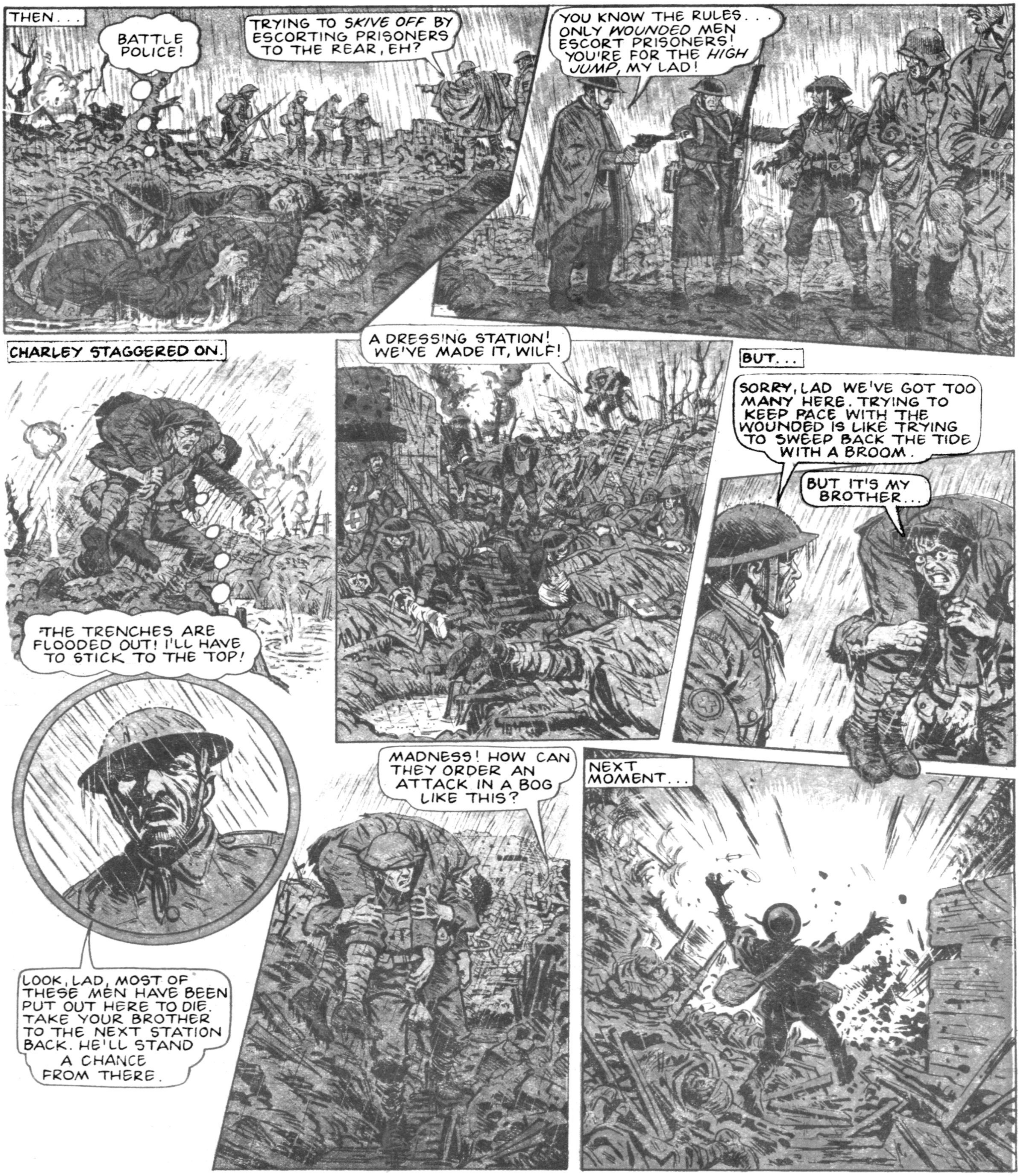
THEN...
BATTLE POLICE!
TRYING TO SKIVE OFF BY ESCORTING PRISONERS TO THE REAR, EH?
YOU KNOW THE RULES... ONLY WOUNDED MEN ESCORT PRISONERS! YOU'RE FOR THE HIGH JUMP, MY LAD!
CHARLEY STAGGERED ON.
THE TRENCHES ARE FLOODED OUT! I'LL HAVE TO STICK TO THE TOP!
A DRESSING STATION! WE'VE MADE IT, WILF!
BUT...
SORRY, LAD WE'VE GOT TOO MANY HERE. TRYING TO KEEP PACE WITH THE WOUNDED IS LIKE TRYING TO SWEEP BACK THE TIDE WITH A BROOM.
BUT IT'S MY BROTHER...
LOOK, LAD, MOST OF THESE MEN HAVE BEEN PUT OUT HERE TO DIE. TAKE YOUR BROTHER TO THE NEXT STATION BACK. HE'LL STAND A CHANCE FROM THERE.
MADNESS! HOW CAN THEY ORDER AN ATTACK IN A BOG LIKE THIS?
NEXT MOMENT...

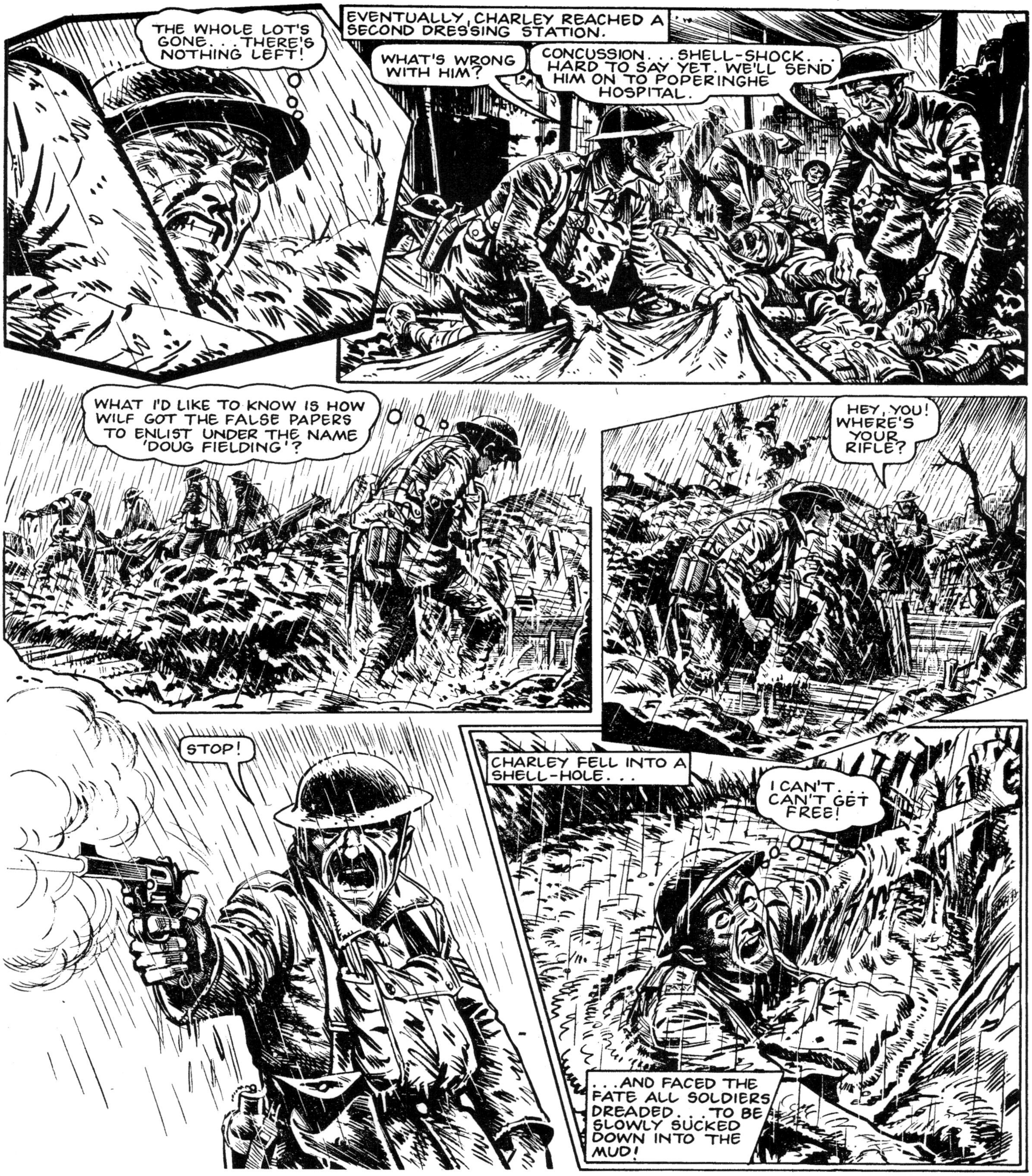
THE WHOLE LOT'S GONE. . . THERE'S NOTHING LEFT!
EVENTUALLY, CHARLEY REACHED A SECOND DRESSING STATION.
WHAT'S WRONG WITH HIM?
CONCUSSION. . . SHELL-SHOCK. . . HARD TO SAY YET. WE'LL SEND HIM ON TO POPERINGHE HOSPITAL.
WHAT I'D LIKE TO KNOW IS HOW WILF GOT THE FALSE PAPERS TO ENLIST UNDER THE NAME 'DOUG FIELDING'?
HEY, YOU! WHERE'S YOUR RIFLE?
STOP!
CHARLEY FELL INTO A SHELL-HOLE. . .
I CAN'T. . . CAN'T GET FREE!
. . .AND FACED THE FATE ALL SOLDIERS DREADED. . . TO BE SLOWLY SUCKED DOWN INTO THE MUD!

CHARLEY'S WAR

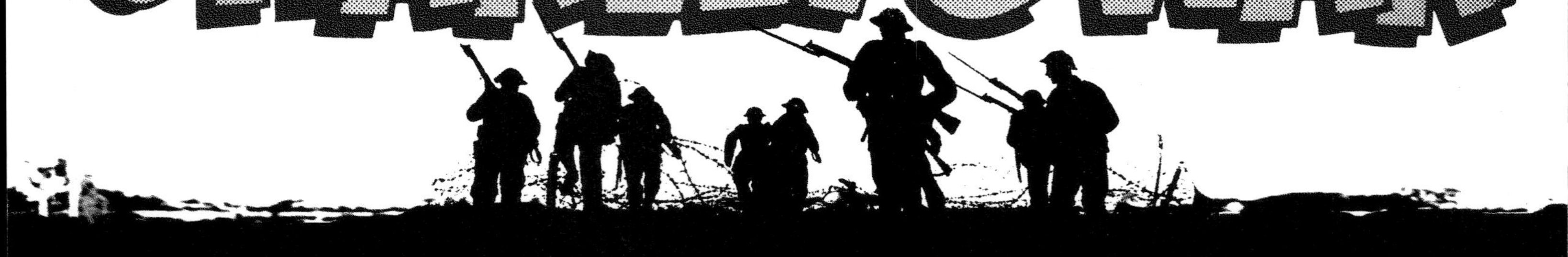

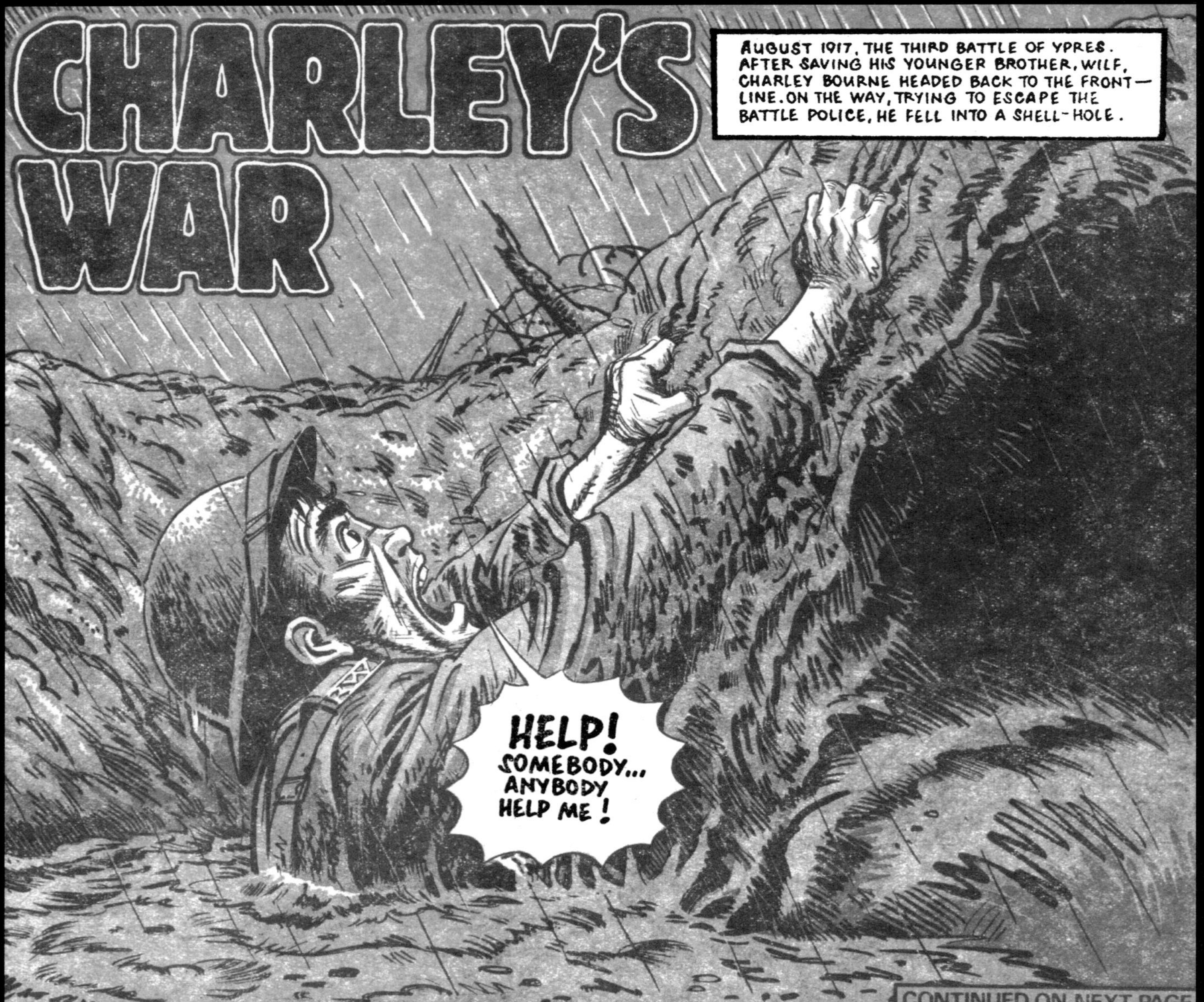
CHARLEY'S WAR
AUGUST 1917, THE THIRD BATTLE OF YPRES. AFTER SAVING HIS YOUNGER BROTHER, WILF, CHARLEY BOURNE HEADED BACK TO THE FRONT-LINE. ON THE WAY, TRYING TO ESCAPE THE BATTLE POLICE, HE FELL INTO A SHELL-HOLE.
HELP! SOMEBODY... ANYBODY HELP ME!

CONTINUED ON NEXT PAGE

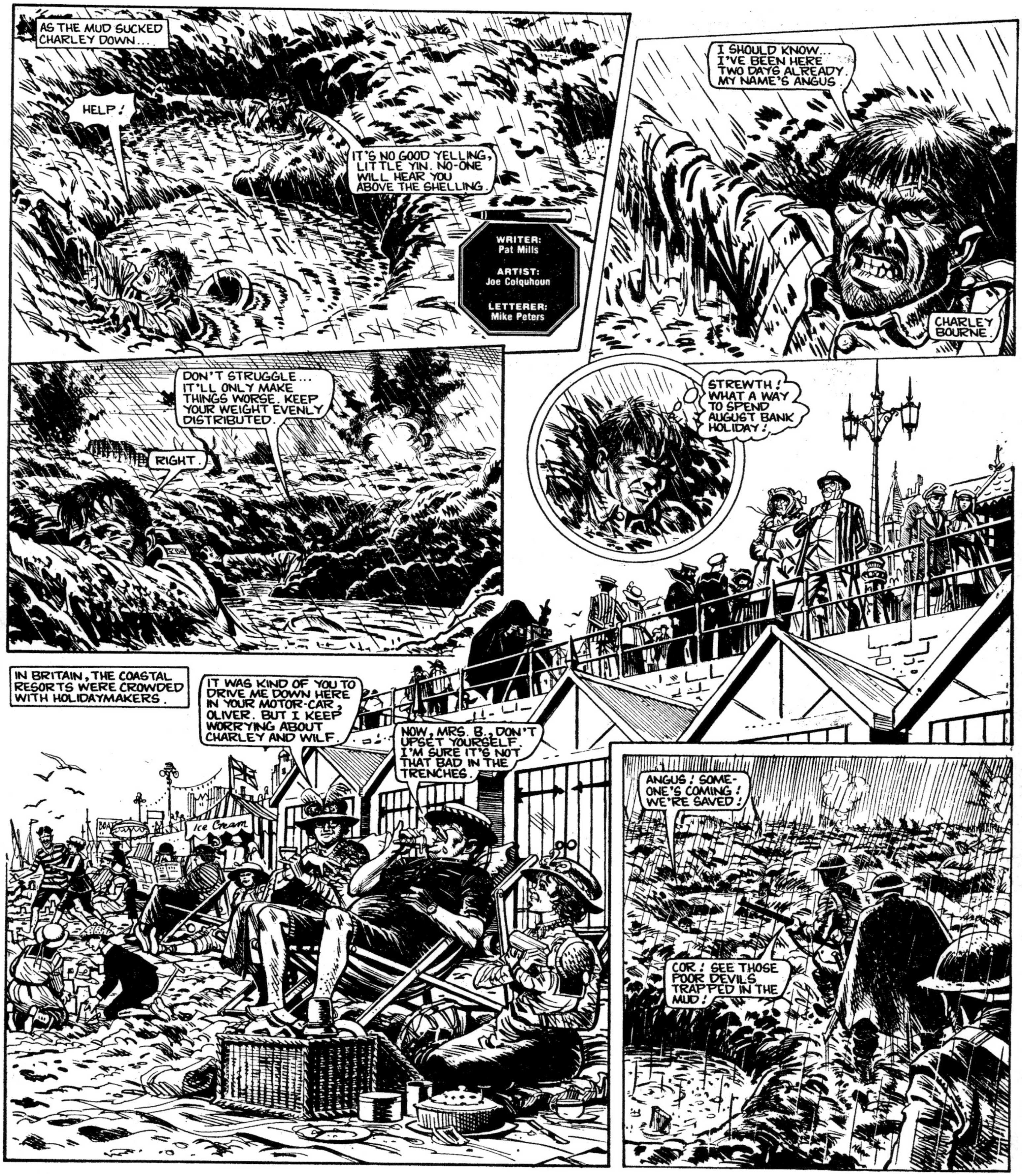
AS THE MUD SUCKED CHARLEY DOWN....
HELP!
IT'S NO GOOD YELLING, LITTLE YIN. NO-ONE WILL HEAR YOU ABOVE THE SHELLING.
WRITER: Pat Mills
ARTIST: Joe Colquhoun
LETTERER: Mike Peters
I SHOULD KNOW... I'VE BEEN HERE TWO DAYS ALREADY. MY NAME'S ANGUS.
CHARLEY BOURNE.
DON'T STRUGGLE... IT'LL ONLY MAKE THINGS WORSE. KEEP YOUR WEIGHT EVENLY DISTRIBUTED.
RIGHT.
STREWTH! WHAT A WAY TO SPEND AUGUST BANK HOLIDAY!
IN BRITAIN, THE COASTAL RESORTS WERE CROWDED WITH HOLIDAYMAKERS.
IT WAS KIND OF YOU TO DRIVE ME DOWN HERE IN YOUR MOTOR-CAR, OLIVER. BUT I KEEP WORRYING ABOUT CHARLEY AND WILF.
NOW, MRS. B., DON'T UPSET YOURSELF. I'M SURE IT'S NOT THAT BAD IN THE TRENCHES.
Ice Cream
ANGUS! SOME-ONE'S COMING! WE'RE SAVED!
COR! SEE THOSE POOR DEVILS TRAPPED IN THE MUD!

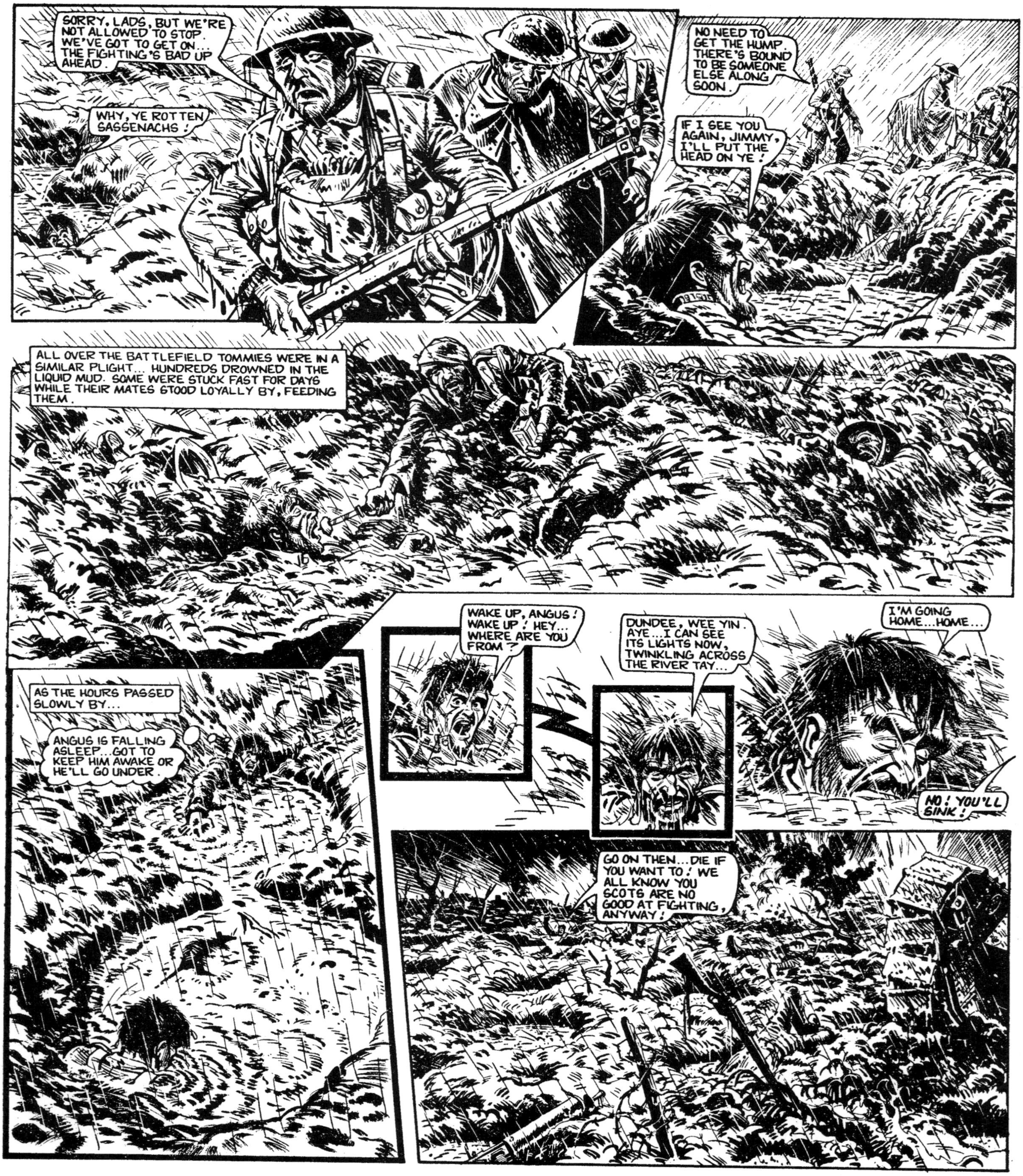
SORRY, LADS, BUT WE'RE NOT ALLOWED TO STOP. WE'VE GOT TO GET ON... THE FIGHTING'S BAD UP AHEAD.
WHY, YE ROTTEN SASSENACHS!
NO NEED TO GET THE HUMP. THERE'S BOUND TO BE SOMEONE ELSE ALONG SOON.
IF I SEE YOU AGAIN, JIMMY, I'LL PUT THE HEAD ON YE!
ALL OVER THE BATTLEFIELD TOMMIES WERE IN A SIMILAR PLIGHT... HUNDREDS DROWNED IN THE LIQUID MUD. SOME WERE STUCK FAST FOR DAYS WHILE THEIR MATES STOOD LOYALLY BY, FEEDING THEM.
AS THE HOURS PASSED SLOWLY BY...
ANGUS IS FALLING ASLEEP...GOT TO KEEP HIM AWAKE OR HE'LL GO UNDER.
WAKE UP, ANGUS! WAKE UP! HEY... WHERE ARE YOU FROM?
DUNDEE, WEE YIN. AYE... I CAN SEE ITS LIGHTS NOW, TWINKLING ACROSS THE RIVER TAY...
I'M GOING HOME...HOME...
NO! YOU'LL SINK!
GO ON THEN... DIE IF YOU WANT TO! WE ALL KNOW YOU SCOTS ARE NO GOOD AT FIGHTING, ANYWAY!

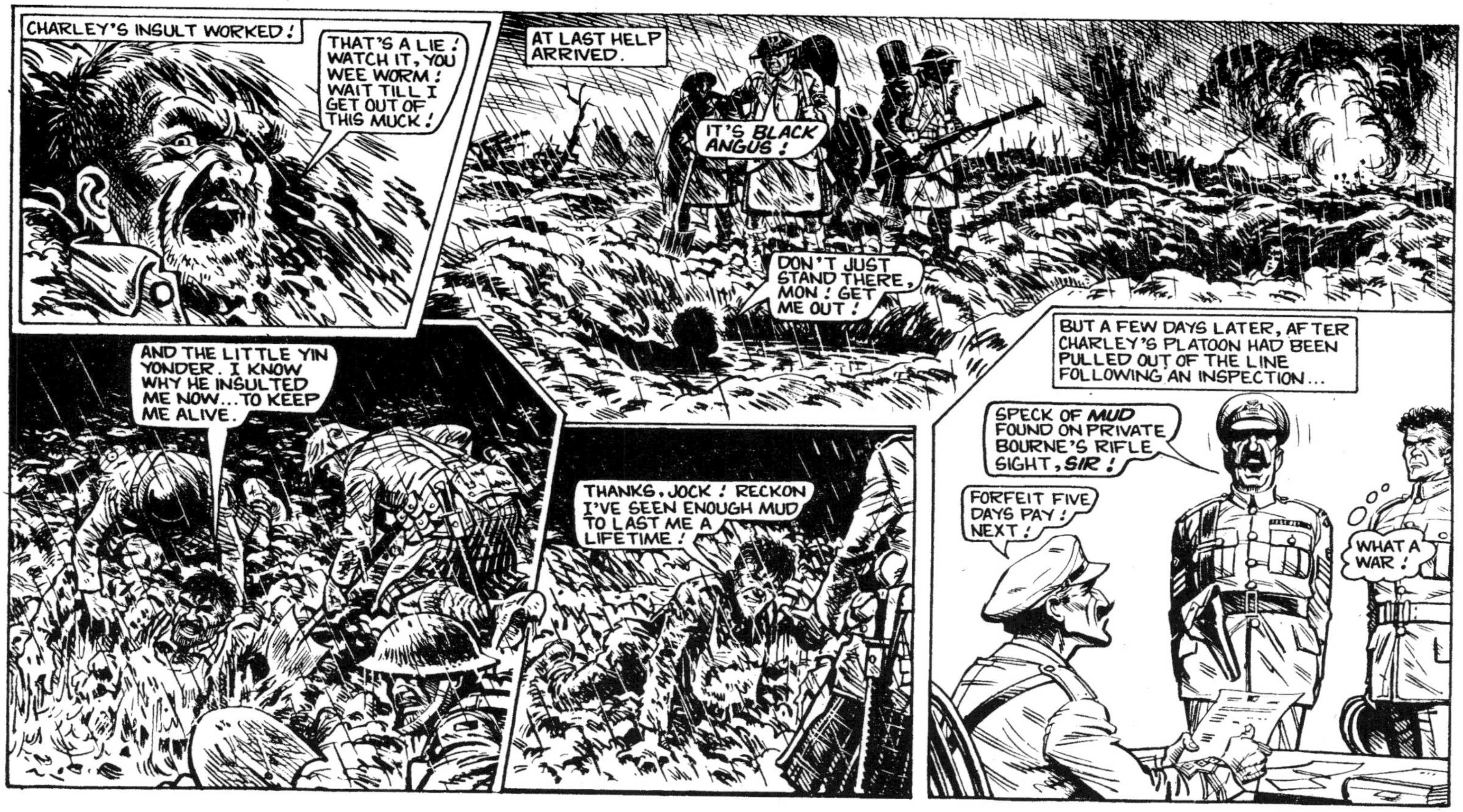
CHARLEY'S INSULT WORKED!
THAT'S A LIE! WATCH IT, YOU WEE WORM! WAIT TILL I GET OUT OF THIS MUCK!
AT LAST HELP ARRIVED.
IT'S BLACK ANGUS!
DON'T JUST STAND THERE, MON! GET ME OUT!
AND THE LITTLE YIN YONDER. I KNOW WHY HE INSULTED ME NOW... TO KEEP ME ALIVE.
THANKS, JOCK! RECKON I'VE SEEN ENOUGH MUD TO LAST ME A LIFETIME!
BUT A FEW DAYS LATER, AFTER CHARLEY'S PLATOON HAD BEEN PULLED OUT OF THE LINE FOLLOWING AN INSPECTION...
SPECK OF MUD FOUND ON PRIVATE BOURNE'S RIFLE SIGHT, SIR!
FORFEIT FIVE DAYS PAY! NEXT!
WHAT A WAR!

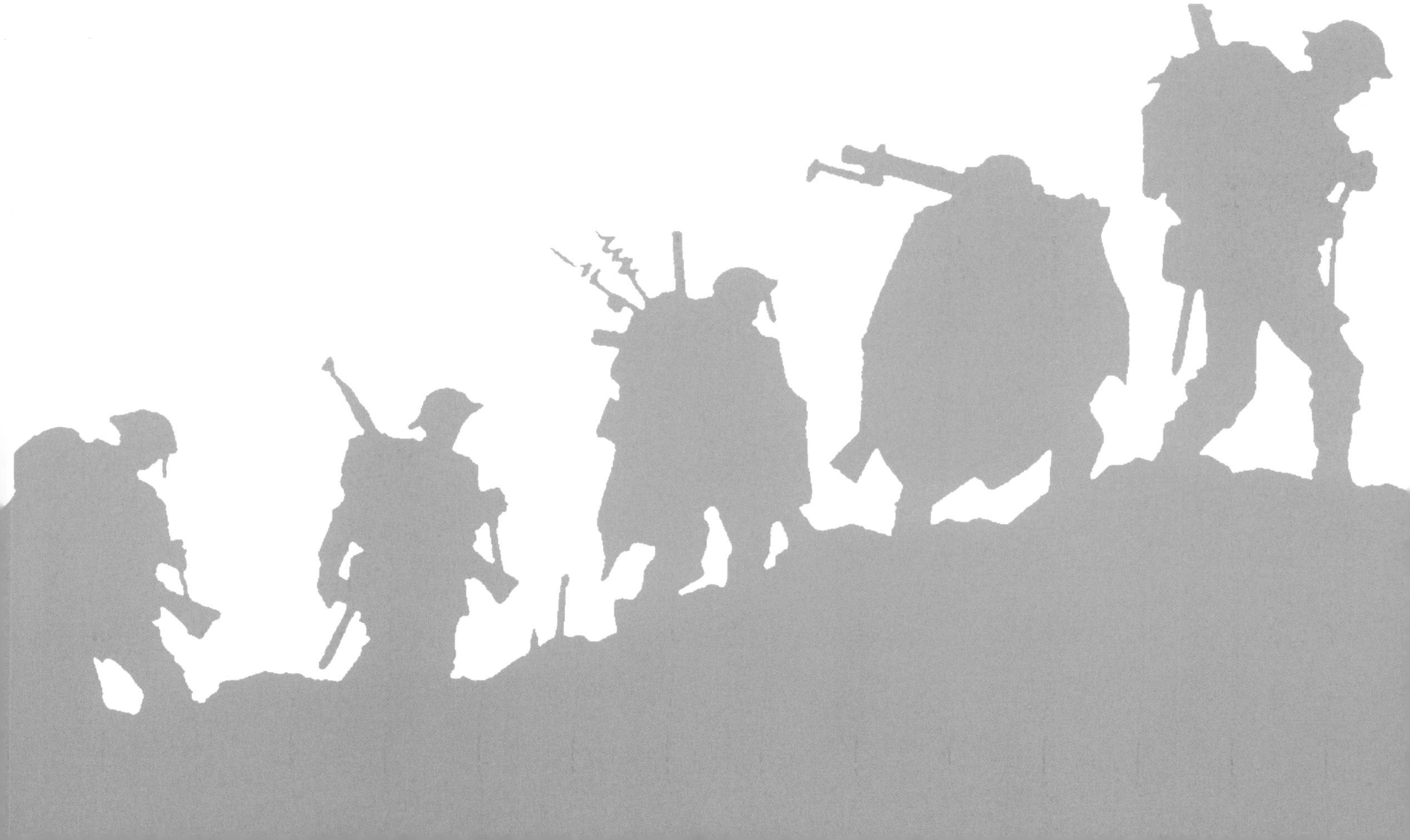

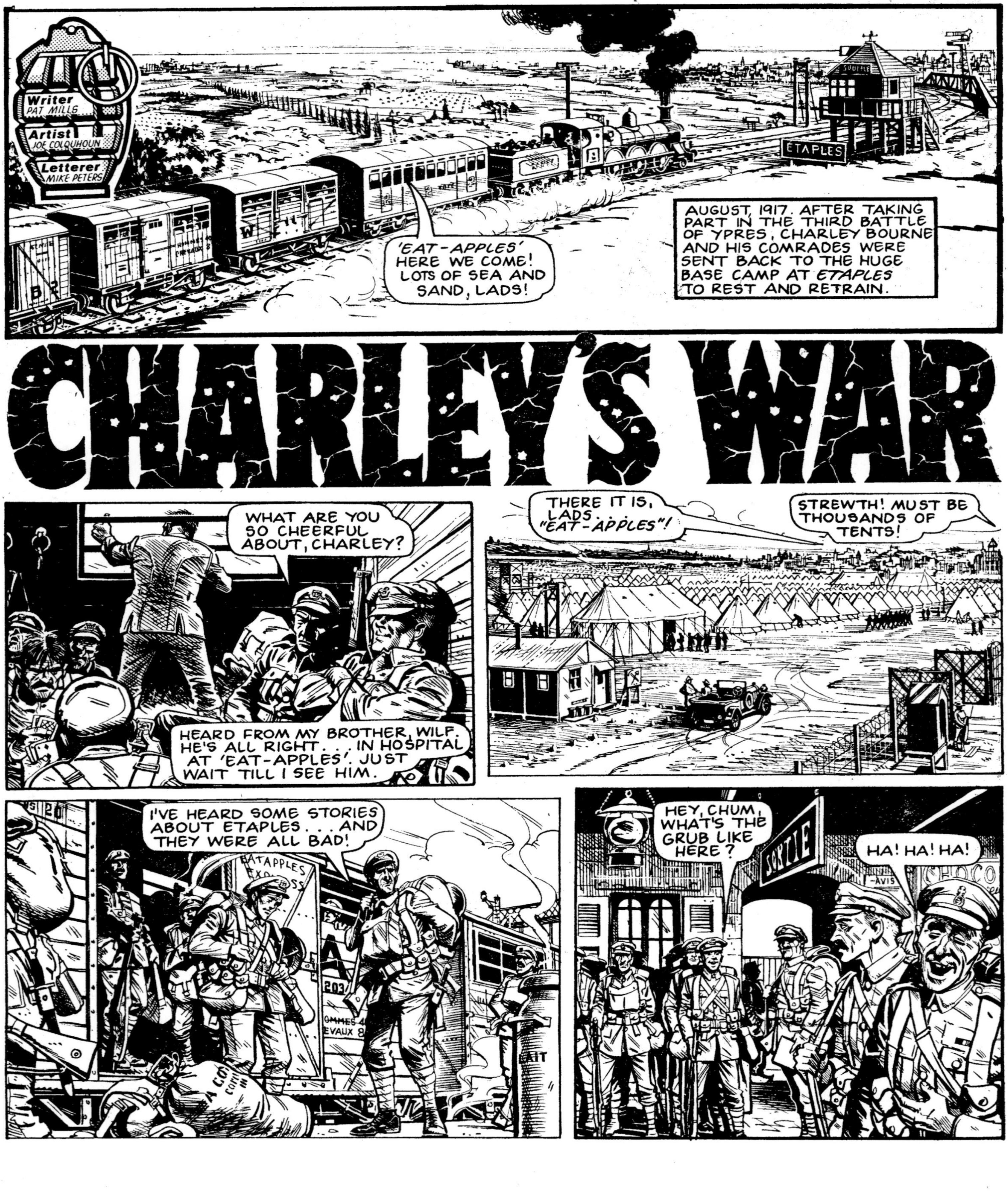
Writer PAT MILLS
Artist JOE COLQUHOUN
Letterer MIKE PETERS
ETAPLES
'EAT-APPLES' HERE WE COME! LOTS OF SEA AND SAND, LADS!
AUGUST, 1917. AFTER TAKING PART IN THE THIRD BATTLE OF YPRES, CHARLEY BOURNE AND HIS COMRADES WERE SENT BACK TO THE HUGE BASE CAMP AT *ETAPLES* TO REST AND RETRAIN.
CHARLEY'S WAR
WHAT ARE YOU SO CHEERFUL ABOUT, CHARLEY?
HEARD FROM MY BROTHER, WILF. HE'S ALL RIGHT . . . IN HOSPITAL AT 'EAT-APPLES'. JUST WAIT TILL I SEE HIM.
THERE IT IS, LADS. "EAT-APPLES"!
STREWTH! MUST BE THOUSANDS OF TENTS!
I'VE HEARD SOME STORIES ABOUT ETAPLES . . . AND THEY WERE ALL BAD!
HEY, CHUM, WHAT'S THE GRUB LIKE HERE?
HA! HA! HA!

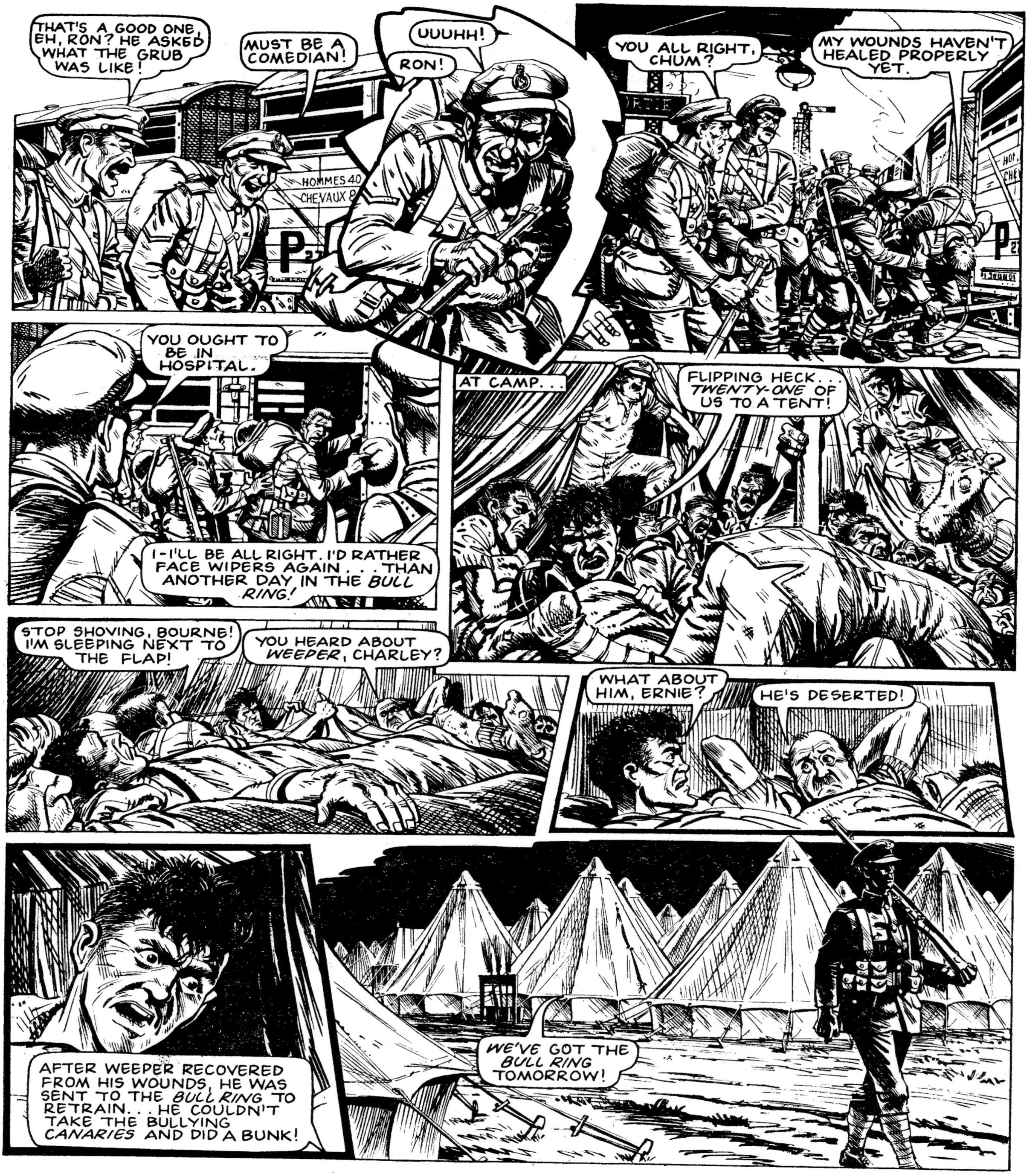
THAT'S A GOOD ONE EH, RON? HE ASKED WHAT THE GRUB WAS LIKE!
MUST BE A COMEDIAN!
RON!
UUUHH!
HOMMES 40
CHEVAUX 8
YOU ALL RIGHT, CHUM?
MY WOUNDS HAVEN'T HEALED PROPERLY YET.
YOU OUGHT TO BE IN HOSPITAL.
I-I'LL BE ALL RIGHT. I'D RATHER FACE WIPERS AGAIN . . . THAN ANOTHER DAY IN THE BULL RING!
AT CAMP. . .
FLIPPING HECK. . . TWENTY-ONE OF US TO A TENT!
STOP SHOVING, BOURNE! I'M SLEEPING NEXT TO THE FLAP!
YOU HEARD ABOUT WEEPER, CHARLEY?
WHAT ABOUT HIM, ERNIE?
HE'S DESERTED!
AFTER WEEPER RECOVERED FROM HIS WOUNDS, HE WAS SENT TO THE BULL RING TO RETRAIN. . HE COULDN'T TAKE THE BULLYING CANARIES AND DID A BUNK!
WE'VE GOT THE BULL RING TOMORROW!

REVEILLE...5.30 A.M...

ONE DOG BISCUIT FOR BREAKFAST!

NOT EVEN A DROP OF BACON FAT TO DIP IT IN!

AFTER "BREAKFAST", THEY BEGAN THE FOUR-MILE MARCH TO THE *BULL RING* TRAINING GROUND THROUGH THE "*CANARY RUN*"... A LINE OF YELLING, CURSING INSTRUCTORS NICKNAMED "*CANARIES*".

THROW YOUR CHEST OUT! YOU'VE GOT A HUMP LIKE A CAMEL! KEEP YOUR EYES OFF THE GROUND...THERE ARE NO COINS LYING ABOUT!

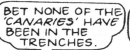

BET NONE OF THE 'CANARIES' HAVE BEEN IN THE TRENCHES.

THEY'RE ALL *BASE WALLAHS*...*YELLOW*, LIKE THEIR ARM BANDS!

THE *BULL RING* WAS A VAST STRETCH OF BEACH...THE TROOPS SAT IN THE SAND UNTIL THEIR INSTRUCTORS ARRIVED.

HERE HE COMES...!*THE FERRET*. THEY SAY HIS LAST JOB WAS A GUARD IN THE COLCHESTER GLASS HOUSE.

ARE YOU NAILED OR FROZE TO THE SAND? ARE YOU *BLOOMING* WAXWORKS...OR A COLLECTION OF STATUES? ON YOUR FEET AND GET FELL IN! YOU'RE IN THE *BULL RING NOW!*

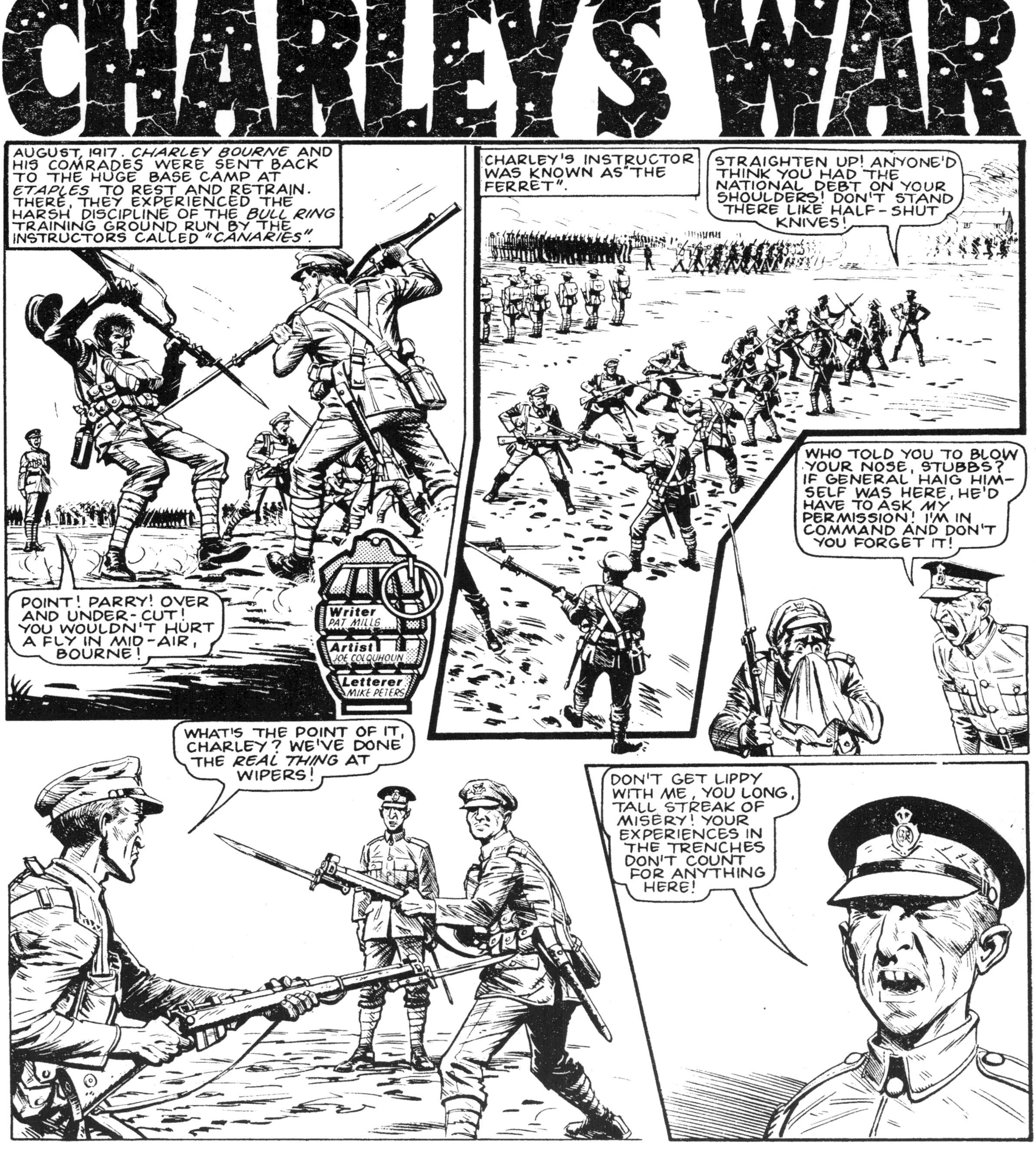
CHARLEY'S WAR
AUGUST, 1917. CHARLEY BOURNE AND HIS COMRADES WERE SENT BACK TO THE HUGE BASE CAMP AT ETAPLES TO REST AND RETRAIN. THERE, THEY EXPERIENCED THE HARSH DISCIPLINE OF THE BULL RING TRAINING GROUND RUN BY THE INSTRUCTORS CALLED "CANARIES".
POINT! PARRY! OVER AND UNDER-CUT! YOU WOULDN'T HURT A FLY IN MID-AIR, BOURNE!
Writer PAT MILLS
Artist JOE COLQUHOUN
Letterer MIKE PETERS
CHARLEY'S INSTRUCTOR WAS KNOWN AS "THE FERRET".
STRAIGHTEN UP! ANYONE'D THINK YOU HAD THE NATIONAL DEBT ON YOUR SHOULDERS! DON'T STAND THERE LIKE HALF-SHUT KNIVES!
WHO TOLD YOU TO BLOW YOUR NOSE, STUBBS? IF GENERAL HAIG HIMSELF WAS HERE, HE'D HAVE TO ASK MY PERMISSION! I'M IN COMMAND AND DON'T YOU FORGET IT!
WHAT'S THE POINT OF IT, CHARLEY? WE'VE DONE THE REAL THING AT WIPERS!
DON'T GET LIPPY WITH ME, YOU LONG, TALL STREAK OF MISERY! YOUR EXPERIENCES IN THE TRENCHES DON'T COUNT FOR ANYTHING HERE!

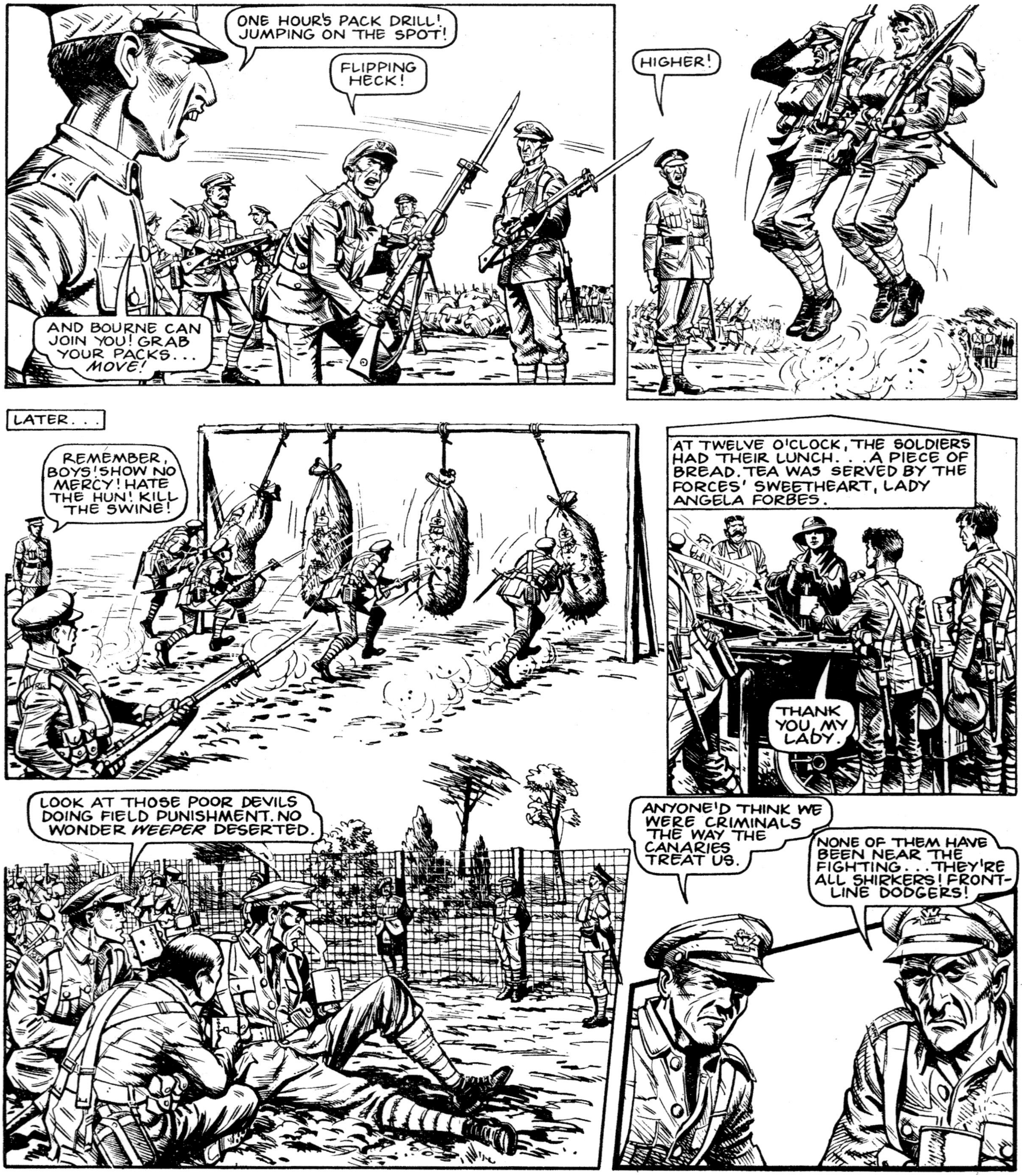
ONE HOUR'S PACK DRILL! JUMPING ON THE SPOT!
FLIPPING HECK!
AND BOURNE CAN JOIN YOU! GRAB YOUR PACKS... *MOVE!*
HIGHER!
LATER...
REMEMBER, BOYS! SHOW NO MERCY! HATE THE HUN! KILL THE SWINE!
AT TWELVE O'CLOCK, THE SOLDIERS HAD THEIR LUNCH... A PIECE OF BREAD. TEA WAS SERVED BY THE FORCES' SWEETHEART, LADY ANGELA FORBES.
THANK YOU, MY LADY.
LOOK AT THOSE POOR DEVILS DOING FIELD PUNISHMENT. NO WONDER *WEEPER* DESERTED.
ANYONE'D THINK WE WERE CRIMINALS THE WAY THE CANARIES TREAT US.
NONE OF THEM HAVE BEEN NEAR THE FIGHTING... THEY'RE ALL SHIRKERS! FRONT-LINE DODGERS!

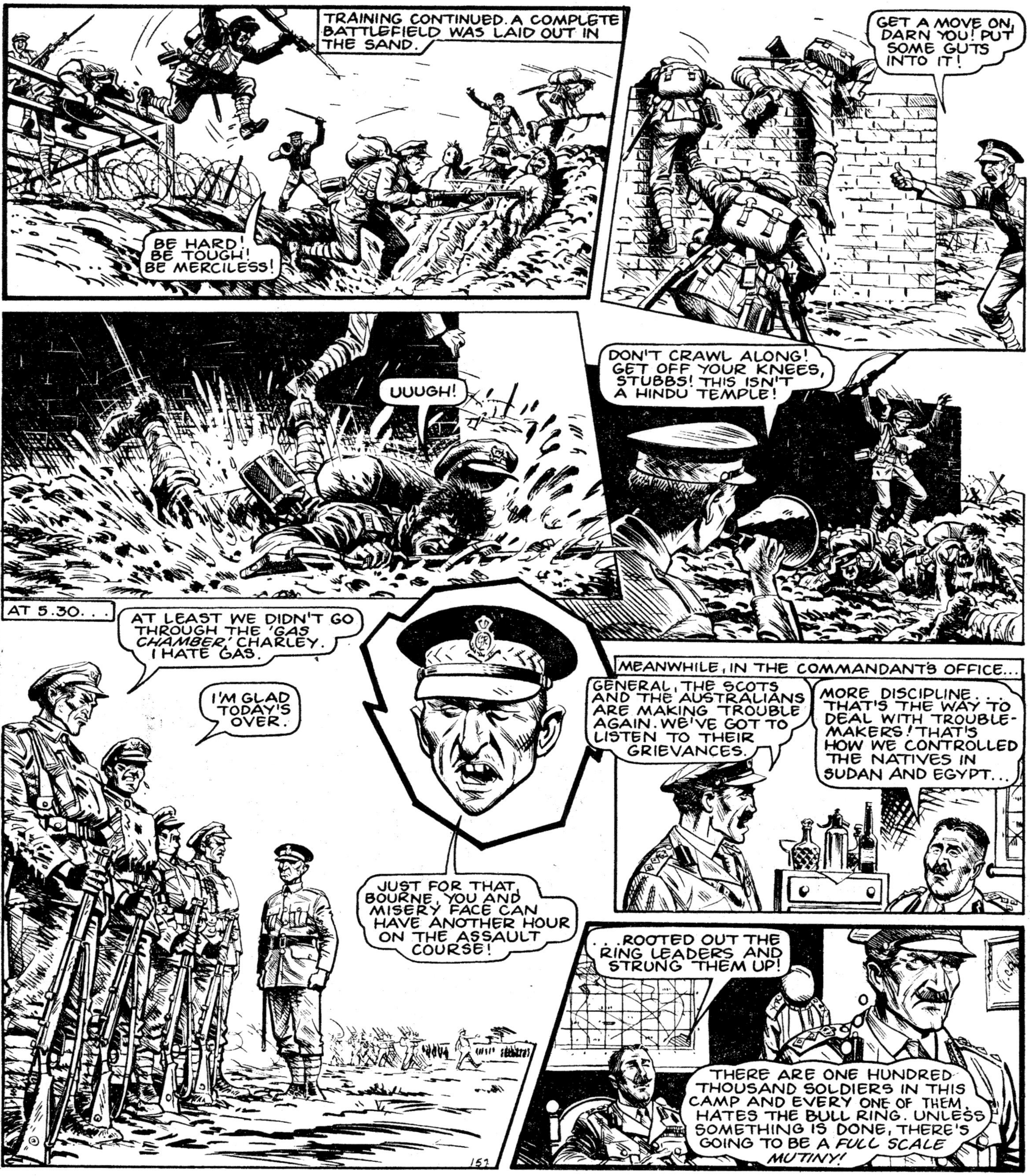
TRAINING CONTINUED. A COMPLETE BATTLEFIELD WAS LAID OUT IN THE SAND.
BE HARD! BE TOUGH! BE MERCILESS!
GET A MOVE ON, DARN YOU! PUT SOME GUTS INTO IT!
UUUGH!
DON'T CRAWL ALONG! GET OFF YOUR KNEES, STUBBS! THIS ISN'T A HINDU TEMPLE!
AT 5.30. . .
AT LEAST WE DIDN'T GO THROUGH THE 'GAS CHAMBER' CHARLEY. I HATE GAS.
I'M GLAD TODAY'S OVER.
JUST FOR THAT, BOURNE, YOU AND MISERY FACE CAN HAVE ANOTHER HOUR ON THE ASSAULT COURSE!
MEANWHILE, IN THE COMMANDANT'S OFFICE...
GENERAL, THE SCOTS AND THE AUSTRALIANS ARE MAKING TROUBLE AGAIN. WE'VE GOT TO LISTEN TO THEIR GRIEVANCES.
MORE DISCIPLINE. . . THAT'S THE WAY TO DEAL WITH TROUBLE-MAKERS! THAT'S HOW WE CONTROLLED THE NATIVES IN SUDAN AND EGYPT. . .
. . .ROOTED OUT THE RING LEADERS AND STRUNG THEM UP!
THERE ARE ONE HUNDRED THOUSAND SOLDIERS IN THIS CAMP AND EVERY ONE OF THEM HATES THE BULL RING. UNLESS SOMETHING IS DONE, THERE'S GOING TO BE A FULL SCALE MUTINY!

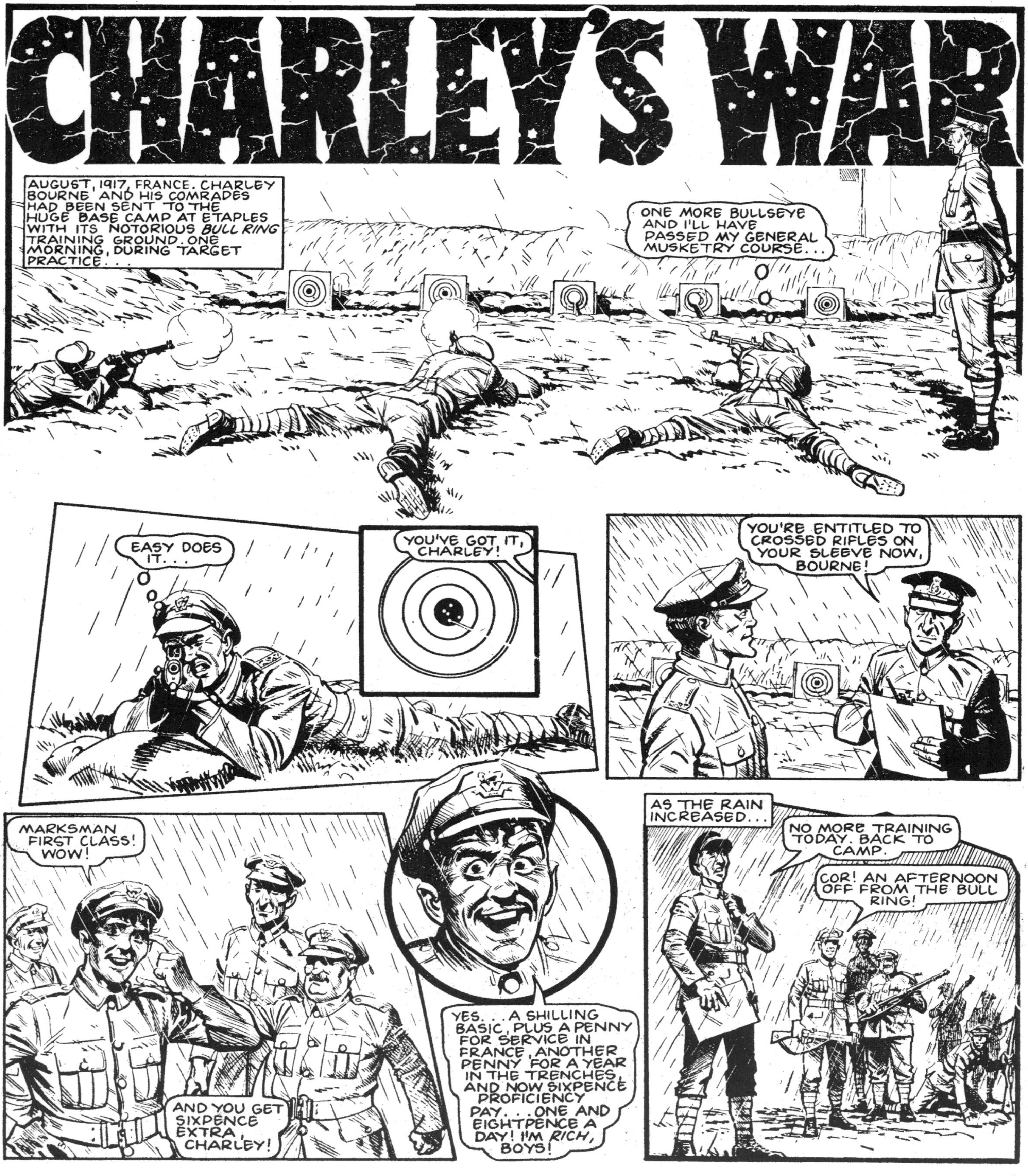
CHARLEY'S WAR
AUGUST, 1917, FRANCE. CHARLEY BOURNE AND HIS COMRADES HAD BEEN SENT TO THE HUGE BASE CAMP AT ETAPLES WITH ITS NOTORIOUS *BULL RING* TRAINING GROUND. ONE MORNING, DURING TARGET PRACTICE. . .
ONE MORE BULLSEYE AND I'LL HAVE PASSED MY GENERAL MUSKETRY COURSE. . .
EASY DOES IT. . .
YOU'VE GOT IT, CHARLEY!
YOU'RE ENTITLED TO CROSSED RIFLES ON YOUR SLEEVE NOW, BOURNE!
MARKSMAN FIRST CLASS! WOW!
AND YOU GET SIXPENCE EXTRA, CHARLEY!
YES. . . A SHILLING BASIC, PLUS A PENNY FOR SERVICE IN FRANCE, ANOTHER PENNY FOR A YEAR IN THE TRENCHES, AND NOW SIXPENCE PROFICIENCY PAY. . . ONE AND EIGHTPENCE A DAY! I'M *RICH*, BOYS!
AS THE RAIN INCREASED. . .
NO MORE TRAINING TODAY. BACK TO CAMP.
COR! AN AFTERNOON OFF FROM THE BULL RING!

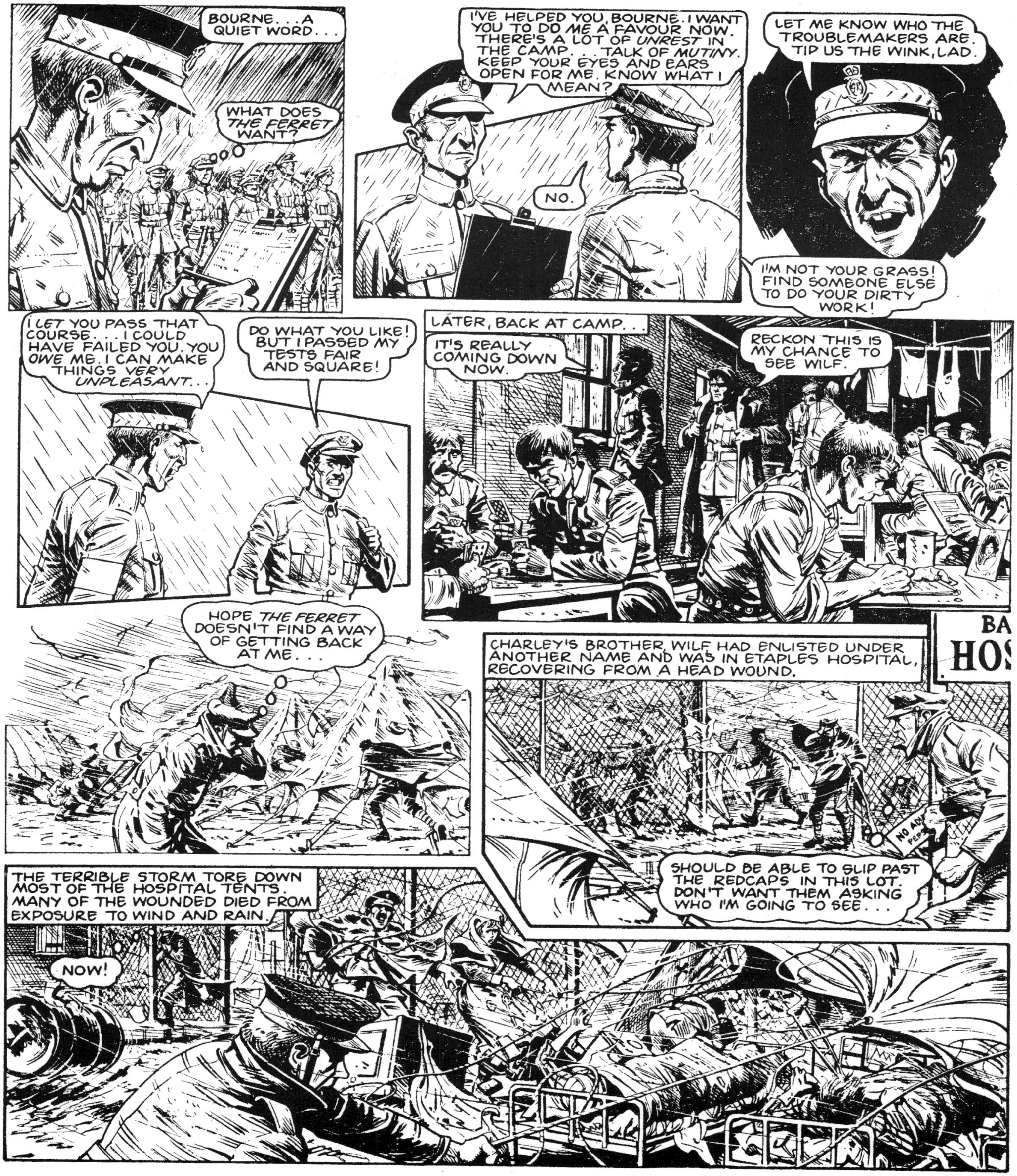
BOURNE. . . A QUIET WORD. . .
WHAT DOES THE FERRET WANT?
I'VE HELPED YOU, BOURNE. I WANT YOU TO DO ME A FAVOUR NOW. THERE'S A LOT OF UNREST IN THE CAMP. . . TALK OF MUTINY. KEEP YOUR EYES AND EARS OPEN FOR ME. KNOW WHAT I MEAN?
NO.
LET ME KNOW WHO THE TROUBLEMAKERS ARE. TIP US THE WINK, LAD.
I'M NOT YOUR GRASS! FIND SOMEONE ELSE TO DO YOUR DIRTY WORK!
I LET YOU PASS THAT COURSE. . . I COULD HAVE FAILED YOU. YOU OWE ME. I CAN MAKE THINGS VERY UNPLEASANT. . .
DO WHAT YOU LIKE! BUT I PASSED MY TESTS FAIR AND SQUARE!
LATER, BACK AT CAMP. . .
IT'S REALLY COMING DOWN NOW.
RECKON THIS IS MY CHANCE TO SEE WILF.
HOPE THE FERRET DOESN'T FIND A WAY OF GETTING BACK AT ME. . .
CHARLEY'S BROTHER, WILF HAD ENLISTED UNDER ANOTHER NAME AND WAS IN ETAPLES HOSPITAL, RECOVERING FROM A HEAD WOUND.
BA
HOS
SHOULD BE ABLE TO SLIP PAST THE REDCAPS IN THIS LOT. DON'T WANT THEM ASKING WHO I'M GOING TO SEE. . .
THE TERRIBLE STORM TORE DOWN MOST OF THE HOSPITAL TENTS. MANY OF THE WOUNDED DIED FROM EXPOSURE TO WIND AND RAIN.
NOW!

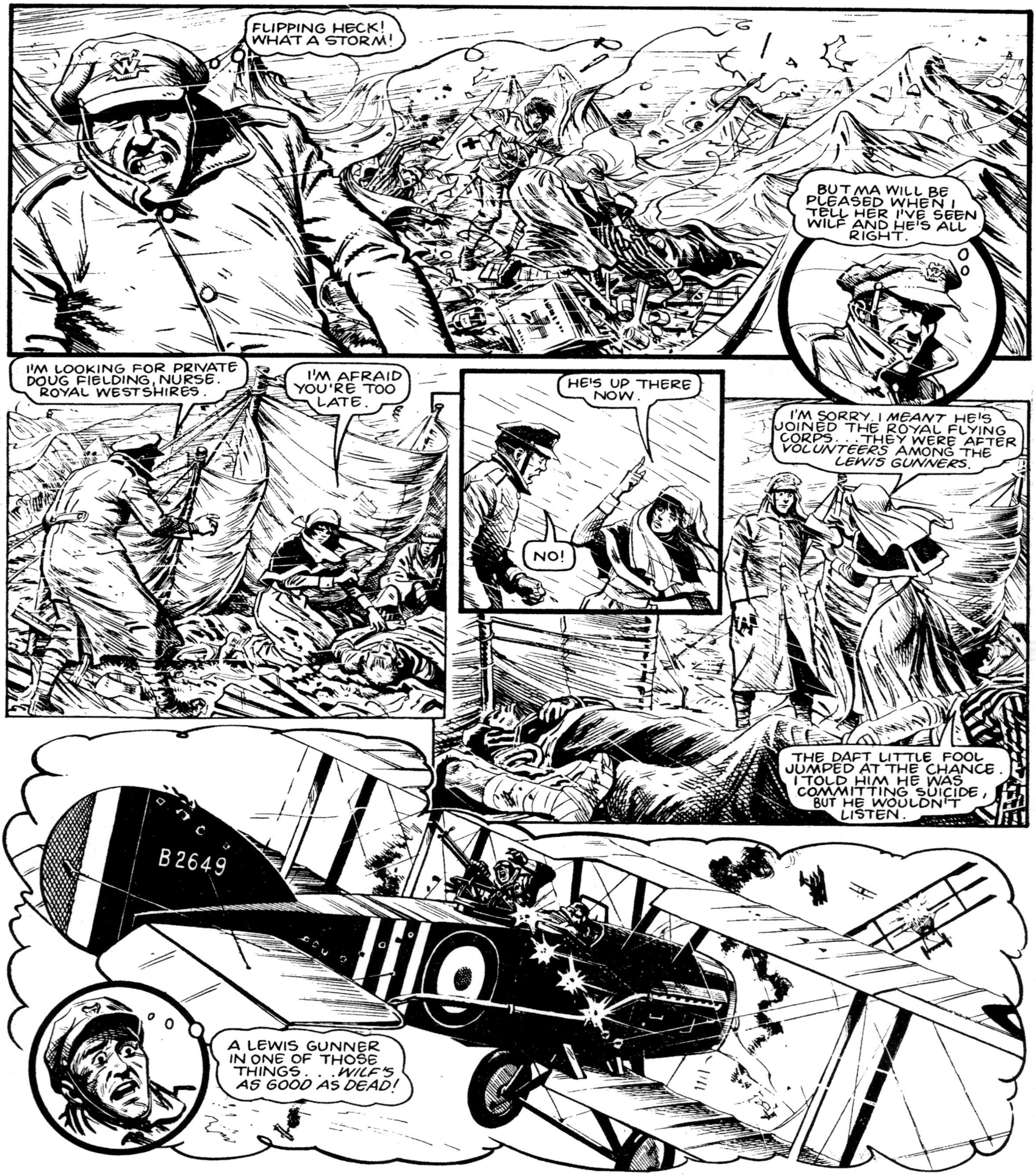
FLIPPING HECK! WHAT A STORM!
BUT MA WILL BE PLEASED WHEN I TELL HER I'VE SEEN WILF AND HE'S ALL RIGHT.
I'M LOOKING FOR PRIVATE DOUG FIELDING, NURSE. ROYAL WESTSHIRES.
I'M AFRAID YOU'RE TOO LATE.
HE'S UP THERE NOW.
NO!
I'M SORRY. I MEANT HE'S JOINED THE ROYAL FLYING CORPS. . . THEY WERE AFTER VOLUNTEERS AMONG THE LEWIS GUNNERS.
THE DAFT LITTLE FOOL JUMPED AT THE CHANCE. I TOLD HIM HE WAS COMMITTING SUICIDE, BUT HE WOULDN'T LISTEN.
B2649
A LEWIS GUNNER IN ONE OF THOSE THINGS. . . WILF'S AS GOOD AS DEAD!

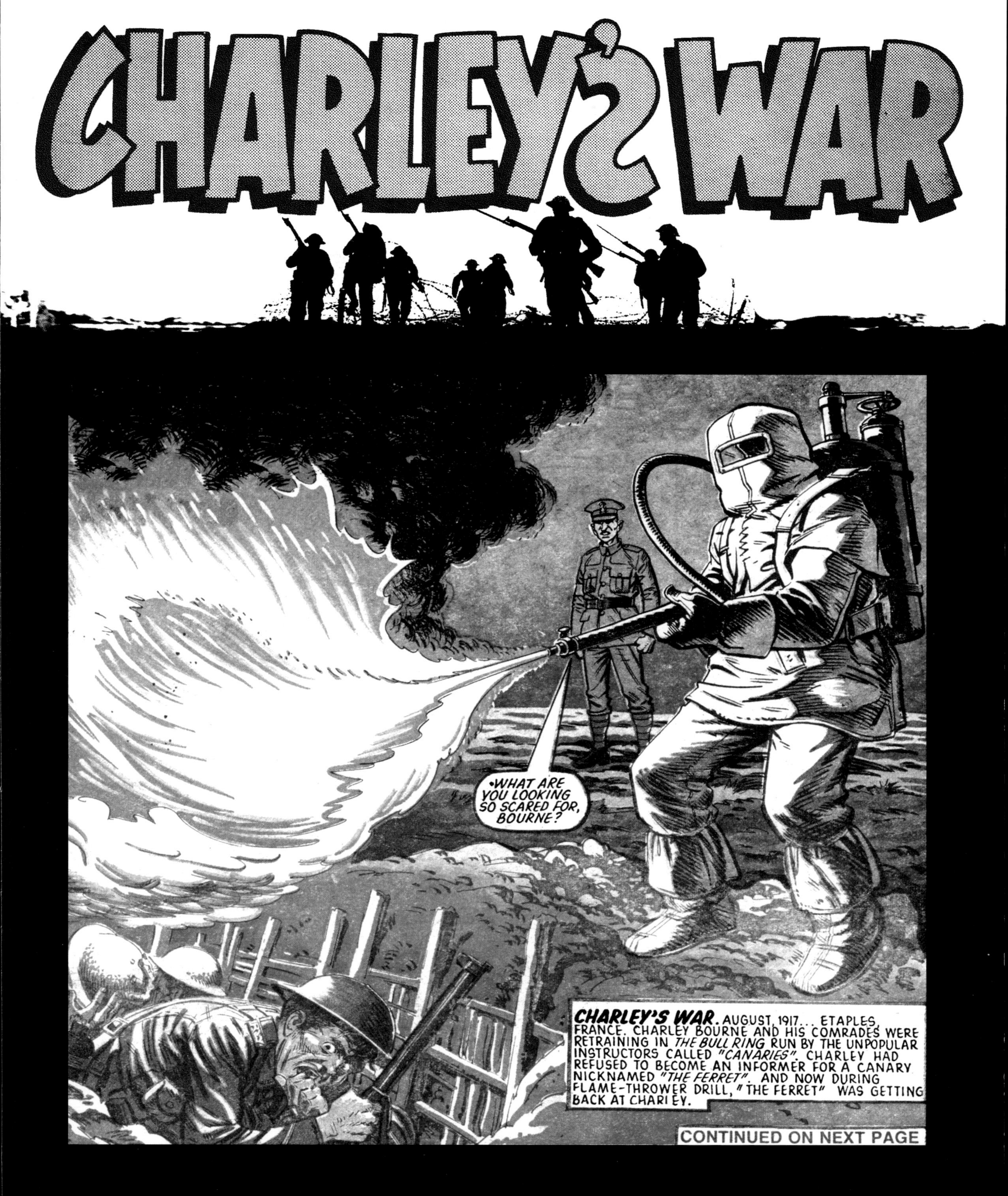
CHARLEY'S WAR
•WHAT ARE YOU LOOKING SO SCARED FOR, BOURNE?
CHARLEY'S WAR. AUGUST, 1917... ETAPLES, FRANCE. CHARLEY BOURNE AND HIS COMRADES WERE RETRAINING IN THE BULL RING RUN BY THE UNPOPULAR INSTRUCTORS CALLED "CANARIES". CHARLEY HAD REFUSED TO BECOME AN INFORMER FOR A CANARY NICKNAMED "THE FERRET". AND NOW DURING FLAME-THROWER DRILL, "THE FERRET" WAS GETTING BACK AT CHARLEY.
CONTINUED ON NEXT PAGE

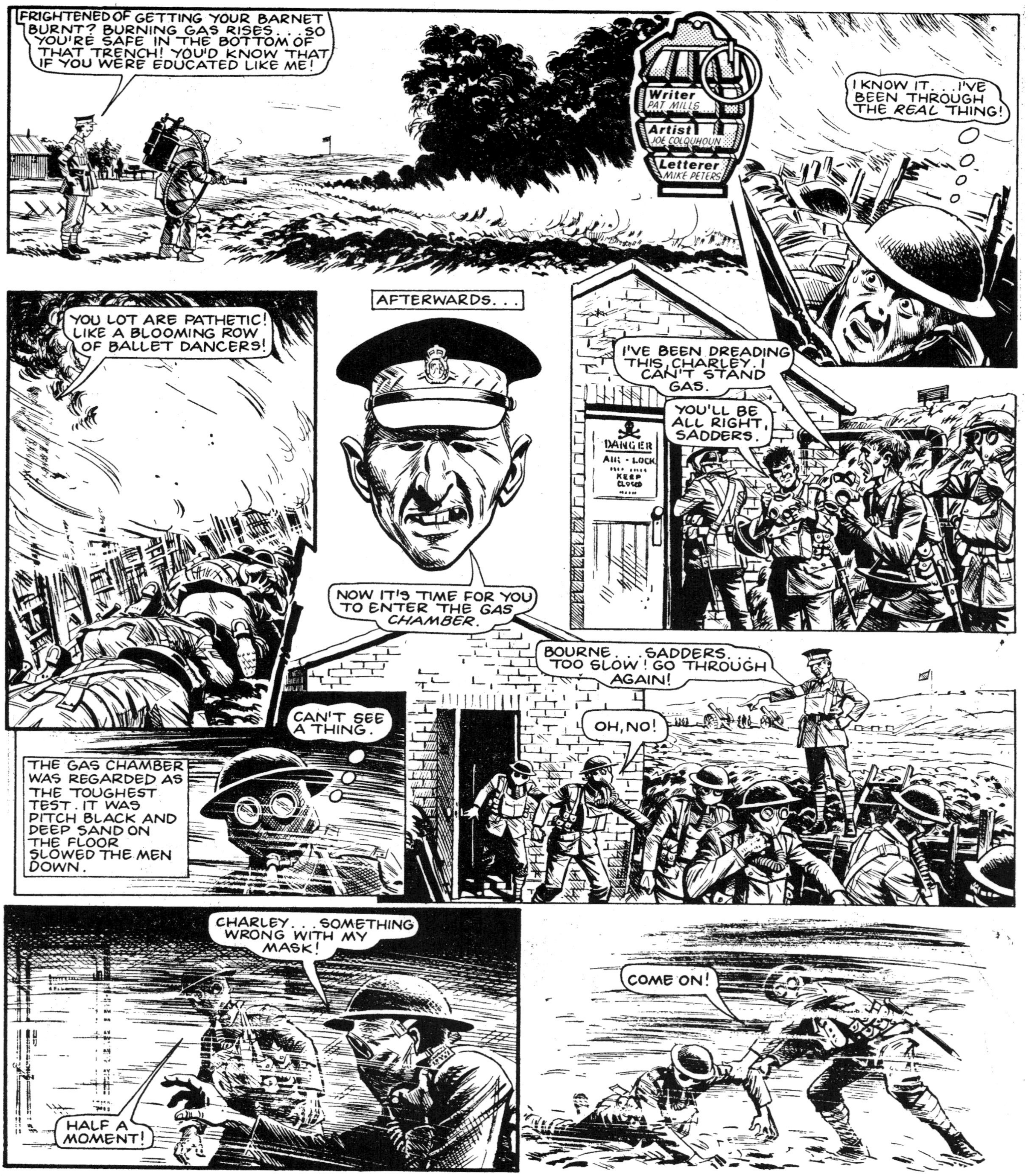

FRIGHTENED OF GETTING YOUR BARNET BURNT? BURNING GAS RISES... SO YOU'RE SAFE IN THE BOTTOM OF THAT TRENCH! YOU'D KNOW THAT IF YOU WERE EDUCATED LIKE ME!
Writer PAT MILLS
Artist JOE COLQUHOUN
Letterer MIKE PETERS
I KNOW IT... I'VE BEEN THROUGH THE REAL THING!
YOU LOT ARE PATHETIC! LIKE A BLOOMING ROW OF BALLET DANCERS!
AFTERWARDS...
NOW IT'S TIME FOR YOU TO ENTER THE GAS CHAMBER.
I'VE BEEN DREADING THIS, CHARLEY. I CAN'T STAND GAS.
YOU'LL BE ALL RIGHT, SADDERS.
DANGER
AIR-LOCK
KEEP CLOSED
BOURNE... SADDERS... TOO SLOW! GO THROUGH AGAIN!
CAN'T SEE A THING.
THE GAS CHAMBER WAS REGARDED AS THE TOUGHEST TEST. IT WAS PITCH BLACK AND DEEP SAND ON THE FLOOR SLOWED THE MEN DOWN.
OH, NO!
CHARLEY... SOMETHING WRONG WITH MY MASK!
HALF A MOMENT!
COME ON!

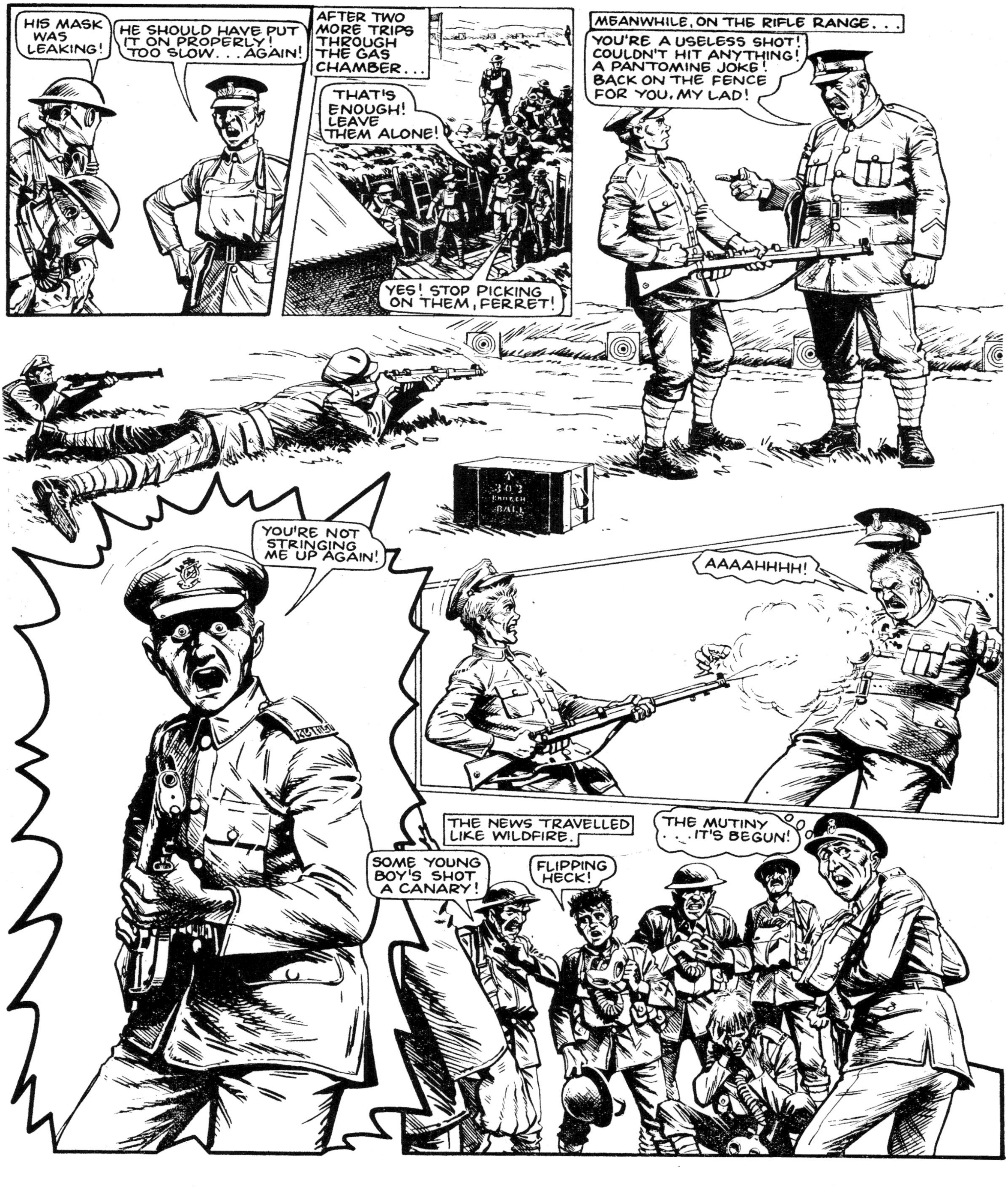
HIS MASK WAS LEAKING!
HE SHOULD HAVE PUT IT ON PROPERLY! TOO SLOW... AGAIN!
AFTER TWO MORE TRIPS THROUGH THE GAS CHAMBER...
THAT'S ENOUGH! LEAVE THEM ALONE!
YES! STOP PICKING ON THEM, FERRET!
MEANWHILE, ON THE RIFLE RANGE...
YOU'RE A USELESS SHOT! COULDN'T HIT ANYTHING! A PANTOMINE JOKE! BACK ON THE FENCE FOR YOU, MY LAD!
YOU'RE NOT STRINGING ME UP AGAIN!
AAAAHHHH!
THE NEWS TRAVELLED LIKE WILDFIRE.
THE MUTINY ...IT'S BEGUN!
SOME YOUNG BOY'S SHOT A CANARY!
FLIPPING HECK!

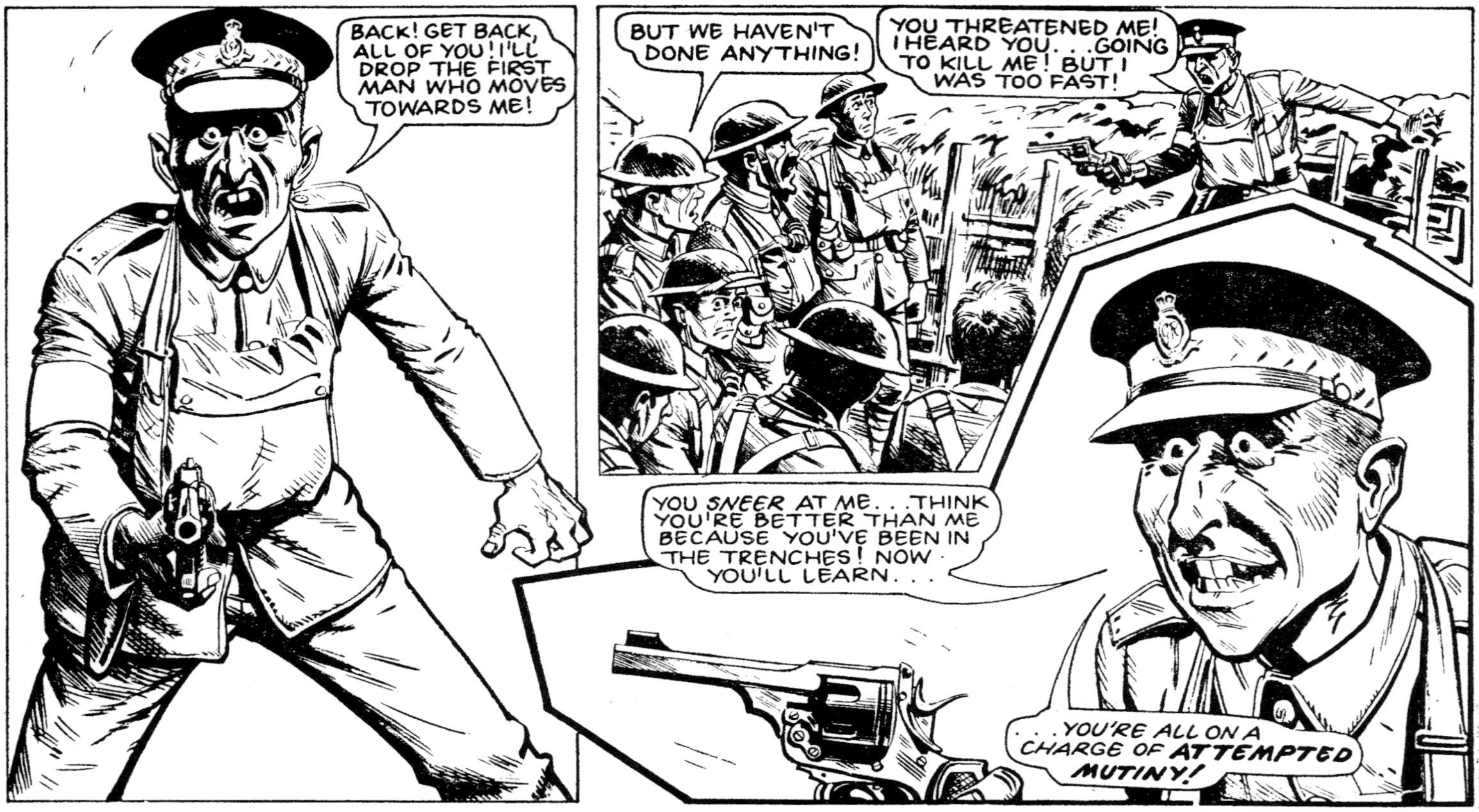
BACK! GET BACK, ALL OF YOU! I'LL DROP THE FIRST MAN WHO MOVES TOWARDS ME!
BUT WE HAVEN'T DONE ANYTHING!
YOU THREATENED ME! I HEARD YOU. . . GOING TO KILL ME! BUT I WAS TOO FAST!
YOU *SNEER* AT ME. . . THINK YOU'RE BETTER THAN ME BECAUSE YOU'VE BEEN IN THE TRENCHES! NOW YOU'LL LEARN. . .
. . . YOU'RE ALL ON A CHARGE OF **ATTEMPTED MUTINY!**

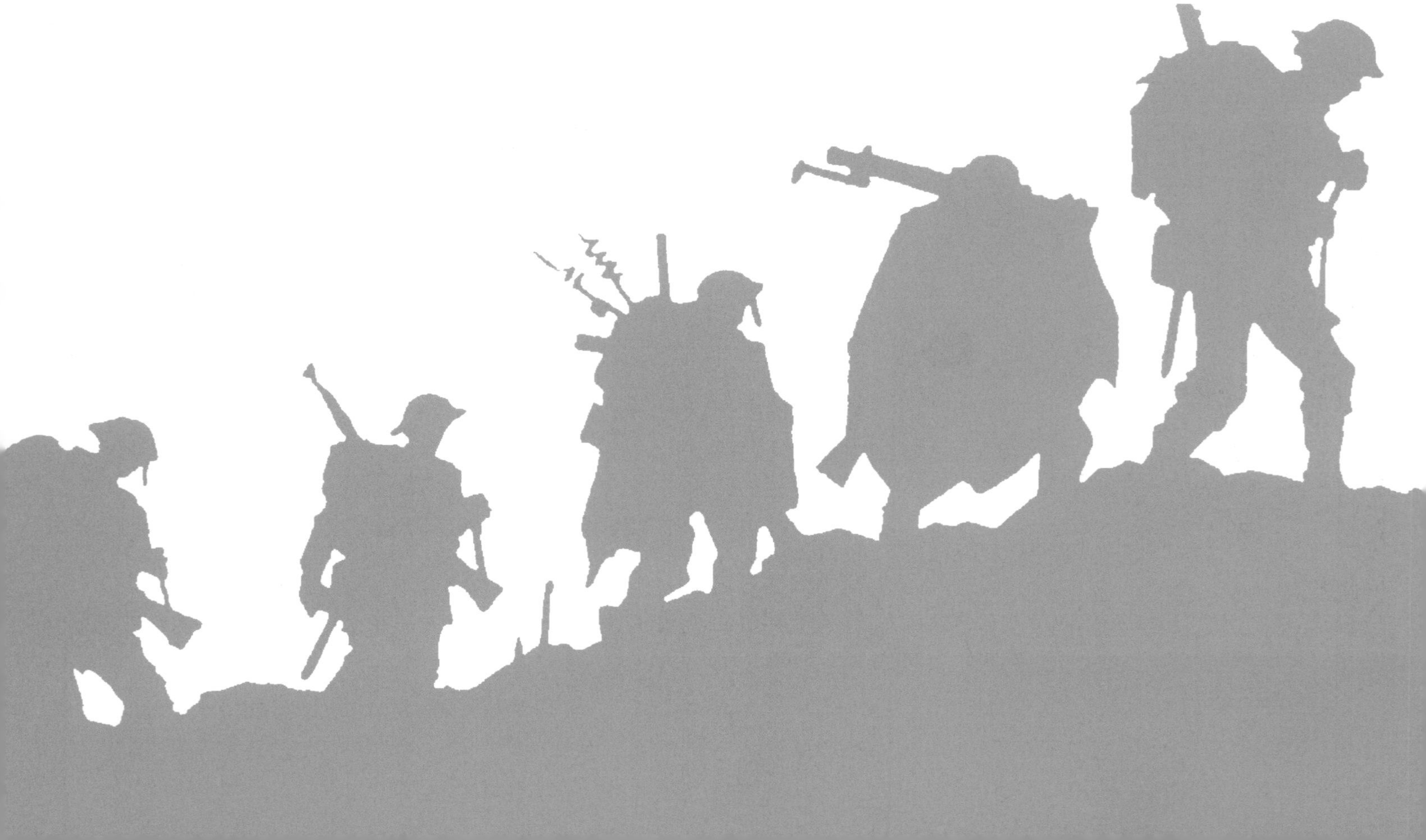

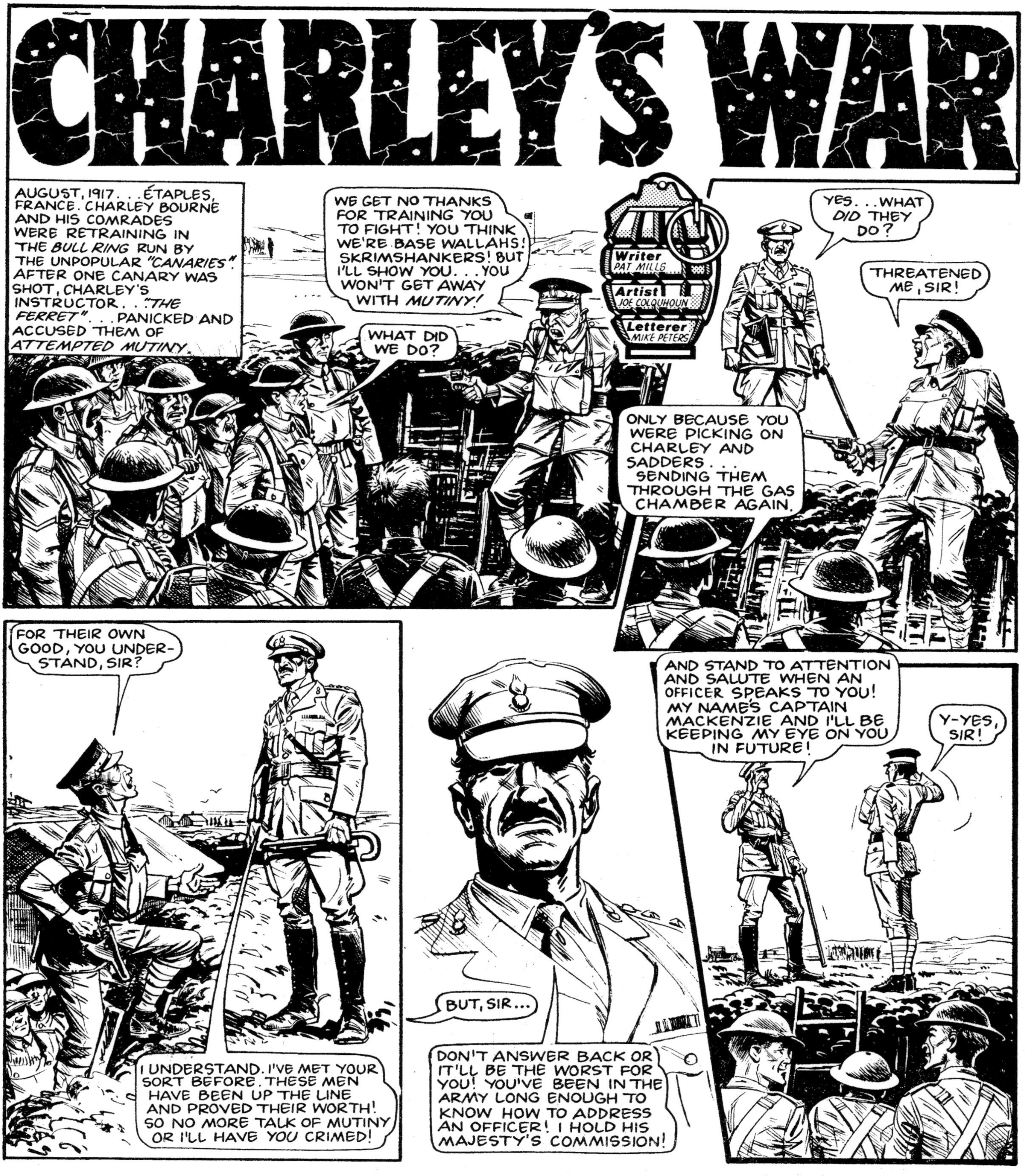
CHARLEY'S WAR
AUGUST, 1917. . . ÉTAPLES, FRANCE. CHARLEY BOURNE AND HIS COMRADES WERE RETRAINING IN THE *BULL RING* RUN BY THE UNPOPULAR *"CANARIES"*. AFTER ONE CANARY WAS SHOT, CHARLEY'S INSTRUCTOR. . . *"THE FERRET"*. . . PANICKED AND ACCUSED THEM OF *ATTEMPTED MUTINY*.
WE GET NO THANKS FOR TRAINING YOU TO FIGHT! YOU THINK WE'RE BASE WALLAHS! SKRIMSHANKERS! BUT I'LL SHOW YOU. . . YOU WON'T GET AWAY WITH *MUTINY!*
WHAT DID WE DO?
Writer PAT MILLS
Artist JOE COLQUHOUN
Letterer MIKE PETERS
YES. . . WHAT *DID* THEY DO?
THREATENED ME, SIR!
ONLY BECAUSE YOU WERE PICKING ON CHARLEY AND SADDERS. . . SENDING THEM THROUGH THE GAS CHAMBER AGAIN.
FOR THEIR OWN GOOD, YOU UNDER-STAND, SIR?
I UNDERSTAND. I'VE MET YOUR SORT BEFORE. THESE MEN HAVE BEEN UP THE LINE AND PROVED THEIR WORTH! SO NO MORE TALK OF MUTINY OR I'LL HAVE *YOU* CRIMED!
BUT, SIR...
DON'T ANSWER BACK OR IT'LL BE THE WORST FOR YOU! YOU'VE BEEN IN THE ARMY LONG ENOUGH TO KNOW HOW TO ADDRESS AN OFFICER! I HOLD HIS MAJESTY'S COMMISSION!
AND STAND TO ATTENTION AND SALUTE WHEN AN OFFICER SPEAKS TO YOU! MY NAME'S CAPTAIN MACKENZIE AND I'LL BE KEEPING MY EYE ON YOU IN FUTURE!
Y-YES, SIR!

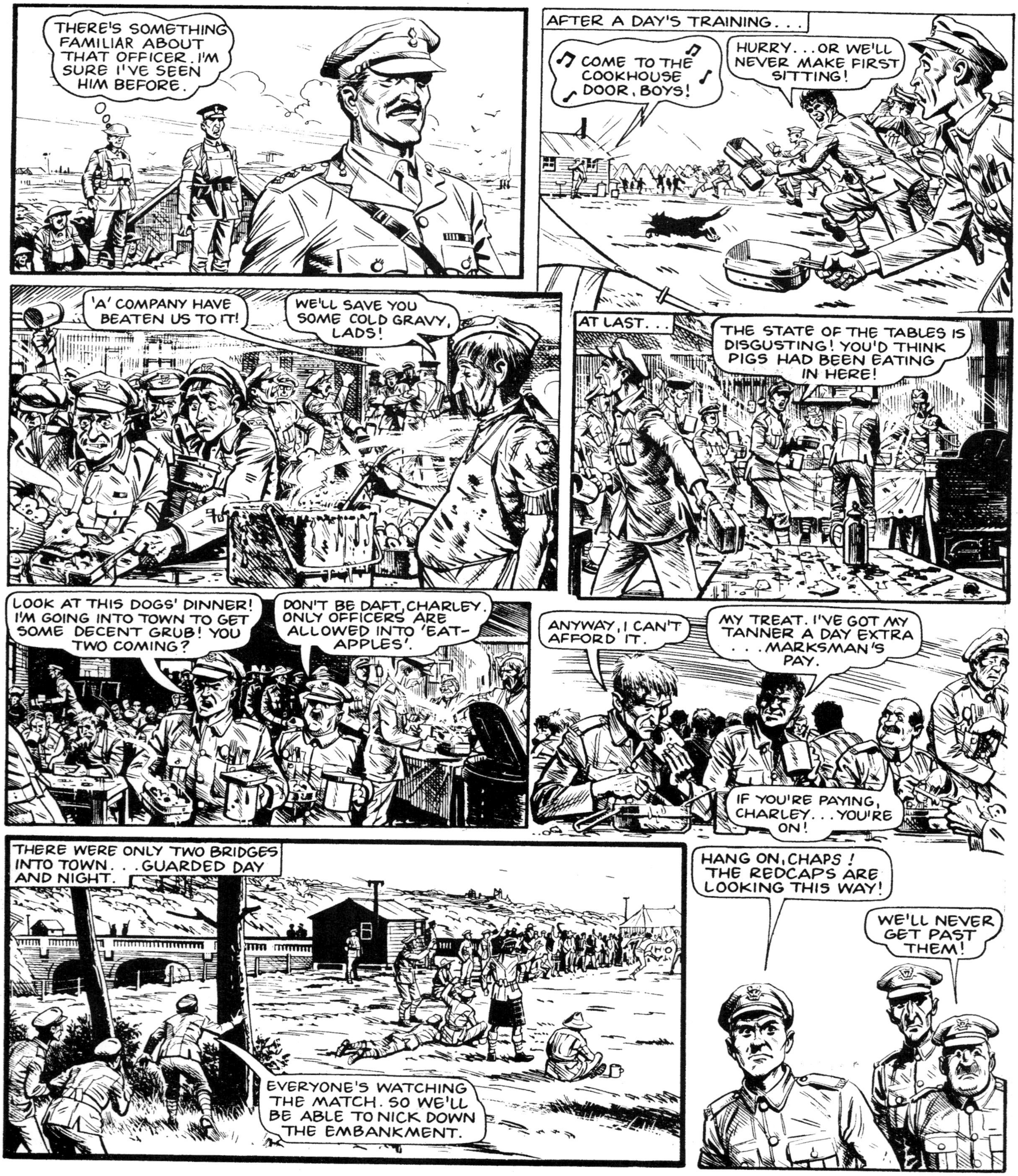

THERE'S SOMETHING FAMILIAR ABOUT THAT OFFICER. I'M SURE I'VE SEEN HIM BEFORE.
AFTER A DAY'S TRAINING...
COME TO THE COOKHOUSE DOOR, BOYS!
HURRY... OR WE'LL NEVER MAKE FIRST SITTING!
'A' COMPANY HAVE BEATEN US TO IT!
WE'LL SAVE YOU SOME COLD GRAVY, LADS!
AT LAST...
THE STATE OF THE TABLES IS DISGUSTING! YOU'D THINK PIGS HAD BEEN EATING IN HERE!
LOOK AT THIS DOGS' DINNER! I'M GOING INTO TOWN TO GET SOME DECENT GRUB! YOU TWO COMING?
DON'T BE DAFT, CHARLEY. ONLY OFFICERS ARE ALLOWED INTO 'EAT-APPLES'.
ANYWAY, I CAN'T AFFORD IT.
MY TREAT. I'VE GOT MY TANNER A DAY EXTRA ... MARKSMAN'S PAY.
IF YOU'RE PAYING, CHARLEY... YOU'RE ON!
THERE WERE ONLY TWO BRIDGES INTO TOWN... GUARDED DAY AND NIGHT.
EVERYONE'S WATCHING THE MATCH. SO WE'LL BE ABLE TO NICK DOWN THE EMBANKMENT.
HANG ON, CHAPS! THE REDCAPS ARE LOOKING THIS WAY!
WE'LL NEVER GET PAST THEM!

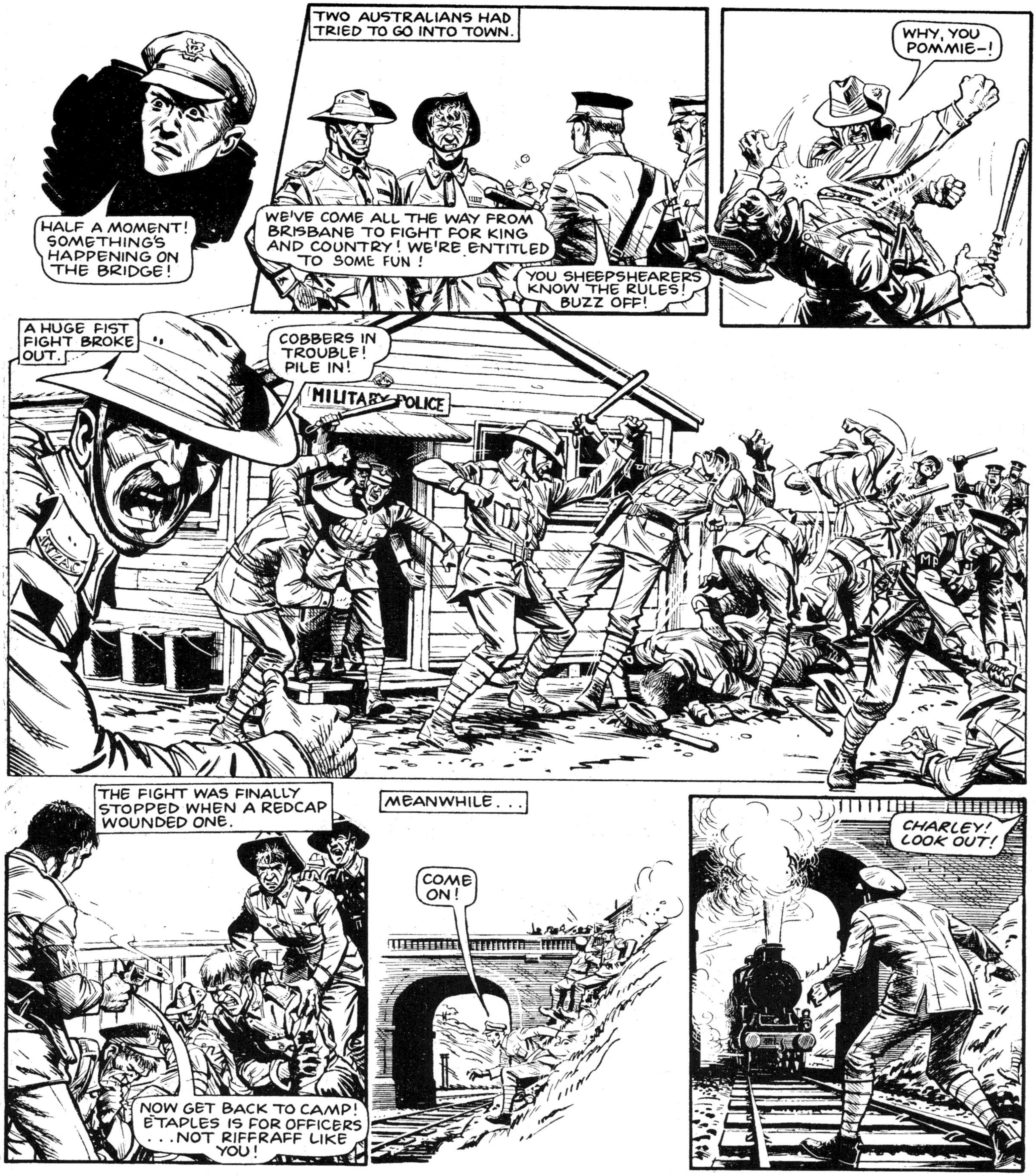
HALF A MOMENT! SOMETHING'S HAPPENING ON THE BRIDGE!
TWO AUSTRALIANS HAD TRIED TO GO INTO TOWN.
WE'VE COME ALL THE WAY FROM BRISBANE TO FIGHT FOR KING AND COUNTRY! WE'RE ENTITLED TO SOME FUN!
YOU SHEEPSHEARERS KNOW THE RULES! BUZZ OFF!
WHY, YOU POMMIE-!
A HUGE FIST FIGHT BROKE OUT.
COBBERS IN TROUBLE! PILE IN!
MILITARY POLICE
THE FIGHT WAS FINALLY STOPPED WHEN A REDCAP WOUNDED ONE.
NOW GET BACK TO CAMP! ETAPLES IS FOR OFFICERS ...NOT RIFFRAFF LIKE YOU!
MEANWHILE...
COME ON!
CHARLEY! LOOK OUT!

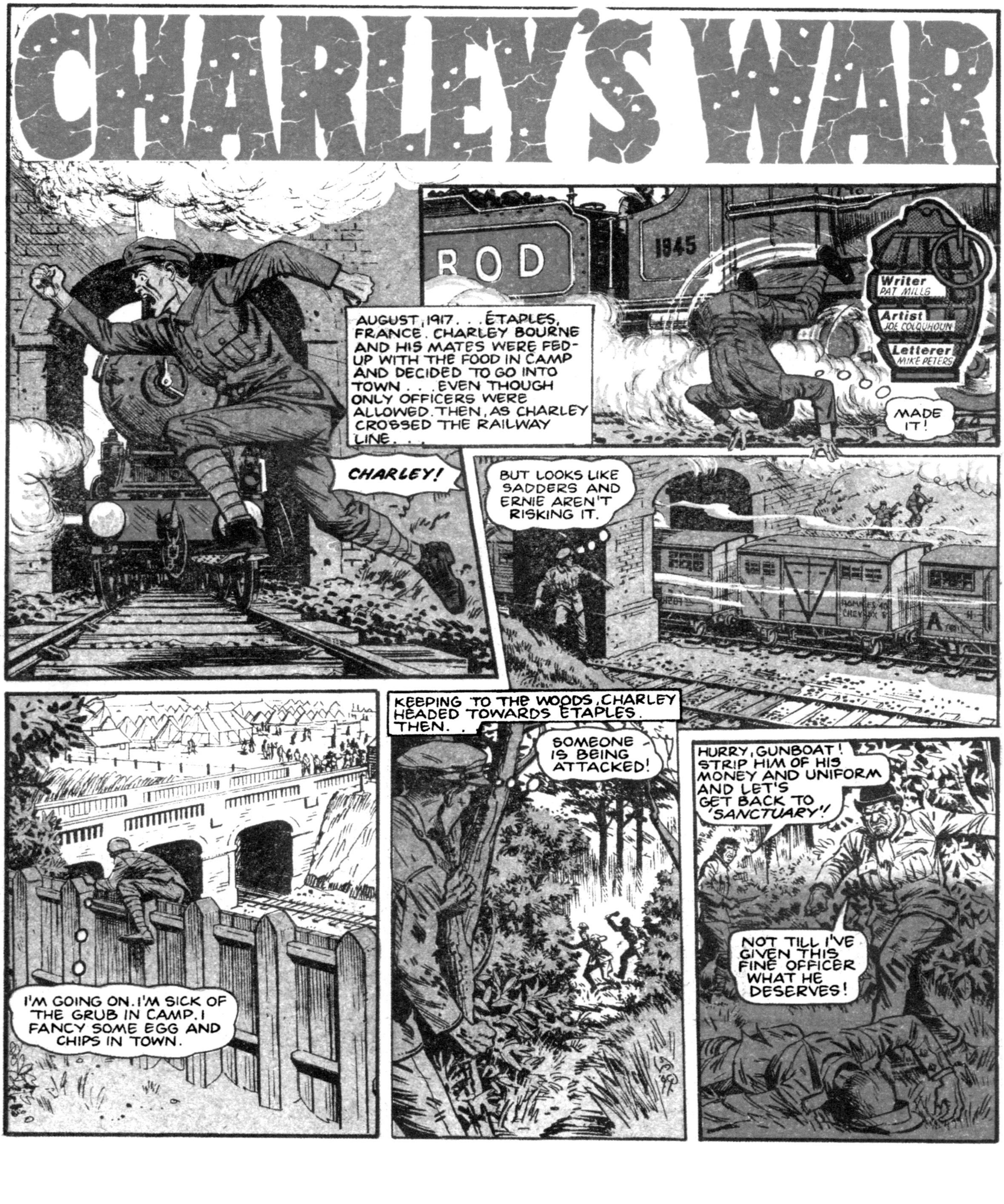
CHARLEY'S WAR
Writer PAT MILLS
Artist JOE COLQUHOUN
Letterer MIKE PETERS
AUGUST 1917. . . ETAPLES, FRANCE. CHARLEY BOURNE AND HIS MATES WERE FED-UP WITH THE FOOD IN CAMP AND DECIDED TO GO INTO TOWN . . . EVEN THOUGH ONLY OFFICERS WERE ALLOWED. THEN, AS CHARLEY CROSSED THE RAILWAY LINE . . .
CHARLEY!
ROD
1945
MADE IT!
BUT LOOKS LIKE SADDERS AND ERNIE AREN'T RISKING IT.
I'M GOING ON. I'M SICK OF THE GRUB IN CAMP. I FANCY SOME EGG AND CHIPS IN TOWN.
KEEPING TO THE WOODS, CHARLEY HEADED TOWARDS ETAPLES. THEN. . .
SOMEONE IS BEING ATTACKED!
HURRY, GUNBOAT! STRIP HIM OF HIS MONEY AND UNIFORM AND LET'S GET BACK TO 'SANCTUARY'!
NOT TILL I'VE GIVEN THIS FINE OFFICER WHAT HE DESERVES!

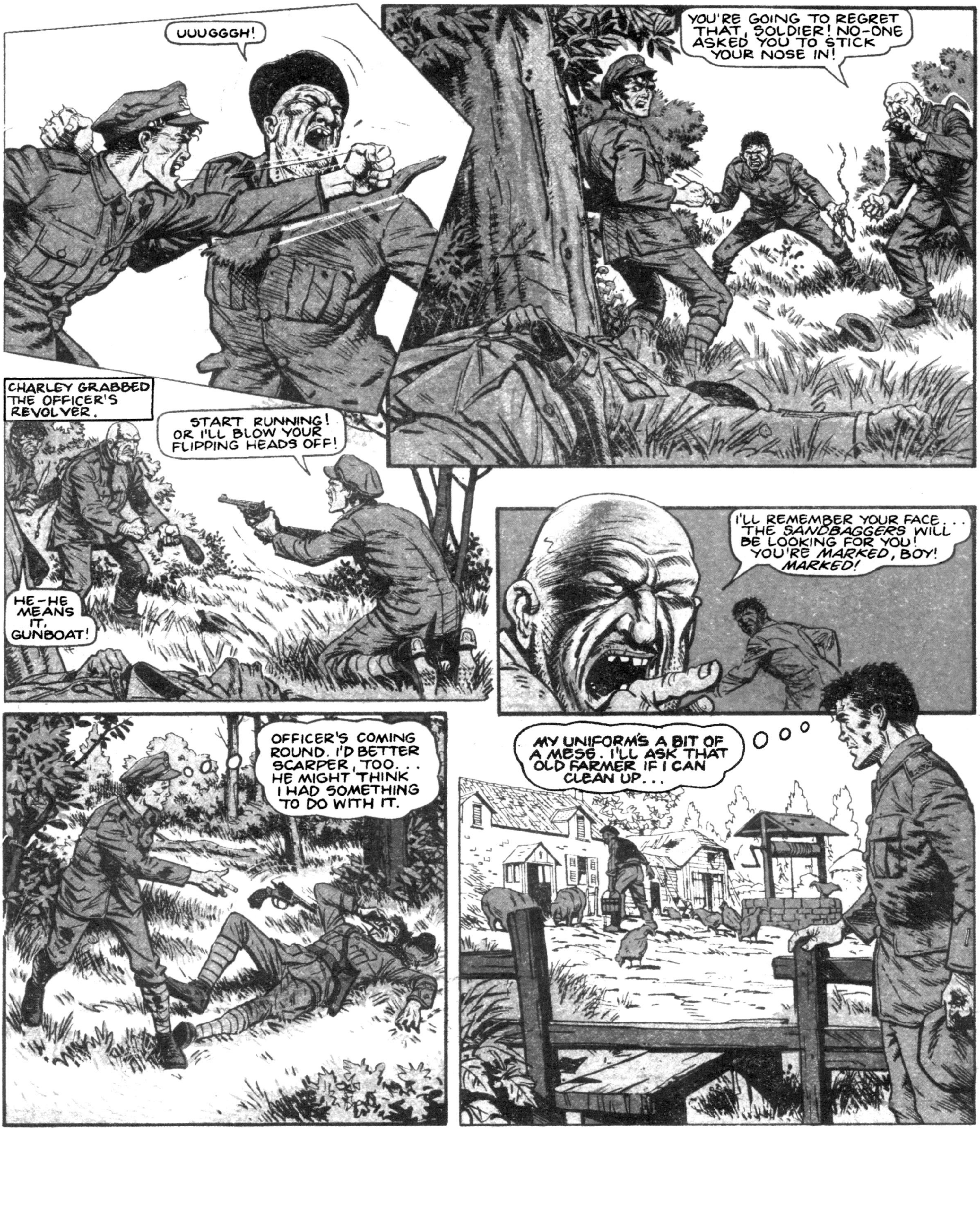
UUUGGGH!
YOU'RE GOING TO REGRET THAT, SOLDIER! NO-ONE ASKED YOU TO STICK YOUR NOSE IN!
CHARLEY GRABBED THE OFFICER'S REVOLVER.
START RUNNING! OR I'LL BLOW YOUR FLIPPING HEADS OFF!
HE-HE MEANS IT, GUNBOAT!
I'LL REMEMBER YOUR FACE... THE SANDBAGGERS WILL BE LOOKING FOR YOU! YOU'RE MARKED, BOY! MARKED!
OFFICER'S COMING ROUND. I'D BETTER SCARPER, TOO... HE MIGHT THINK I HAD SOMETHING TO DO WITH IT.
MY UNIFORM'S A BIT OF A MESS. I'LL ASK THAT OLD FARMER IF I CAN CLEAN UP...

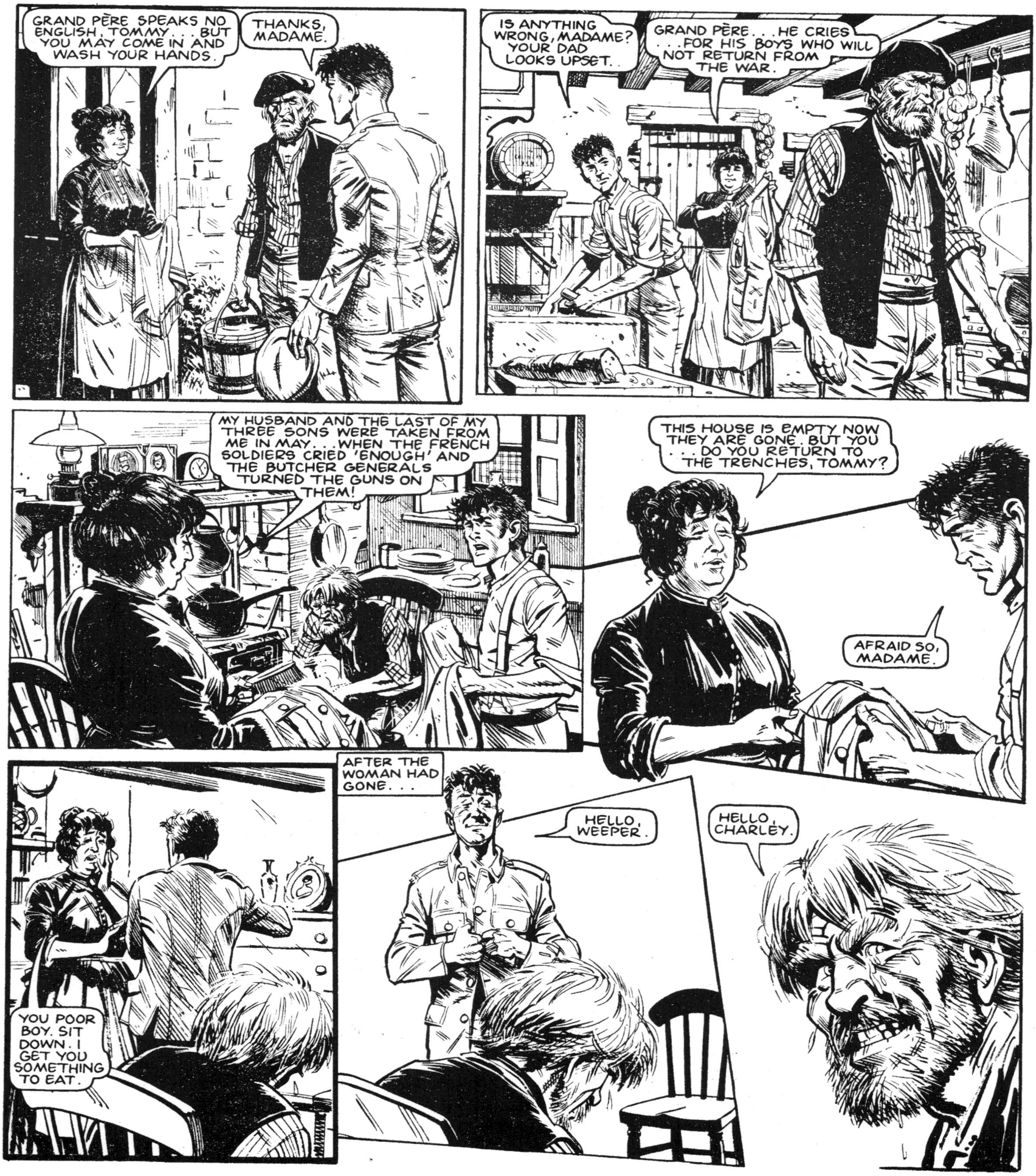
GRAND PÈRE SPEAKS NO ENGLISH, TOMMY . . . BUT YOU MAY COME IN AND WASH YOUR HANDS.
THANKS, MADAME.
IS ANYTHING WRONG, MADAME? YOUR DAD LOOKS UPSET.
GRAND PÈRE . . . HE CRIES . . . FOR HIS BOYS WHO WILL NOT RETURN FROM THE WAR.
MY HUSBAND AND THE LAST OF MY THREE SONS WERE TAKEN FROM ME IN MAY . . . WHEN THE FRENCH SOLDIERS CRIED 'ENOUGH' AND THE BUTCHER GENERALS TURNED THE GUNS ON THEM!
THIS HOUSE IS EMPTY NOW THEY ARE GONE. BUT YOU . . . DO YOU RETURN TO THE TRENCHES, TOMMY?
AFRAID SO, MADAME.
YOU POOR BOY. SIT DOWN. I GET YOU SOMETHING TO EAT.
AFTER THE WOMAN HAD GONE . . .
HELLO, WEEPER.
HELLO, CHARLEY.

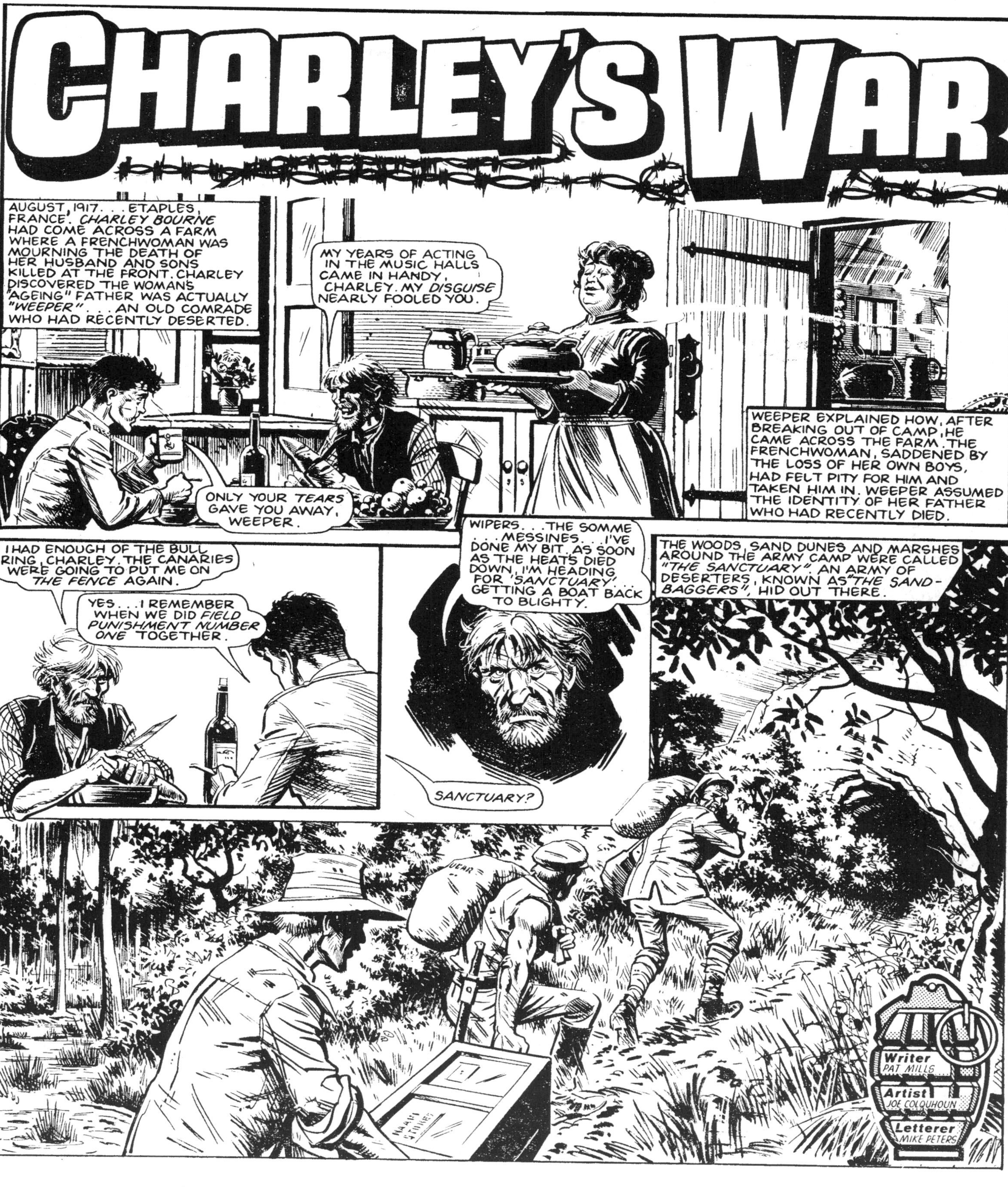
CHARLEY'S WAR
AUGUST, 1917. . . ETAPLES, FRANCE. CHARLEY BOURNE HAD COME ACROSS A FARM WHERE A FRENCHWOMAN WAS MOURNING THE DEATH OF HER HUSBAND AND SONS KILLED AT THE FRONT. CHARLEY DISCOVERED THE WOMAN'S "AGEING" FATHER WAS ACTUALLY "WEEPER" . . . AN OLD COMRADE WHO HAD RECENTLY DESERTED.
MY YEARS OF ACTING IN THE MUSIC HALLS CAME IN HANDY, CHARLEY. MY DISGUISE NEARLY FOOLED YOU.
ONLY YOUR TEARS GAVE YOU AWAY, WEEPER.
WEEPER EXPLAINED HOW, AFTER BREAKING OUT OF CAMP, HE CAME ACROSS THE FARM. THE FRENCHWOMAN, SADDENED BY THE LOSS OF HER OWN BOYS, HAD FELT PITY FOR HIM AND TAKEN HIM IN. WEEPER ASSUMED THE IDENTITY OF HER FATHER WHO HAD RECENTLY DIED.
I HAD ENOUGH OF THE BULL RING, CHARLEY. THE CANARIES WERE GOING TO PUT ME ON THE FENCE AGAIN.
YES. . . I REMEMBER WHEN WE DID FIELD PUNISHMENT NUMBER ONE TOGETHER.
WIPERS. . . THE SOMME . . . MESSINES. . . I'VE DONE MY BIT. AS SOON AS THE HEAT'S DIED DOWN, I'M HEADING FOR 'SANCTUARY' . . . GETTING A BOAT BACK TO BLIGHTY.
SANCTUARY?
THE WOODS, SAND DUNES AND MARSHES AROUND THE ARMY CAMP WERE CALLED "THE SANCTUARY". AN ARMY OF DESERTERS, KNOWN AS "THE SAND-BAGGERS", HID OUT THERE.
Writer PAT MILLS
Artist JOE COLQUHOUN
Letterer MIKE PETERS

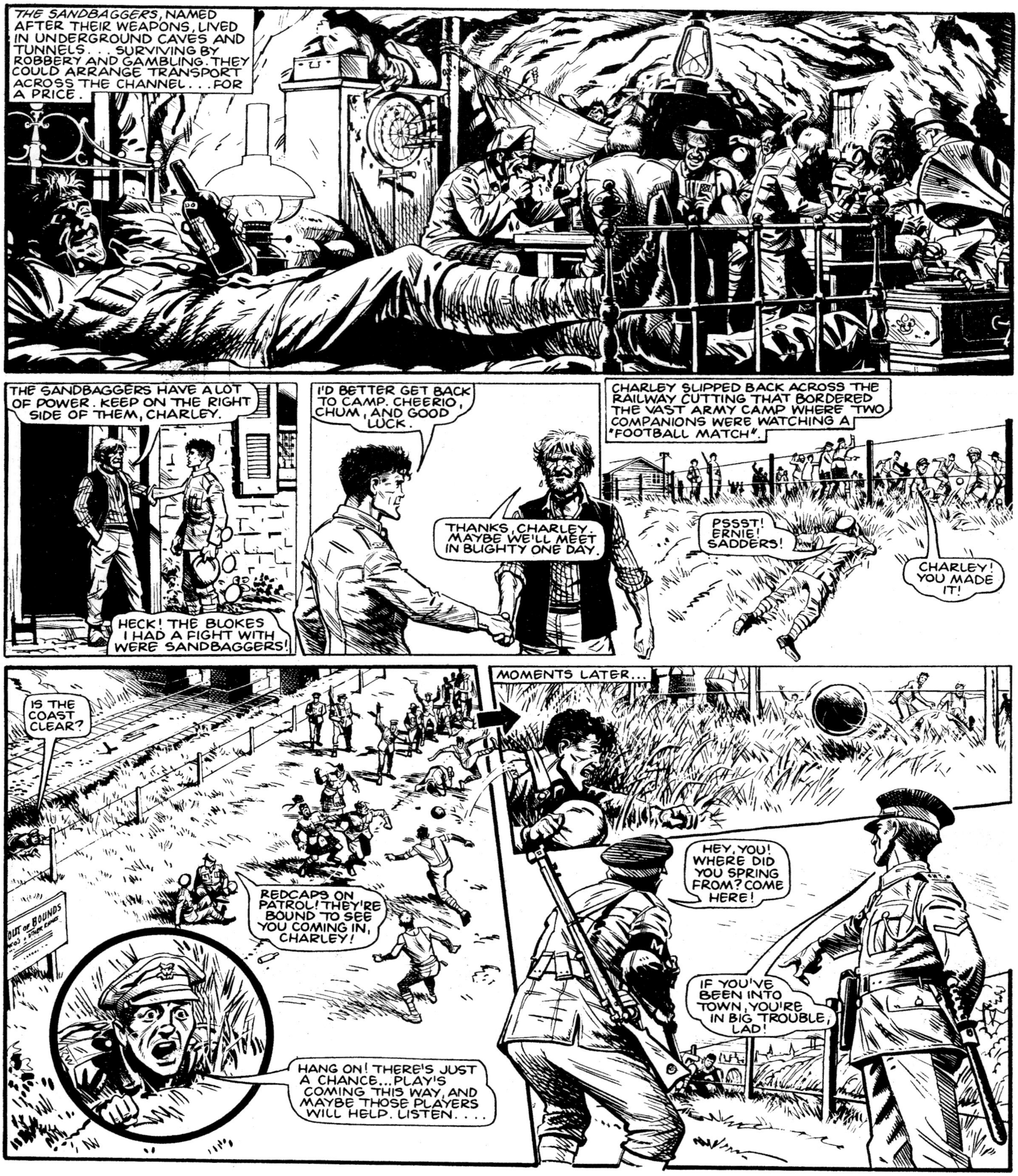
THE SANDBAGGERS, NAMED AFTER THEIR WEAPONS, LIVED IN UNDERGROUND CAVES AND TUNNELS . . . SURVIVING BY ROBBERY AND GAMBLING. THEY COULD ARRANGE TRANSPORT ACROSS THE CHANNEL . . . FOR A PRICE.
THE SANDBAGGERS HAVE A LOT OF POWER. KEEP ON THE RIGHT SIDE OF THEM, CHARLEY.
HECK! THE BLOKES I HAD A FIGHT WITH WERE SANDBAGGERS!
I'D BETTER GET BACK TO CAMP. CHEERIO, CHUM, AND GOOD LUCK.
THANKS, CHARLEY. MAYBE WE'LL MEET IN BLIGHTY ONE DAY.
CHARLEY SLIPPED BACK ACROSS THE RAILWAY CUTTING THAT BORDERED THE VAST ARMY CAMP WHERE TWO COMPANIONS WERE WATCHING A "FOOTBALL MATCH".
PSSST! ERNIE! SADDERS!
CHARLEY! YOU MADE IT!
IS THE COAST CLEAR?
REDCAPS ON PATROL! THEY'RE BOUND TO SEE YOU COMING IN, CHARLEY!
OUT OF BOUNDS
HANG ON! THERE'S JUST A CHANCE... PLAY'S COMING THIS WAY, AND MAYBE THOSE PLAYERS WILL HELP. LISTEN. . . .
MOMENTS LATER...
HEY, YOU! WHERE DID YOU SPRING FROM? COME HERE!
IF YOU'VE BEEN INTO TOWN, YOU'RE IN BIG TROUBLE, LAD!

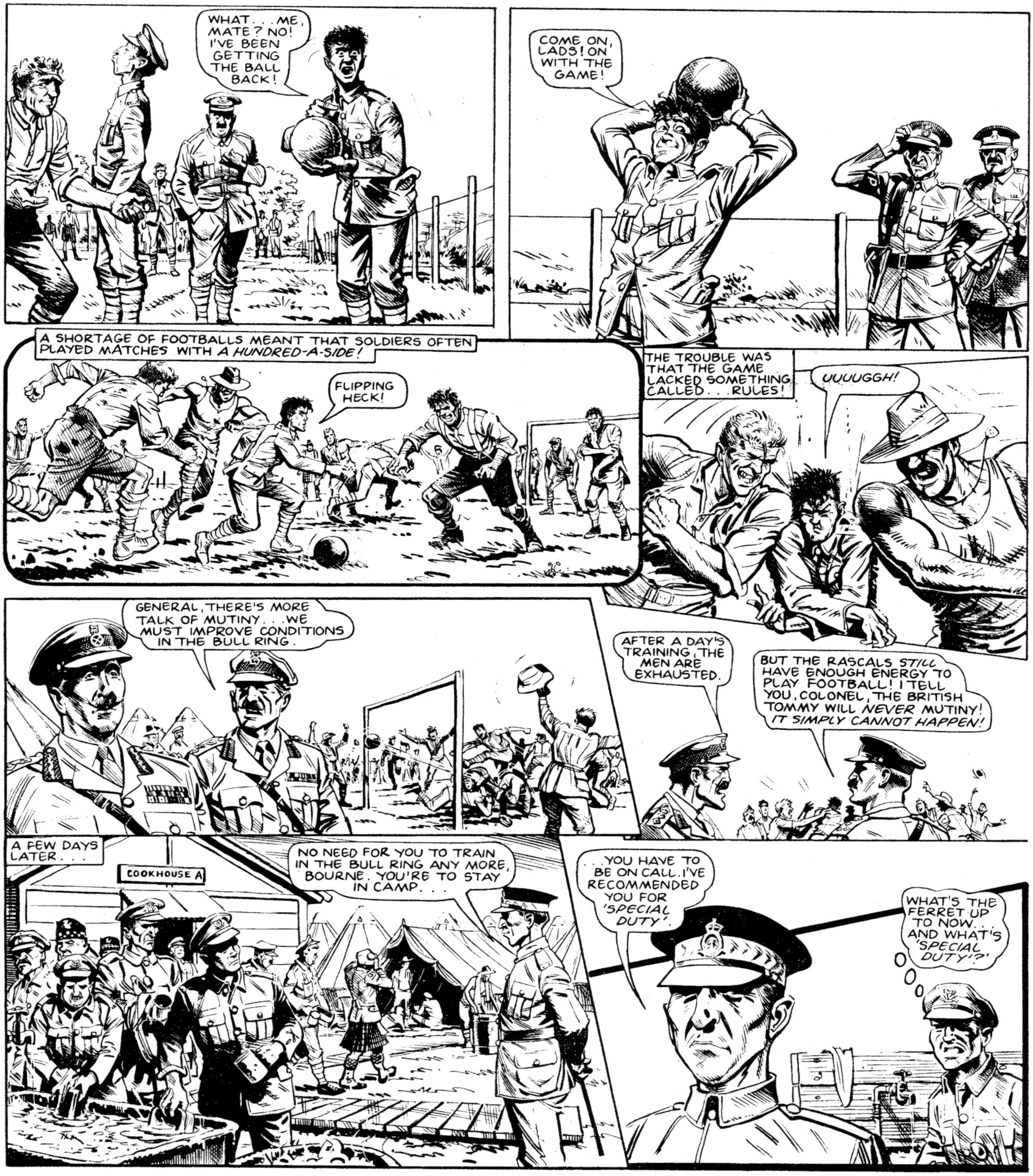
WHAT. . . ME, MATE? NO! I'VE BEEN GETTING THE BALL BACK!
COME ON, LADS! ON WITH THE GAME!
A SHORTAGE OF FOOTBALLS MEANT THAT SOLDIERS OFTEN PLAYED MATCHES WITH A HUNDRED-A-SIDE!
FLIPPING HECK!
THE TROUBLE WAS THAT THE GAME LACKED SOMETHING CALLED. . . RULES!
UUUUGGH!
GENERAL, THERE'S MORE TALK OF MUTINY. . . WE MUST IMPROVE CONDITIONS IN THE BULL RING.
AFTER A DAY'S TRAINING, THE MEN ARE EXHAUSTED.
BUT THE RASCALS STILL HAVE ENOUGH ENERGY TO PLAY FOOTBALL! I TELL YOU, COLONEL, THE BRITISH TOMMY WILL NEVER MUTINY! IT SIMPLY CANNOT HAPPEN!
A FEW DAYS LATER. . .
COOKHOUSE A
NO NEED FOR YOU TO TRAIN IN THE BULL RING ANY MORE, BOURNE. YOU'RE TO STAY IN CAMP. . .
. . .YOU HAVE TO BE ON CALL. I'VE RECOMMENDED YOU FOR 'SPECIAL DUTY'.
WHAT'S THE FERRET UP TO NOW. . . AND WHAT'S 'SPECIAL DUTY'?'

CHARLEY'S WAR

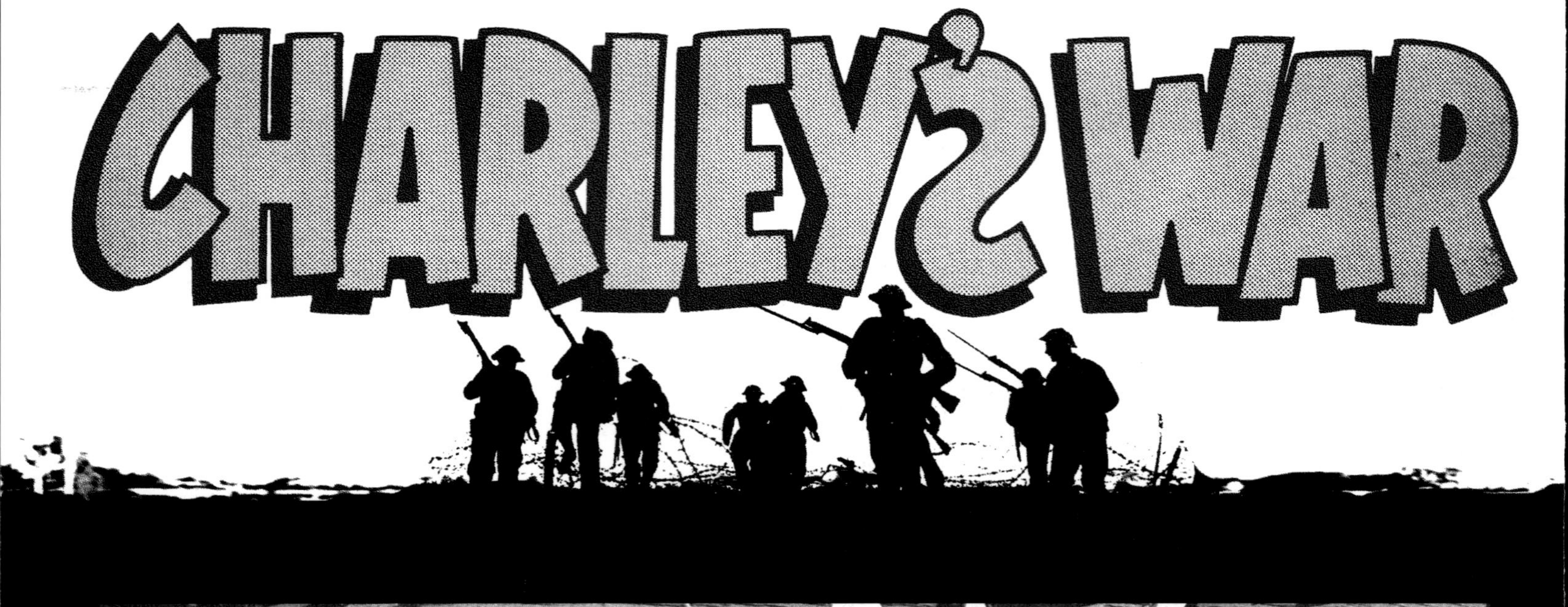

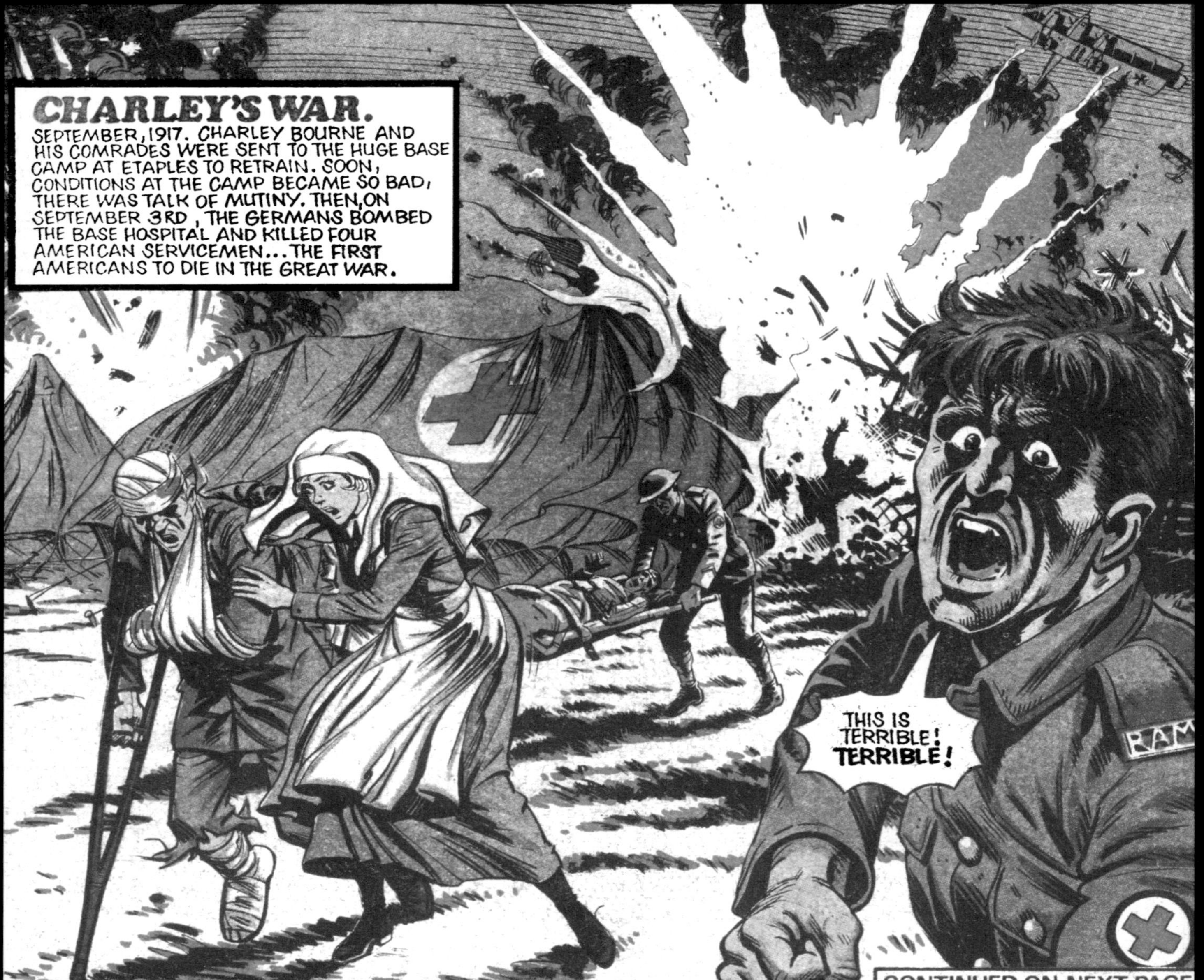
CHARLEY'S WAR.
SEPTEMBER, 1917. CHARLEY BOURNE AND HIS COMRADES WERE SENT TO THE HUGE BASE CAMP AT ETAPLES TO RETRAIN. SOON, CONDITIONS AT THE CAMP BECAME SO BAD, THERE WAS TALK OF MUTINY. THEN, ON SEPTEMBER 3RD, THE GERMANS BOMBED THE BASE HOSPITAL AND KILLED FOUR AMERICAN SERVICEMEN... THE FIRST AMERICANS TO DIE IN THE GREAT WAR.
THIS IS TERRIBLE! TERRIBLE!
RAM

CONTINUED ON NEXT PAGE

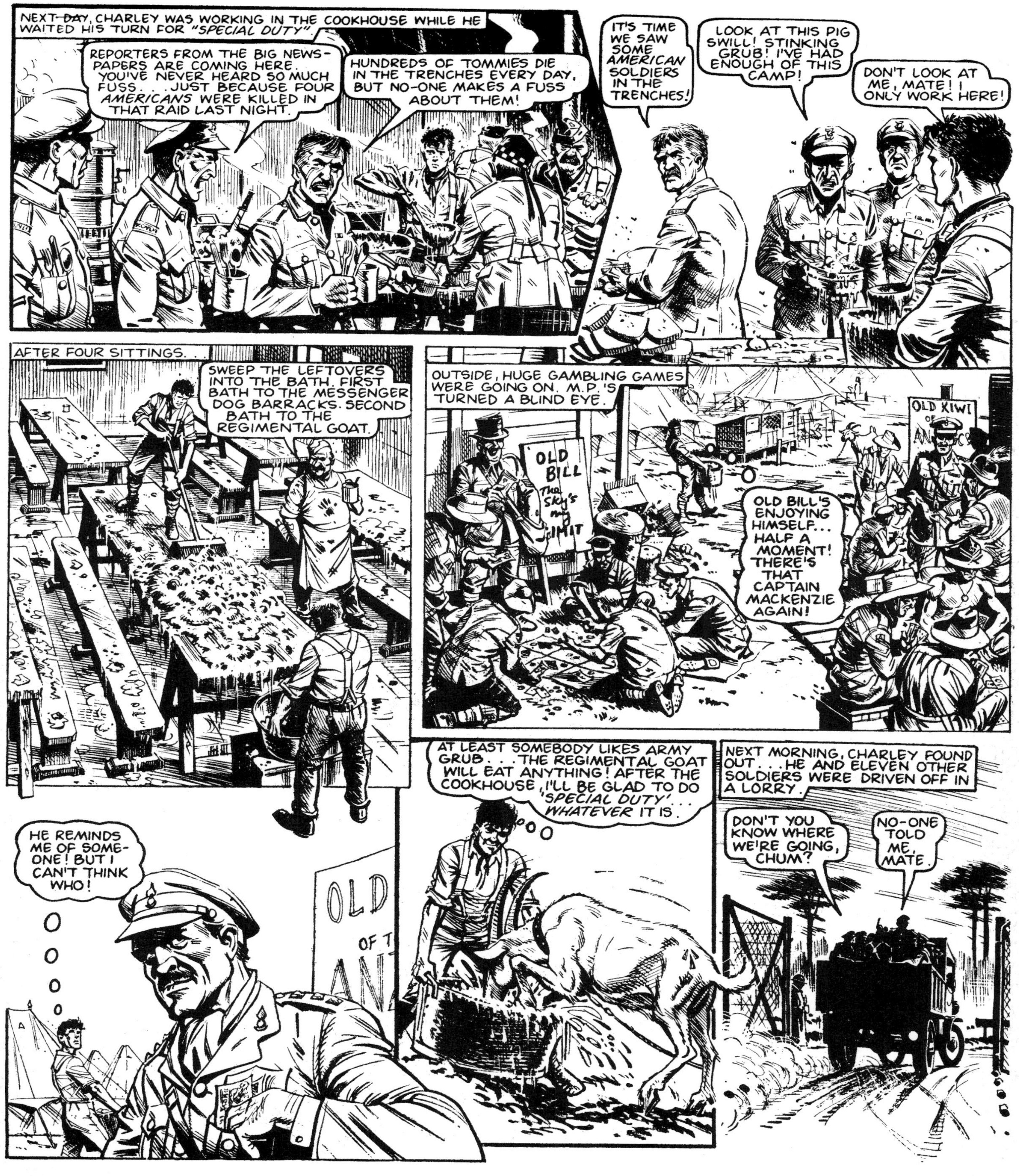
NEXT DAY, CHARLEY WAS WORKING IN THE COOKHOUSE WHILE HE WAITED HIS TURN FOR "SPECIAL DUTY".
REPORTERS FROM THE BIG NEWSPAPERS ARE COMING HERE. YOU'VE NEVER HEARD SO MUCH FUSS... JUST BECAUSE FOUR AMERICANS WERE KILLED IN THAT RAID LAST NIGHT.
HUNDREDS OF TOMMIES DIE IN THE TRENCHES EVERY DAY, BUT NO-ONE MAKES A FUSS ABOUT THEM!
IT'S TIME WE SAW SOME AMERICAN SOLDIERS IN THE TRENCHES!
LOOK AT THIS PIG SWILL! STINKING GRUB! I'VE HAD ENOUGH OF THIS CAMP!
DON'T LOOK AT ME, MATE! I ONLY WORK HERE!
AFTER FOUR SITTINGS...
SWEEP THE LEFTOVERS INTO THE BATH. FIRST BATH TO THE MESSENGER DOG BARRACKS. SECOND BATH TO THE REGIMENTAL GOAT.
OUTSIDE, HUGE GAMBLING GAMES WERE GOING ON. M.P.'S TURNED A BLIND EYE.
OLD BILL The Sky's my LIMIT
OLD KIWI
OLD BILL'S ENJOYING HIMSELF... HALF A MOMENT! THERE'S THAT CAPTAIN MACKENZIE AGAIN!
HE REMINDS ME OF SOMEONE! BUT I CAN'T THINK WHO!
AT LEAST SOMEBODY LIKES ARMY GRUB... THE REGIMENTAL GOAT WILL EAT ANYTHING! AFTER THE COOKHOUSE, I'LL BE GLAD TO DO 'SPECIAL DUTY'... WHATEVER IT IS.
NEXT MORNING, CHARLEY FOUND OUT... HE AND ELEVEN OTHER SOLDIERS WERE DRIVEN OFF IN A LORRY.
DON'T YOU KNOW WHERE WE'RE GOING, CHUM?
NO-ONE TOLD ME, MATE.

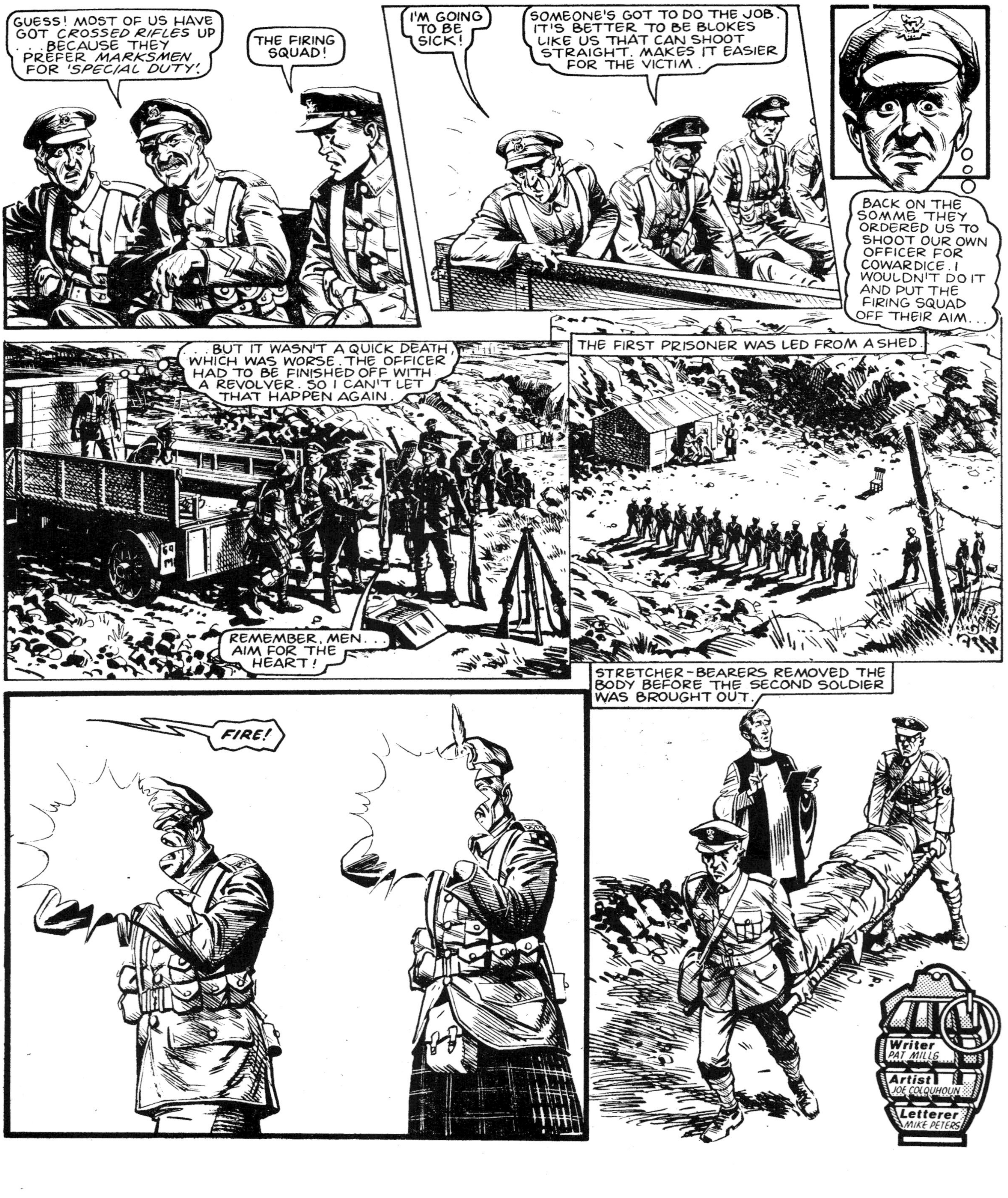
GUESS! MOST OF US HAVE GOT CROSSED RIFLES UP . . . BECAUSE THEY PREFER MARKSMEN FOR 'SPECIAL DUTY'.
THE FIRING SQUAD!
I'M GOING TO BE SICK!
SOMEONE'S GOT TO DO THE JOB. IT'S BETTER TO BE BLOKES LIKE US THAT CAN SHOOT STRAIGHT. MAKES IT EASIER FOR THE VICTIM.
BACK ON THE SOMME THEY ORDERED US TO SHOOT OUR OWN OFFICER FOR COWARDICE. I WOULDN'T DO IT AND PUT THE FIRING SQUAD OFF THEIR AIM. . .
. . BUT IT WASN'T A QUICK DEATH, WHICH WAS WORSE. THE OFFICER HAD TO BE FINISHED OFF WITH A REVOLVER. SO I CAN'T LET THAT HAPPEN AGAIN.
REMEMBER, MEN. . . AIM FOR THE HEART!
THE FIRST PRISONER WAS LED FROM A SHED.
FIRE!
STRETCHER-BEARERS REMOVED THE BODY BEFORE THE SECOND SOLDIER WAS BROUGHT OUT.
Writer PAT MILLS
Artist JOE COLQUHOUN
Letterer MIKE PETERS

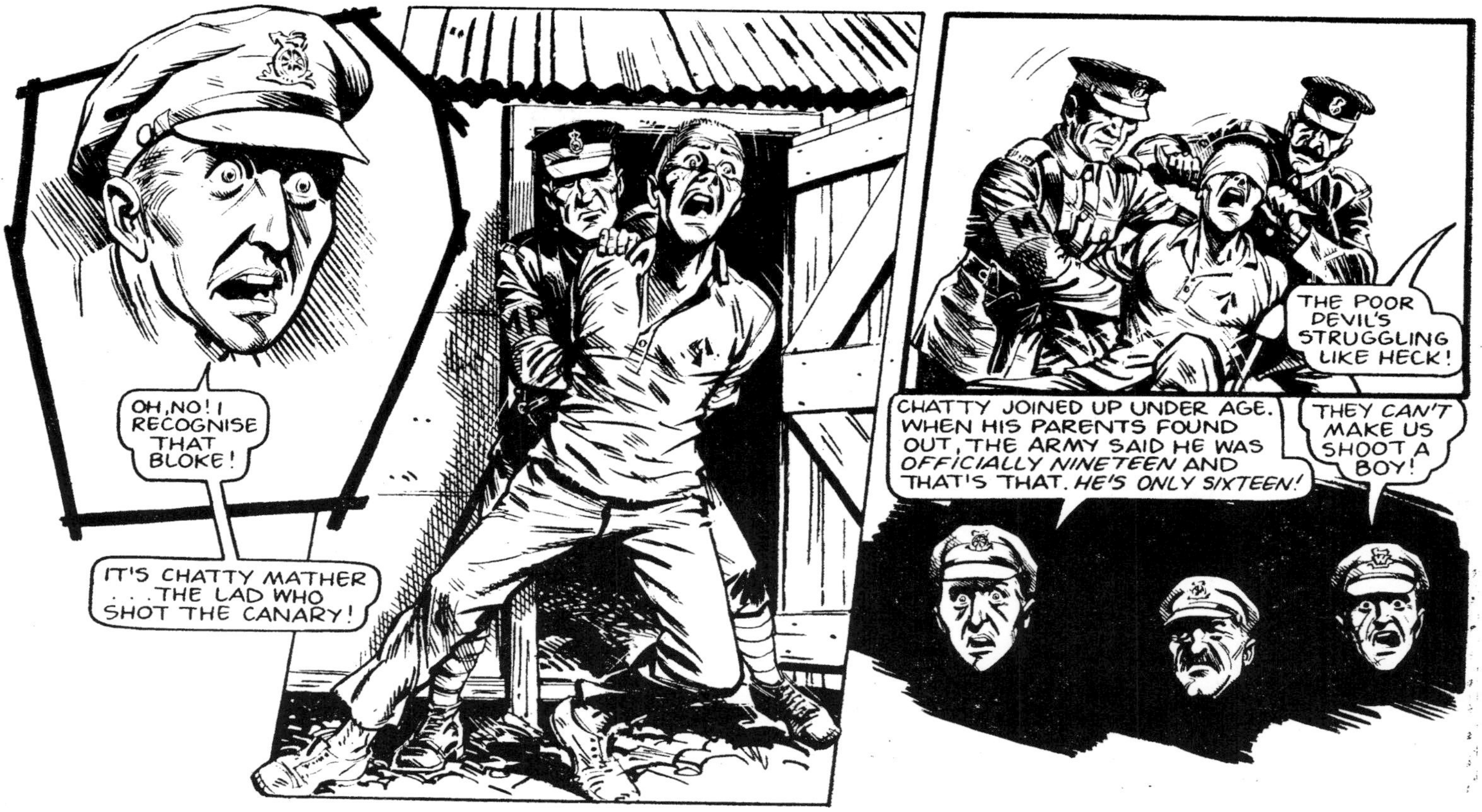
OH, NO! I RECOGNISE THAT BLOKE!
IT'S CHATTY MATHER . . . THE LAD WHO SHOT THE CANARY!
THE POOR DEVIL'S STRUGGLING LIKE HECK!
CHATTY JOINED UP UNDER AGE. WHEN HIS PARENTS FOUND OUT, THE ARMY SAID HE WAS *OFFICIALLY NINETEEN* AND THAT'S THAT. *HE'S ONLY SIXTEEN!*
THEY *CAN'T* MAKE US SHOOT A BOY!

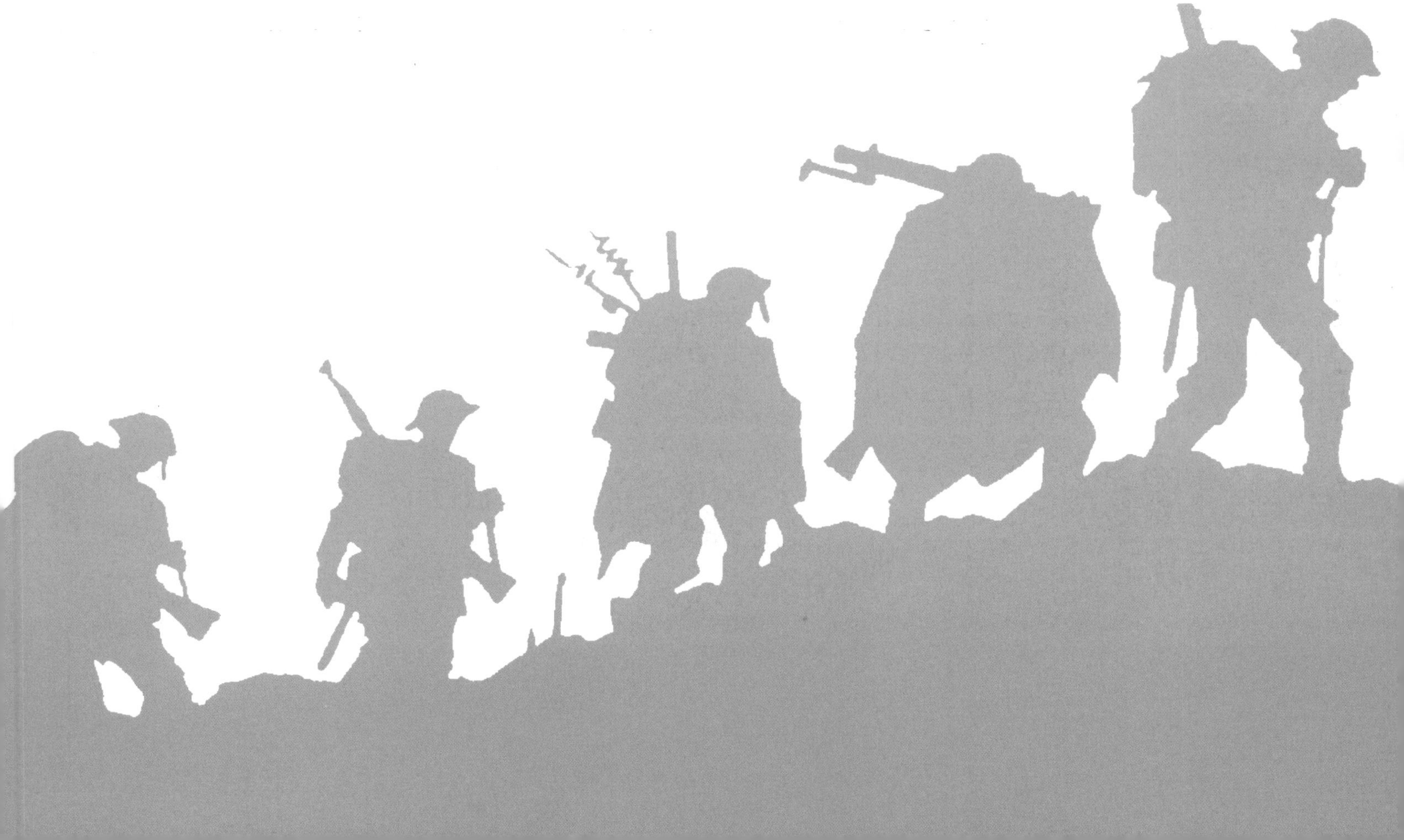

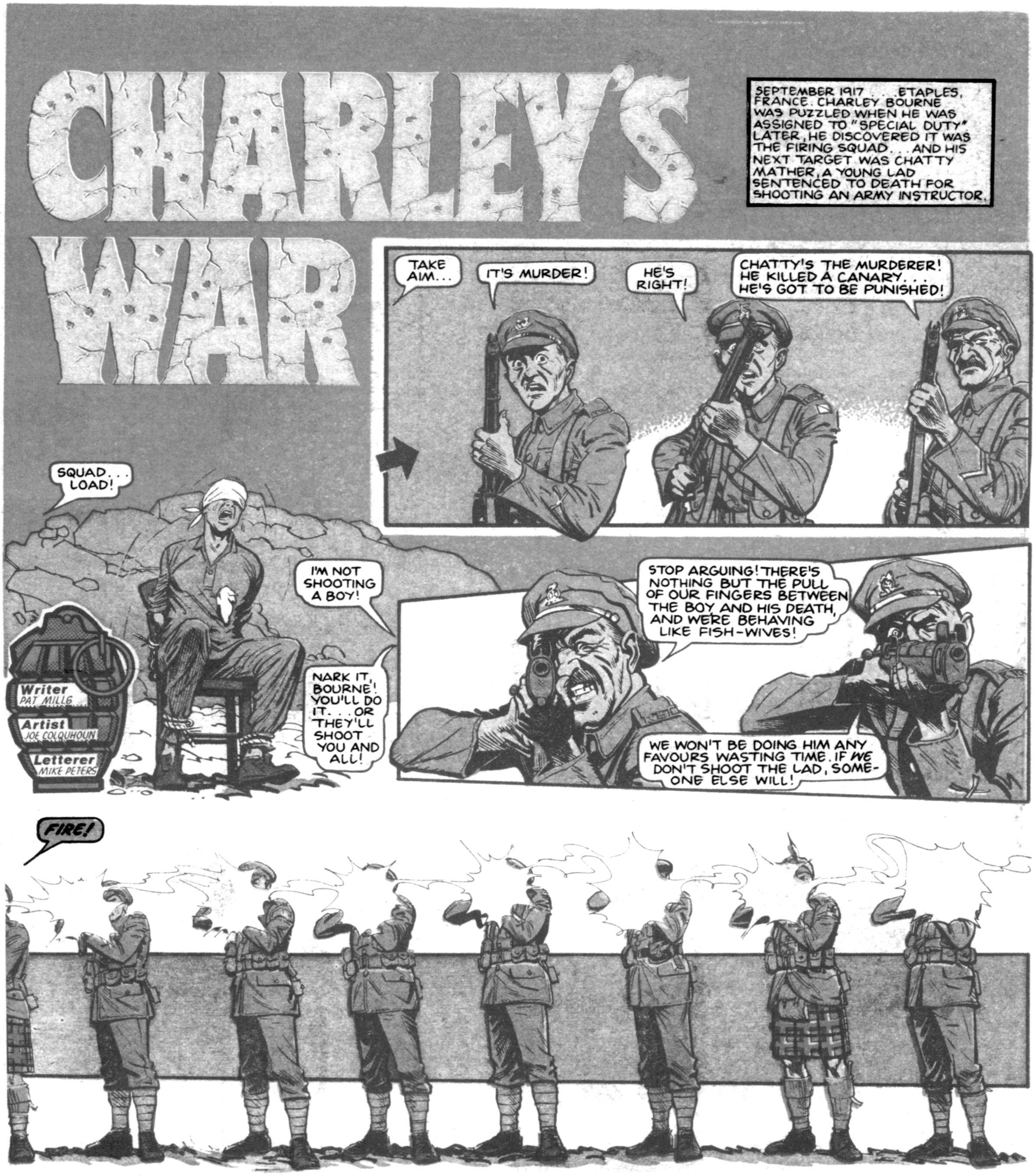
CHARLEY'S WAR
SEPTEMBER 1917 . . . ETAPLES, FRANCE. CHARLEY BOURNE WAS PUZZLED WHEN HE WAS ASSIGNED TO "SPECIAL DUTY". LATER, HE DISCOVERED IT WAS THE FIRING SQUAD . . . AND HIS NEXT TARGET WAS CHATTY MATHER, A YOUNG LAD SENTENCED TO DEATH FOR SHOOTING AN ARMY INSTRUCTOR.
SQUAD . . . LOAD!
TAKE AIM . . .
IT'S MURDER!
HE'S RIGHT!
CHATTY'S THE MURDERER! HE KILLED A CANARY . . . HE'S GOT TO BE PUNISHED!
Writer PAT MILLS
Artist JOE COLQUHOUN
Letterer MIKE PETERS
I'M NOT SHOOTING A BOY!
NARK IT, BOURNE! YOU'LL DO IT . . . OR THEY'LL SHOOT YOU AND ALL!
STOP ARGUING! THERE'S NOTHING BUT THE PULL OF OUR FINGERS BETWEEN THE BOY AND HIS DEATH, AND WE'RE BEHAVING LIKE FISH-WIVES!
WE WON'T BE DOING HIM ANY FAVOURS WASTING TIME. IF WE DON'T SHOOT THE LAD, SOME-ONE ELSE WILL!
FIRE!

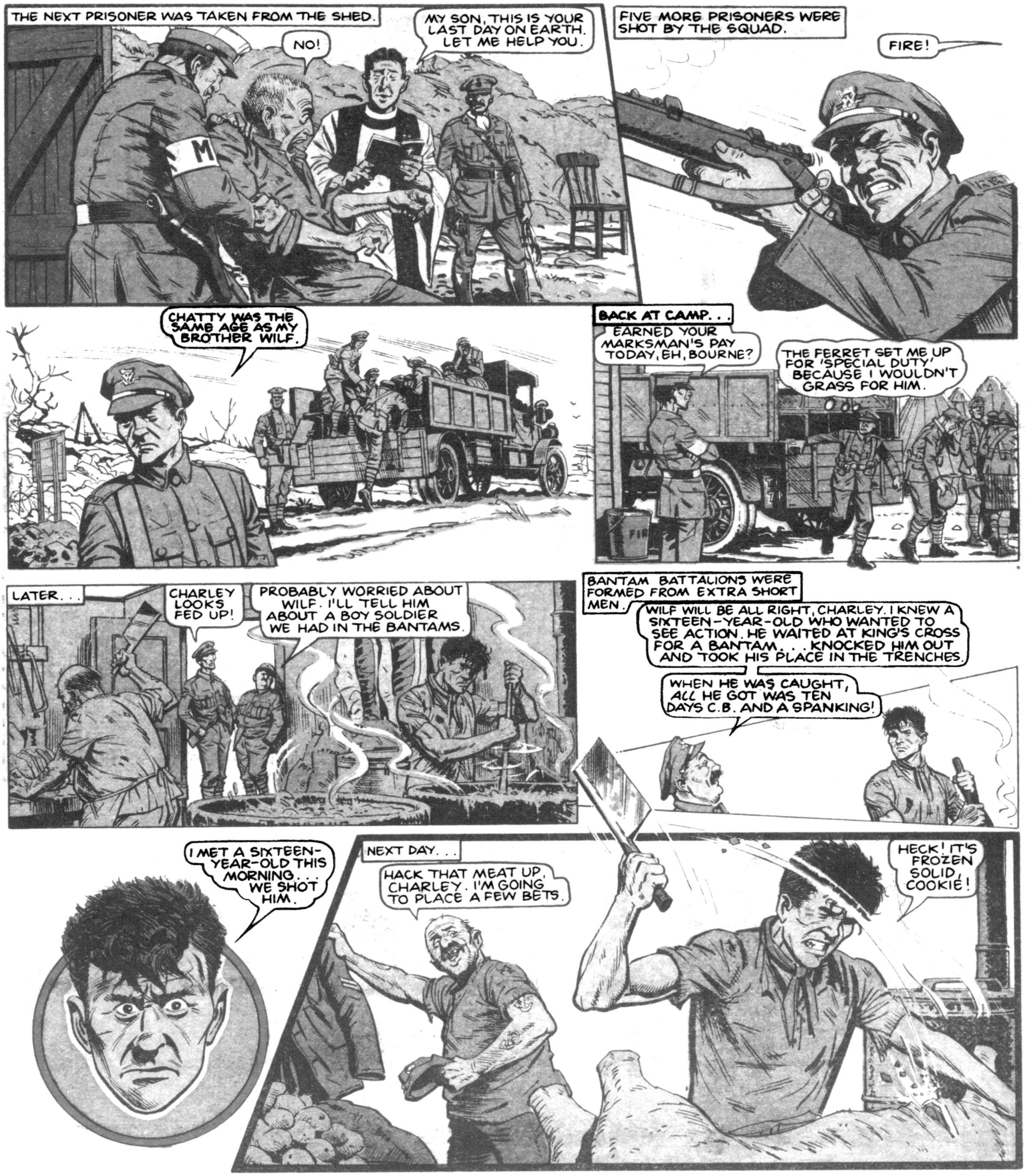
THE NEXT PRISONER WAS TAKEN FROM THE SHED.
NO!
MY SON, THIS IS YOUR LAST DAY ON EARTH. LET ME HELP YOU.
FIVE MORE PRISONERS WERE SHOT BY THE SQUAD.
FIRE!
CHATTY WAS THE SAME AGE AS MY BROTHER WILF.
BACK AT CAMP. . .
EARNED YOUR MARKSMAN'S PAY TODAY, EH, BOURNE?
THE FERRET SET ME UP FOR 'SPECIAL DUTY' BECAUSE I WOULDN'T GRASS FOR HIM.
LATER. . .
CHARLEY LOOKS FED UP!
PROBABLY WORRIED ABOUT WILF. I'LL TELL HIM ABOUT A BOY SOLDIER WE HAD IN THE BANTAMS.
BANTAM BATTALIONS WERE FORMED FROM EXTRA SHORT MEN.
WILF WILL BE ALL RIGHT, CHARLEY. I KNEW A SIXTEEN-YEAR-OLD WHO WANTED TO SEE ACTION. HE WAITED AT KING'S CROSS FOR A BANTAM. . . KNOCKED HIM OUT AND TOOK HIS PLACE IN THE TRENCHES.
WHEN HE WAS CAUGHT, ALL HE GOT WAS TEN DAYS C.B. AND A SPANKING!
I MET A SIXTEEN-YEAR-OLD THIS MORNING. . . WE SHOT HIM.
NEXT DAY. . .
HACK THAT MEAT UP, CHARLEY. I'M GOING TO PLACE A FEW BETS.
HECK! IT'S FROZEN SOLID, COOKIE!

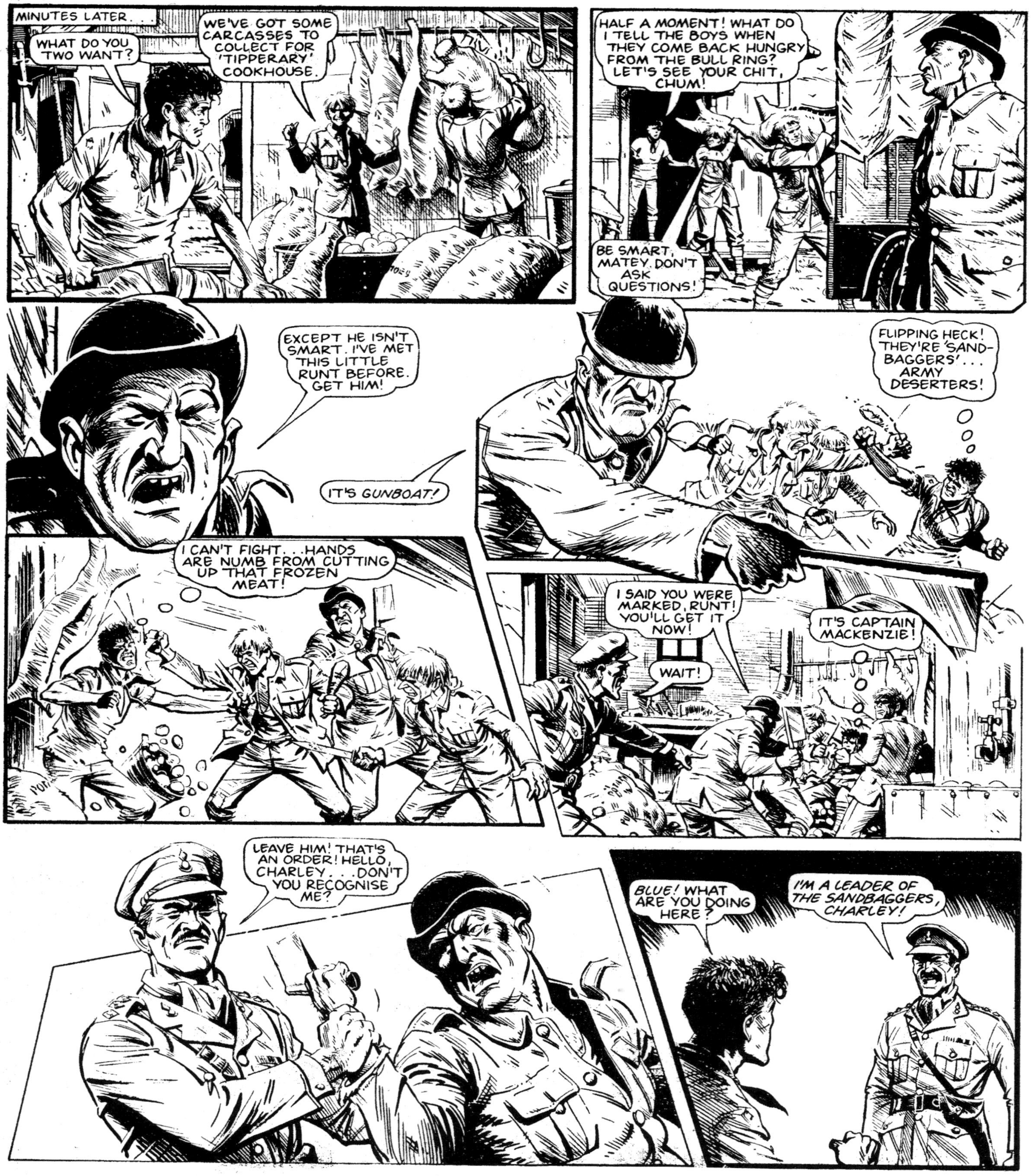

MINUTES LATER...
WHAT DO YOU TWO WANT?
WE'VE GOT SOME CARCASSES TO COLLECT FOR 'TIPPERARY' COOKHOUSE.
HALF A MOMENT! WHAT DO I TELL THE BOYS WHEN THEY COME BACK HUNGRY FROM THE BULL RING? LET'S SEE YOUR CHIT, CHUM!
BE SMART, MATEY. DON'T ASK QUESTIONS!
EXCEPT HE ISN'T SMART. I'VE MET THIS LITTLE RUNT BEFORE. GET HIM!
IT'S GUNBOAT!
FLIPPING HECK! THEY'RE 'SANDBAGGERS'... ARMY DESERTERS!
I CAN'T FIGHT... HANDS ARE NUMB FROM CUTTING UP THAT FROZEN MEAT!
I SAID YOU WERE MARKED, RUNT! YOU'LL GET IT NOW!
WAIT!
IT'S CAPTAIN MACKENZIE!
LEAVE HIM! THAT'S AN ORDER! HELLO, CHARLEY... DON'T YOU RECOGNISE ME?
BLUE! WHAT ARE YOU DOING HERE?
I'M A LEADER OF THE SANDBAGGERS, CHARLEY!

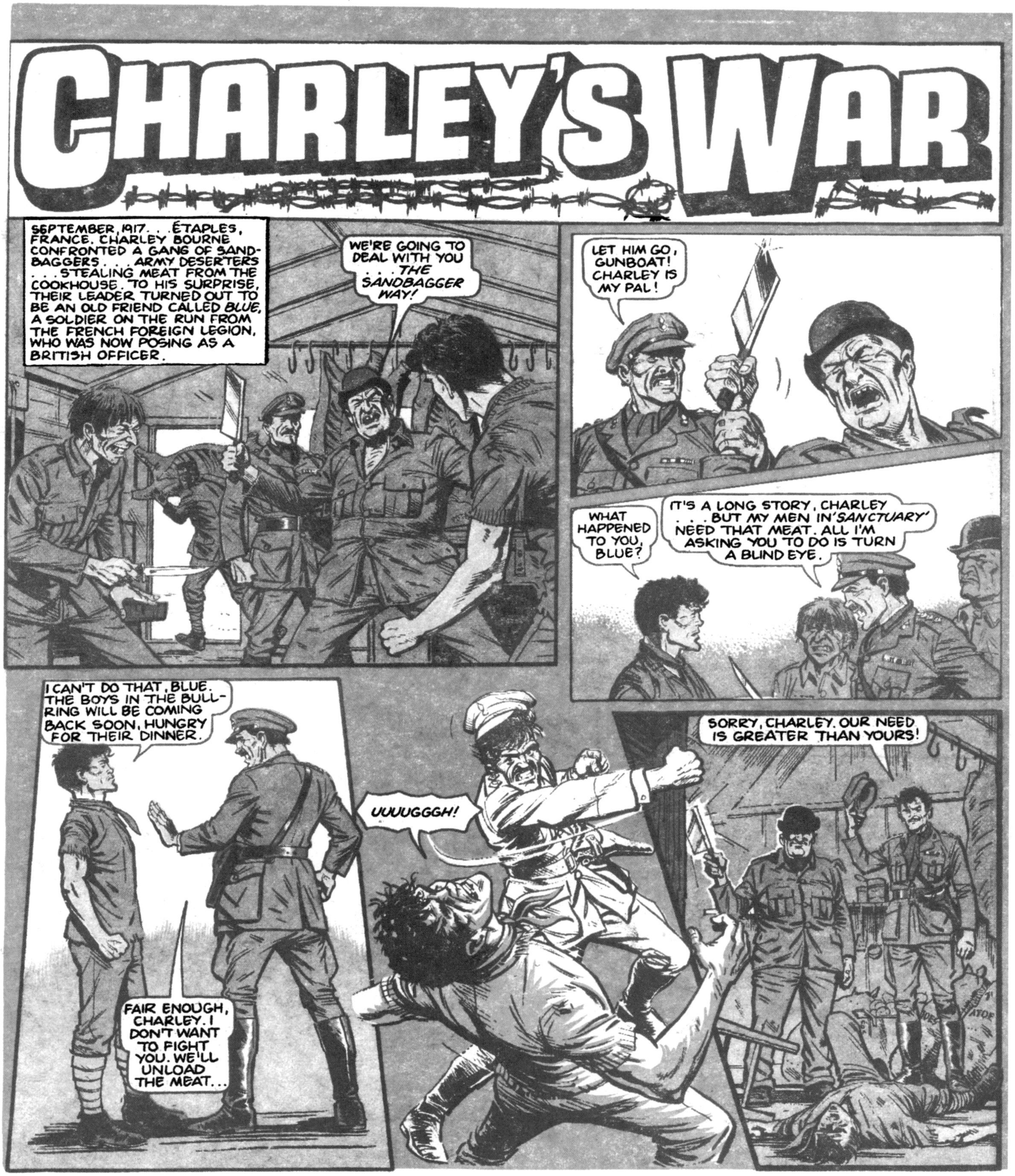
CHARLEY'S WAR
SEPTEMBER, 1917. . . ÉTAPLES, FRANCE. CHARLEY BOURNE CONFRONTED A GANG OF SAND-BAGGERS . . . ARMY DESERTERS . . . STEALING MEAT FROM THE COOKHOUSE. TO HIS SURPRISE, THEIR LEADER TURNED OUT TO BE AN OLD FRIEND CALLED BLUE, A SOLDIER ON THE RUN FROM THE FRENCH FOREIGN LEGION, WHO WAS NOW POSING AS A BRITISH OFFICER.
WE'RE GOING TO DEAL WITH YOU . . . THE SANDBAGGER WAY!
LET HIM GO, GUNBOAT! CHARLEY IS MY PAL!
WHAT HAPPENED TO YOU, BLUE?
IT'S A LONG STORY, CHARLEY . . . BUT MY MEN IN 'SANCTUARY' NEED THAT MEAT. ALL I'M ASKING YOU TO DO IS TURN A BLIND EYE.
I CAN'T DO THAT, BLUE. THE BOYS IN THE BULL-RING WILL BE COMING BACK SOON, HUNGRY FOR THEIR DINNER.
FAIR ENOUGH, CHARLEY. I DON'T WANT TO FIGHT YOU. WE'LL UNLOAD THE MEAT...
UUUUGGGH!
SORRY, CHARLEY. OUR NEED IS GREATER THAN YOURS!

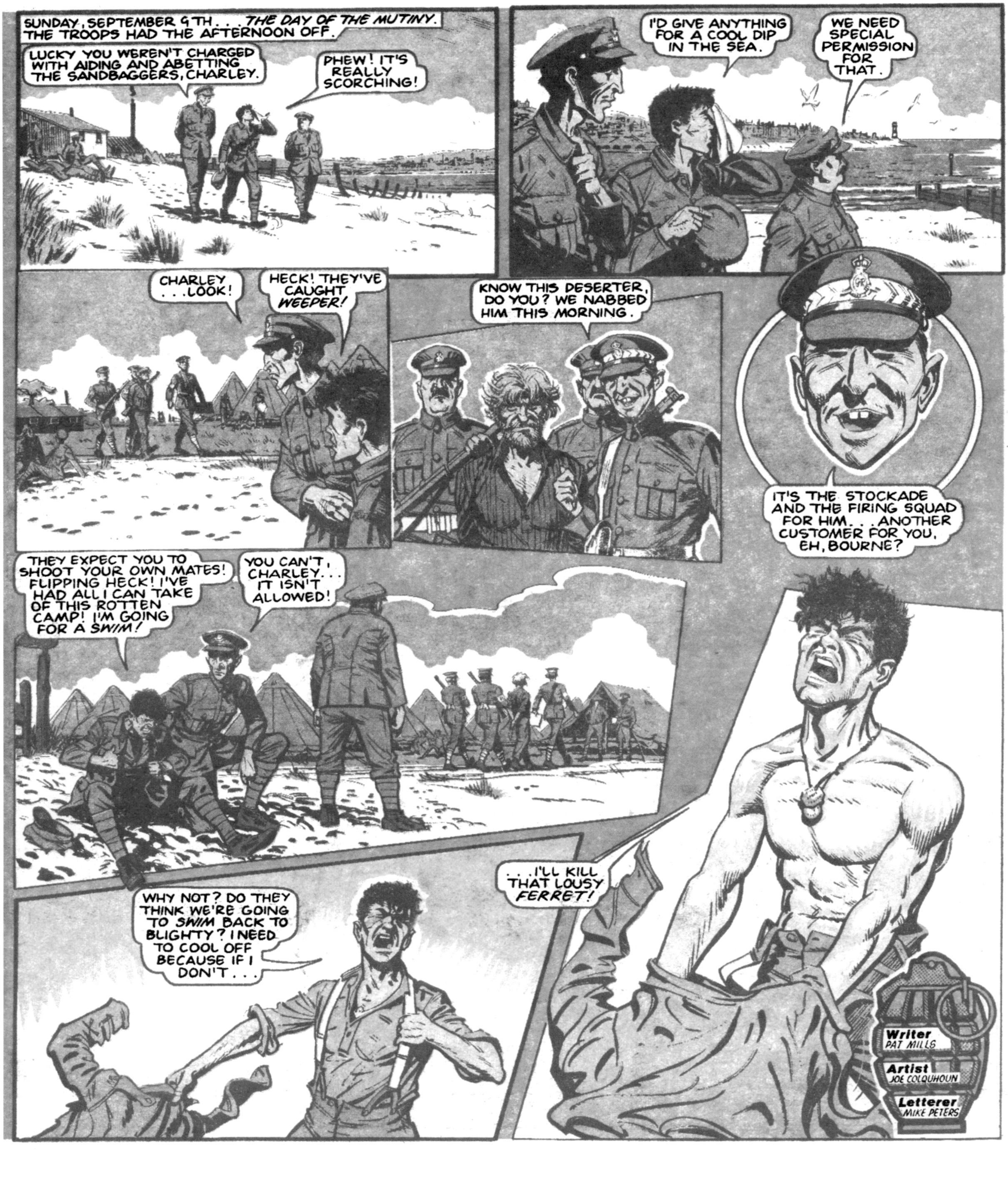
SUNDAY, SEPTEMBER 9TH . . . THE DAY OF THE MUTINY. THE TROOPS HAD THE AFTERNOON OFF.
LUCKY YOU WEREN'T CHARGED WITH AIDING AND ABETTING THE SANDBAGGERS, CHARLEY.
PHEW! IT'S REALLY SCORCHING!
I'D GIVE ANYTHING FOR A COOL DIP IN THE SEA.
WE NEED SPECIAL PERMISSION FOR THAT.
CHARLEY . . . LOOK!
HECK! THEY'VE CAUGHT WEEPER!
KNOW THIS DESERTER, DO YOU? WE NABBED HIM THIS MORNING.
IT'S THE STOCKADE AND THE FIRING SQUAD FOR HIM. . . ANOTHER CUSTOMER FOR YOU, EH, BOURNE?
THEY EXPECT YOU TO SHOOT YOUR OWN MATES! FLIPPING HECK! I'VE HAD ALL I CAN TAKE OF THIS ROTTEN CAMP! I'M GOING FOR A SWIM!
YOU CAN'T, CHARLEY. . . IT ISN'T ALLOWED!
WHY NOT? DO THEY THINK WE'RE GOING TO SWIM BACK TO BLIGHTY? I NEED TO COOL OFF BECAUSE IF I DON'T . . .
. . . I'LL KILL THAT LOUSY FERRET!
Writer PAT MILLS
Artist JOE COLQUHOUN
Letterer MIKE PETERS

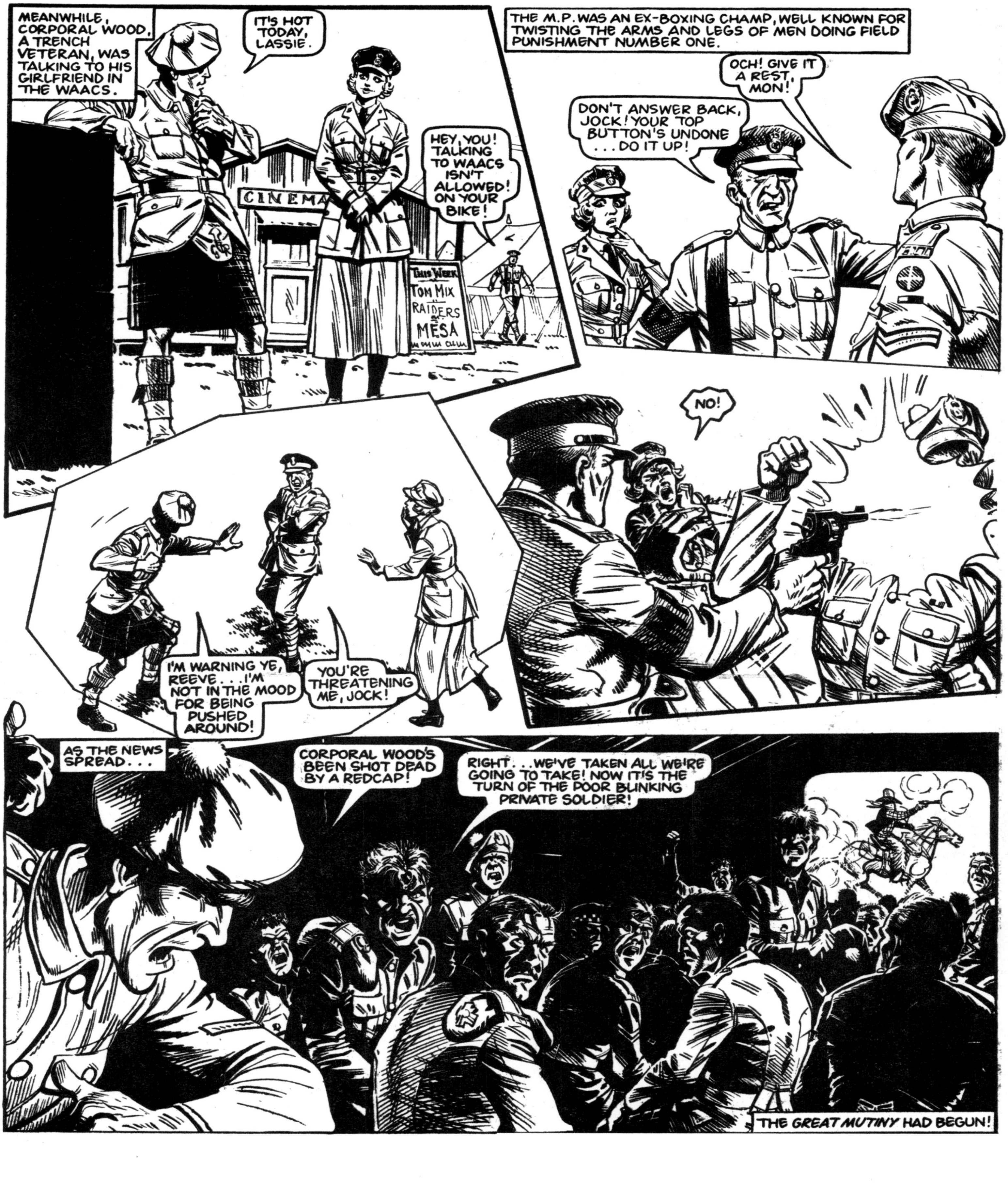
MEANWHILE, CORPORAL WOOD, A TRENCH VETERAN, WAS TALKING TO HIS GIRLFRIEND IN THE WAACS.
IT'S HOT TODAY, LASSIE.
CINEMA
THIS WEEK TOM MIX RAIDERS MESA
HEY, YOU! TALKING TO WAACS ISN'T ALLOWED! ON YOUR BIKE!
THE M.P. WAS AN EX-BOXING CHAMP, WELL KNOWN FOR TWISTING THE ARMS AND LEGS OF MEN DOING FIELD PUNISHMENT NUMBER ONE.
DON'T ANSWER BACK, JOCK! YOUR TOP BUTTON'S UNDONE . . . DO IT UP!
OCH! GIVE IT A REST, MON!
I'M WARNING YE, REEVE . . . I'M NOT IN THE MOOD FOR BEING PUSHED AROUND!
YOU'RE THREATENING ME, JOCK!
NO!
AS THE NEWS SPREAD . . .
CORPORAL WOOD'S BEEN SHOT DEAD BY A REDCAP!
RIGHT . . . WE'VE TAKEN ALL WE'RE GOING TO TAKE! NOW IT'S THE TURN OF THE POOR BLINKING PRIVATE SOLDIER!
THE GREAT MUTINY HAD BEGUN!

STRIP COMMENTARY

by Pat Mills

EPISODE ONE

In this first episode of the underground war, Smith regales us with curious details on how the enemy's tunnels can be detected. I recently came across some magazines from World War One which I am sure Smith would have read avidly, featuring science fiction machines as bizarre as the huge war machine he designed in an earlier volume of this series. In *The Electrical Experimenter* magazine, first published in 1913 and edited by Hugo Gernsback (who would later edit the SF magazine *Amazing Stories*, among others), there is a giant two-wheeled "Trench Destroyer"; Allied soldiers storming the German trenches to electrocute the enemy; and an "Electric Gyro-Cruiser" – a two-wheeled motorbike tank! Another issue features "Old Battleships to the Front" – a vast ship tank that is the ultimate in steampunk. Yet the secret war Charley and his mates are now about to embark upon as "clay-kickers" is just as fantastic as any of these machines – and just as nightmarish.

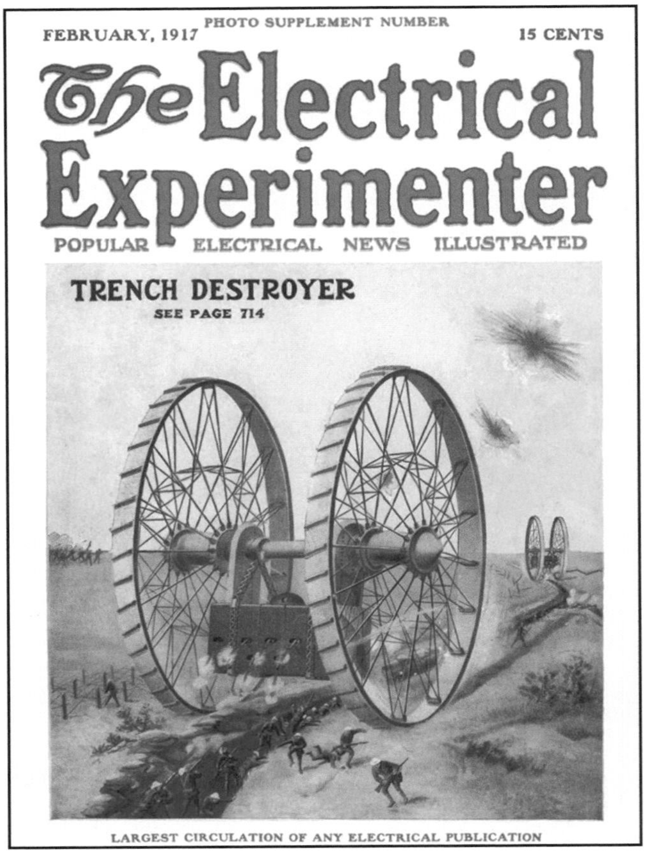

FEBRUARY, 1917
PHOTO SUPPLEMENT NUMBER
15 CENTS
The Electrical Experimenter
POPULAR ELECTRICAL NEWS ILLUSTRATED
TRENCH DESTROYER
SEE PAGE 714
LARGEST CIRCULATION OF ANY ELECTRICAL PUBLICATION

EPISODE THREE

Because of its popularity, *Charley's War* continued to be featured on the cover of *Battle* from time to time. This caused me some considerable problems, as most of the action takes place underground and was hardly conducive to striking images. Here, however, a German observation balloon provides an eye-catching visual.

Joe's cross-section drawing on the next page is amazing and shows yet again what a superb storyteller he was. I found myself drawn into the tension and drama of the story by just looking at this striking image and imagining what the tunnellers must have gone through.

EPISODE FOUR

I was delighted to see I had featured a heroic conscientious objector here. It's remarkable that this particular episode features soldiers sitting around waiting to die; there is no action whatsoever; and a pacifist is portrayed as a hero; and yet it was the number one story in a war comic. This says a great deal about the maturity of the readers who could appreciate the sub-text, the characterisation and the underlying tension. But, despite this, *Charley's War* has never been a role model for new anti-war stories and the plotting and characterisation techniques exampled here have never influenced other comic writers.

EPISODE SIX

Once again the title logo is still in that inappropriate Teutonic style, although it finally changes later in this volume. And on the third page of this episode, Charley's expression "'alf a mo" (a famous phrase in World War One) has been amended by *Battle* editorial to "Half a Moment". Would anyone really say that?! Ludicrous! Please try and ignore the subsequent "Half a Moment"s in later episodes.

EPISODE TEN

The dramatic conclusion to the tunnel adventure, but it's a pity that the *Battle* editorial team added those two enormous arrows on the final page of the episode. I think the readers could have figured out the pictures go from left to right without them! There is a similar huge unnecessary arrow on the next episode. They demonstrate, yet again, how they underestimated the intelligence of the readers.

In correspondence with a leading *2000AD* fan a few weeks ago, the fan commented that the traditional pacing of *Charley's War* – as exampled here – was too fast and he suggested that I must wish now that I'd written the serial at the slower, more measured pace of today's stories. But if I had written it with modern pacing, I would have needed six pages an episode and Joe could only draw three pages a week. This would have meant the story would have been out of *Battle* for six months of a year and readers and editorial needed the story to be in the comic all the time.

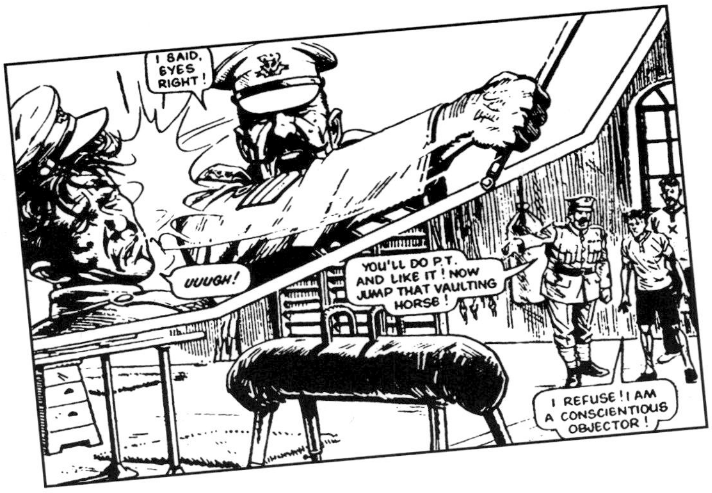
I SAID, EYES RIGHT!
UUUGH!
YOU'LL DO P.T. AND LIKE IT! NOW JUMP THAT VAULTING HORSE!
I REFUSE! I AM A CONSCIENTIOUS OBJECTOR!

Also, *Charley's War* was written for *Battle* readers and I think it inappropriate to view it through the lens of a different comic and different readership. But it is fair to say that *Charley's War* – both in story and art – sometimes put content ahead of style, which I am still comfortable with. Better this than all style and no content.

EPISODE ELEVEN

With a superb image of the tanks advancing, it's a pity editorial had to add those balloons from the fleeing Germans: they do very little for me. On the next page, Charley comments on the mammoth remains uncovered by the blast and how we have come a long way from our caveman ancestors. I found that image very effective. If I had written this sequence today, it probably would have occupied a page, rather than be covered in just three pictures. But I still feel it was more important to pack as much content into three pages as possible because some *Battle* readers were buying the comic just for *Charley's War*, and had no interest in the other stories – so my three pages really had to "deliver".

EPISODE TWELVE

The postcard featured at the end of the episode is authentic. A good example of self-deprecating British humour which has changed little in the last ninety years.

EPISODE THIRTEEN

The harsh reality of the Third Battle of Ypres is graphically portrayed here with a soldier committing suicide rather than going over the top. I recently watched the superb film *Redacted* and was struck by its similar approach to war. Directed by Brian De Palma, it portrays American soldiers in Iraq with a story so disturbing and critical of the conflict he has been called a traitor in the States. In the early episodes of *Charley's War*, I featured letters and postcards Charley was sending home, while in *Redacted* De Palma uses the modern equivalent, with a soldier keeping a video diary. The American soldiers are also blue collar workers, have a similar black sense of humour, and are aware they are fighting a pointless hellish war and comparable tragedies occur. Sadly, there is no British film equivalent about our country's role in the Iraq and Afghanistan occupations.

EPISODE FOURTEEN

This has an excellent image of the Tommies going over the top, weighed down with equipment. Given the disaster on the Somme the previous year, when the troops were similarly loaded down and massacred, it must have been obvious to the British generals that there would be a huge and unnecessary loss of life. By any sane criteria, this is surely a war crime.

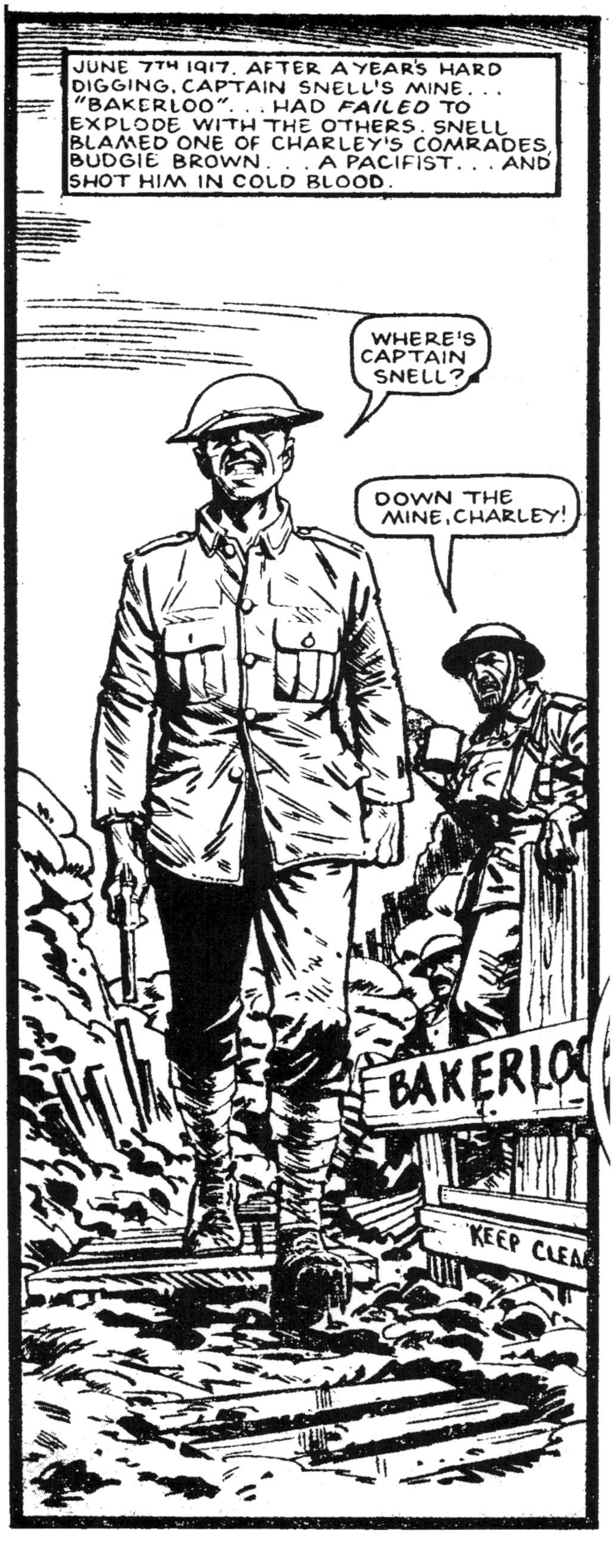
JUNE 7TH 1917. AFTER A YEAR'S HARD DIGGING, CAPTAIN SNELL'S MINE... "BAKERLOO"... HAD FAILED TO EXPLODE WITH THE OTHERS. SNELL BLAMED ONE OF CHARLEY'S COMRADES, BUDGIE BROWN... A PACIFIST... AND SHOT HIM IN COLD BLOOD.
WHERE'S CAPTAIN SNELL?
DOWN THE MINE, CHARLEY!
BAKERLO
KEEP CLEA

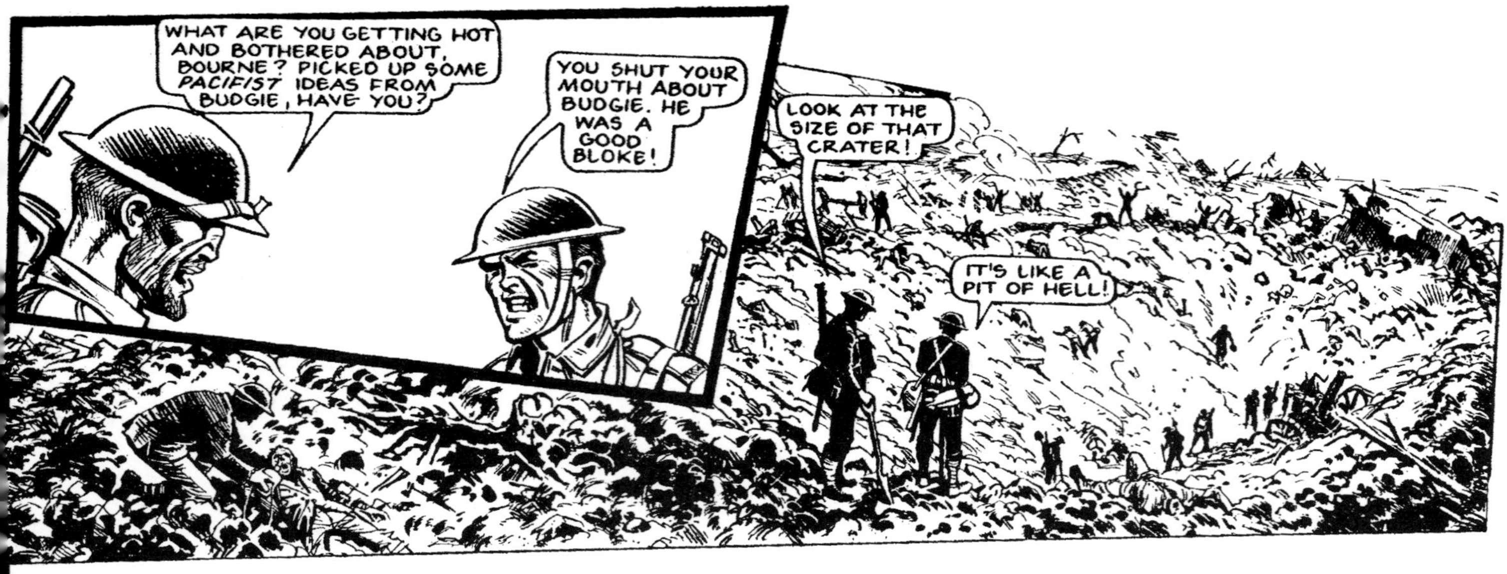
WHAT ARE YOU GETTING HOT AND BOTHERED ABOUT, BOURNE? PICKED UP SOME PACIFIST IDEAS FROM BUDGIE, HAVE YOU?
YOU SHUT YOUR MOUTH ABOUT BUDGIE. HE WAS A GOOD BLOKE!
LOOK AT THE SIZE OF THAT CRATER!
IT'S LIKE A PIT OF HELL!

EPISODE SIXTEEN

This episode, where Ypres is turned into a vast swamp, would surely put any one off going to war. I recall an ex-squaddie once telling me that he joined the army because he grew up reading war comics; so I like to think *Charley's War* goes some way to having the opposite effect – a necessary "penance", if you like, as I was the co-creator, with John Wagner, of *Battle*. I recall when we started, we both had doubts about doing a war comic. After all, we were both from the anti-war generation of the 1960s, but because we had a free hand, we decided to stay with it. Consequently, *Battle* was often anti-authority, with stories like *Rat Pack* (criminal soldiers in the style of the *Inglorious Bastards*) and working class heroes like the *Bootneck Boy* (a prototype for *Charley's War*). The stories were also fairly realistic for their time, so it had several redeeming features. And it laid the ground for *Charley's War* and Joe's *Johnny Red* to appear later. After all, featuring Russian communists as heroes in *Johnny Red* was somewhat unusual at the height of the Cold War.

But the impact an anti-war story can have was confirmed when I did a talk at the Cartoon Museum last year. Two readers came up to me afterwards and said that they both came from traditional military families – but didn't enlist because of reading *Charley's War*.

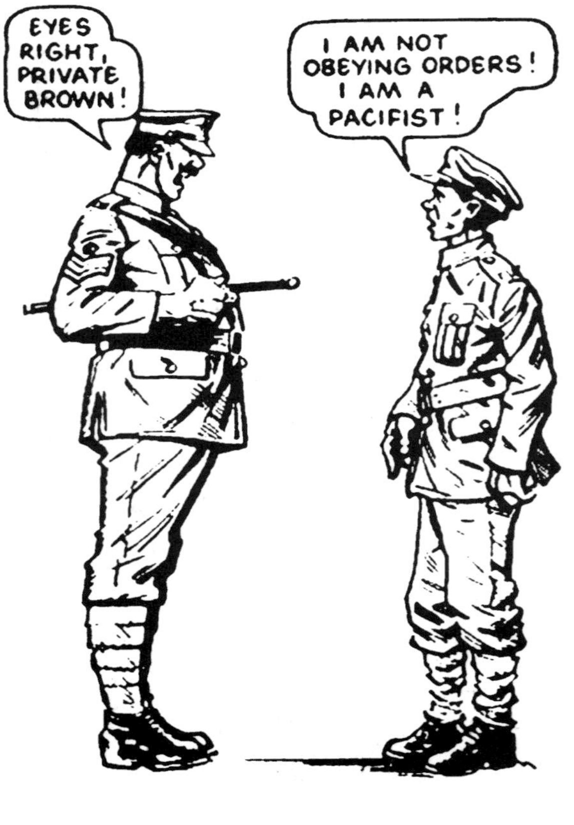
EYES RIGHT, PRIVATE BROWN!
I AM NOT OBEYING ORDERS! I AM A PACIFIST!

EPISODE EIGHTEEN

Another episode that would, surely, put anyone off going to war. If you feel I am exaggerating the significance of war comics, consider the importance the Ministry of Defence attaches to war toys. In January 2009, the MOD announced their own Action Man-like range of toys to boost the profile of the armed forces. Three soldier toys were featured, one of them in desert uniform based closely on our combat troops in Afghanistan. "Senior commanders who gave their blessing to the project are hoping that the figures will capture the imagination of a new generation of children," ran a press release. Sold under the HM Armed Forces brand name, some of the profits will go back to the MOD.

"Capturing the imagination of a new generation of children"… The recruiting implications of this statement are quite disturbing.

EPISODE TWENTY

The beginning of the Etaples story which culminates in a British army mutiny involving 100,000 men, the grim details of which have still not been fully revealed to this day.

EPISODE TWENTY-TWO

Wilf, Charley's brother, enlists as a Royal Flying Corps Lewis Gunner. The choice was deliberate; usually the pilot is the hero in stories, but I wanted to show the heroic nature of other personnel. In due course Wilf's story appears within the *Charley's War* saga and the readers accepted the detour away from Charley. Encouraged by this, I subsequently wrote about Charley's cousin as a stoker in the naval Battle of the Falklands. But the readers did not approve on this occasion and I had to drop the cousin from the saga. It was a pity as I was keen to write about the titanic naval Battle of Jutland from his point of view.

Recently, I mentioned in a talk at the Cartoon Museum that no one has ever produced a popular ship story in comics. Anita O'Brian, the museum's Curator, wittily responded that this was not so. There has been one extremely popular ship story – the brilliant Ken Reid's cartoon strip in the *Beano*, *Jonah*, featuring a goofy-looking sailor who manages to sink every ship he boards!

EPISODE TWENTY-FOUR

Tensions rise and the mutiny draws ever closer. Undoubtedly the French army mutiny and the Russian revolution would have made the authorities fearful that the British might also revolt. It's part of the talent of our establishment historians that they play down any connection between the British mutiny and political revolution. Thus when the mutiny began and British soldiers were turning back troop trains, waving them down with red flags, according to one such historian this was simply because "there were only red flags available".

EPISODE TWENTY-FIVE

A very cool last page to this episode. I had forgotten the twist ending that the "old man" was really Charley's friend Weeper and it took me totally by surprise. I love the expression on Charley's face. Very subtle.

EPISODE TWENTY-SIX

Like other script writers, I wrote *Charley's War* as a full script. It might be occasionally edited or censored, but essentially the words were left intact. These days, the artwork is sent to me and I edit the story myself against the images. I will then improve the dialogue, think about whether a character looks like he is actually saying what I have him saying, move balloons around and cut or add dialogue to suit. Some artists don't like this but – on balance – I feel it makes for a smoother and sharper read. This episode is one that I would have liked to have edited. For instance, there is too much text on the first picture: I would have probably cut the introduction and moved the second text box up to replace it. Subsequently I would have added more text for the two large Sandbagger pictures, which are visually engrossing but look like they need some dialogue.

EPISODE TWENTY-SEVEN

The story returns to the cover of *Battle* and it's a very effective image. But what a pointless balloon: "This is terrible! Terrible!" That would certainly have been added by editorial. Far better to say nothing.

However, the interior shots are amazing. There's so much detail in Joe's art. I think he particularly enjoyed drawing canteen pictures as they always look horrible, perhaps inspired by his own wartime recollections?!

The episode concludes with a firing squad scene. The dance impresario Victor Sylvester was an underage soldier in World War One and he describes such events in his memoirs. They are deeply disturbing. Joe's rendering of the hypocritical establishment vicar looking on, facilitating legal murder, is excellent.

EPISODE TWENTY-EIGHT

Charley actually takes part in the legal murder of prisoners sentenced to death. Of course he would have done so in real life; he had no choice; but it is unusual for a comic book character to do something so unsympathetic. I'm glad I didn't pull any punches here and I hope Joe understood the necessity for the scene. Over the years he never once complained about anything I asked him to draw, but he might have felt he had reason here.

I recall when I had my character, Slaine, take part in the massacre of men, women and children in Colchester during Boudicca's revolt, the artist, Glenn Fabry, was uncomfortable about him acting so unheroically. I understand his point of view, but to do anything else – for me – would have been a cop-out. Slaine was a Celtic warrior and the Celts showed no mercy to the Roman colonists who had over-run their land. It's difficult, but if comics are ever to truly grow up, we cannot whitewash our heroes.

It's great to see the return of Blue, one of my favourite characters in *Charley's War*. When he featured in the earlier episodes, I didn't see through his disguise at first as I had forgotten the story. Blue is inspired by Percy Toplis, the Monocled Mutineer, the subject of the excellent TV series that outraged Conservative MPs.

EPISODE TWENTY-NINE

The first two pages would have been in colour, like the previous episode. I'm not sure I can see the sense in that, because the reader would then have turned over to a solitary black and white page. Also the subject matter hardly lends itself to colour. It would have been coloured by a colourist using blue line guides, so you really haven't missed much. Of course if Joe himself had coloured it, it would have been another matter. See, for example, his *Kid Chameleon* (which appeared in *Cor!*) and *Football Family Robinson* (in *Tiger*), both beautifully coloured by him.

It's astonishing to think the soldiers needed special permission to swim in the sea. It's so heartless. They really were regarded as cannon fodder by the military, which is why I find modern historians' rehabilitation of generals like Haig and disasters like the Somme so appalling.

I have to admit this is one episode which I should have made into two episodes in order to show more reactions from Charley. Firstly, an extra page for his confrontation with Blue. Then, an extra page over the realisation that he will have to shoot his best friend Weeper. And, finally, another page detailing the start of the mutiny.

But finally the Great Mutiny kicks off. My blood is boiling after that build-up and I can't wait to see what happens in the next volume. ✛

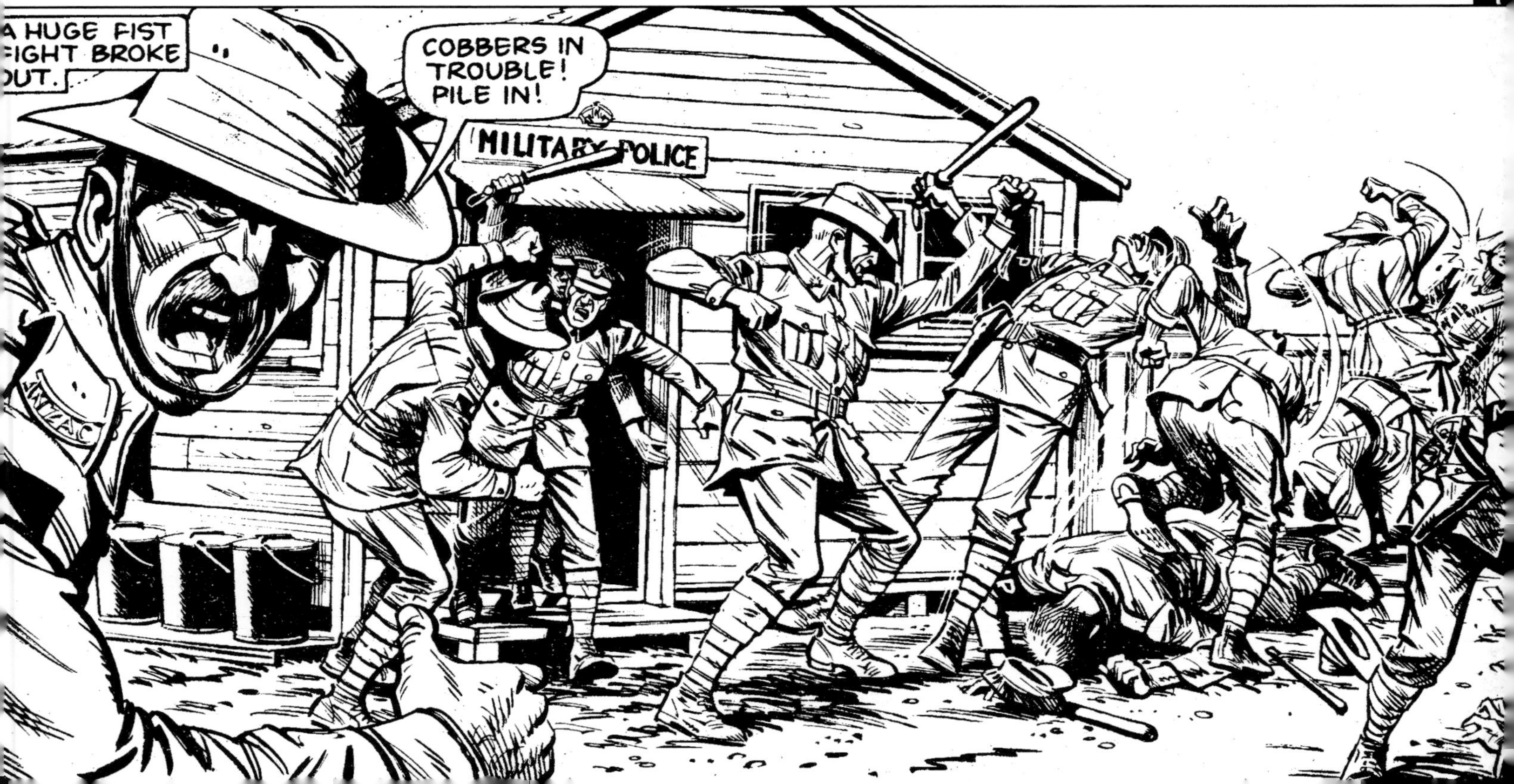
A HUGE FIST FIGHT BROKE OUT. . .
COBBERS IN TROUBLE! PILE IN!
MILITARY POLICE
ANZAC

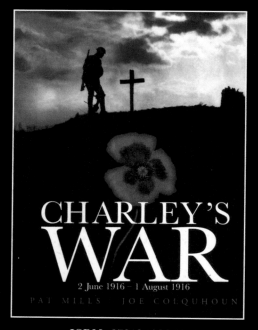
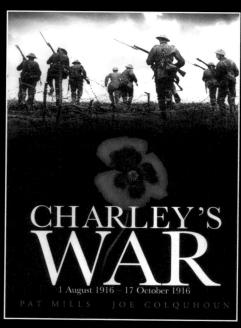
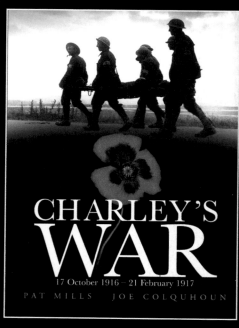
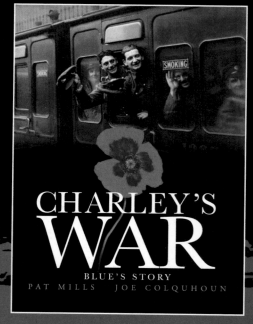
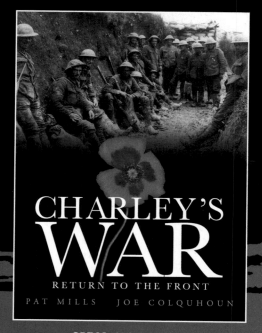